Alwyn Crawshaw

THE COMPLETE PAINTING COURSE

Alwyn Crawshaw

THE COMPLETE PAINTING COURSE

This material first published in paperback by HarperCollins Publishers as
Learn to Paint Sketch
Learn to Paint Watercolours
Learn to Paint Acrylics
Learn to Paint Oils for the Beginner

This edition produced exclusively for W. H. Smith in 1995
by HarperCollins Publishers, London

A catalogue record for this book is available from the British Library

Photography: Michael Petts and Nigel Cheffers-Heard
Design: Bev Speight and Nigel Wright

ISBN 0 583 31890 8

Printed and bound in Spain

Pages 2 and 3: *A Carpet of Bluebells*, watercolour, 380 x 500mm (15 x 20in)

CONTENTS

A Tuscan Farm, oil on hardboard, 250 x 300 mm (10 x 12 in)

INTRODUCTION

Have you ever thought what it is that makes us want to paint? If we stop to think, this urge to paint has been with us for a long time. Over twenty-five thousand years ago our ancestors painted on cave walls, but no one knows exactly why they painted. It could have been for the education and instruction of their children, for decorating their caves, or as a creative pastime. Before the camera was invented, painting was the only way of communicating visually with others, so it was not only important, it was to a great extent necessary. But even with the camera and new technology, there seem to be more people painting now than ever before.

I believe the reason for this is that we all have a creative urge inside us and painting is one exciting way of fulfilling it. Painting is available to us all. It has no social boundaries; there is no age limit; there is no restriction as to when you paint. You can choose to work indoors when the weather is miserable or outdoors when it is fine. You can work for half an hour on a small sketch or take weeks to finish a large oil painting. The choice is yours.

One of the statements most frequently made to me is: 'I wish I could paint.' My reply is: 'Have you tried?' and invariably the answer is: 'Oh no, I'm not an artist, and I wouldn't know where or how to start.' How can anyone say they cannot paint if they have never tried?

If you are a beginner in painting, you have bought this book because you are curious and your creative instinct has been aroused. What you will find here are the simple but successful techniques and methods explained in my best-selling *Learn to Paint* books. This *Complete Painting Course* brings together, for the first time, my methods for using all the main painting media – watercolours, acrylics and oils – together with a comprehensive beginner's guide to the essential art of sketching. I have followed a definite plan of progression throughout each section so that you can compare techniques and exercises in the different media, from drawing your composition and mixing your colours to painting a detailed landscape.

Following the whole sequence of the book page by page, you will find a complete instruction course on drawing and painting. But if you choose to go straight to the painting medium that interests you most – say, watercolour – you will also find in those pages everything you need to get you started and encourage you to progress quickly. Then, as your confidence builds, you will discover that once you can paint in watercolours, you can just as easily master acrylics and oils.

I recommend one thing – relax and read before you start. When you begin the lessons and exercises, enjoy them. If you find some parts difficult, don't become obsessed with the problem, go on a stage further and then come back. Seeing the difficulty with a fresh eye will make it easier to solve. Go on, have a go – and good luck!

Alwyn Crawshaw

ALWYN CRAWSHAW

PORTRAIT OF AN ARTIST

Alwyn Crawshaw in his studio

Successful painter, author and teacher Alwyn Crawshaw was born at Mirfield, Yorkshire, and studied at Hastings School of Art. He now lives in Dawlish, Devon, with his wife June, where they have their own gallery.

Alwyn is a Fellow of the Royal Society of Arts, and a member of the British Watercolour Society and the Society of Equestrian Artists. He is also President of the National Acrylic Painters Association and is listed in the current edition of *Who's Who in Art*.

Alwyn works in watercolour, oil, acrylic and occasionally pastel. He chooses to paint landscapes, seascapes, buildings and anything else that inspires him. Heavy working horses and elm trees are frequently featured in his paintings and may be considered the artist's trademark.

Alwyn has written eight titles for the HarperCollins *Learn to Paint* series. His other books for HarperCollins include: *The Artist at Work* (an autobiography of his painting

career), *Sketching with Alwyn Crawshaw, The Half-Hour Painter, Alwyn Crawshaw's Watercolour Painting Course, Alwyn Crawshaw's Oil Painting Course* and *Alwyn Crawshaw's Acrylic Painting Course.*

To date Alwyn has made five television series: *A Brush with Art, Crawshaw Paints on Holiday, Crawshaw Paints Oils, Crawshaw's Watercolour Studio* and *Crawshaw Paints Acrylics,* and for each of these he has written a book of the same title to accompany the series.

Alwyn has been a guest on local and national radio programmes and has appeared on various television programmes. In addition, his television programmes have been shown in the USA. He has made several successful videos on painting and in 1991 was listed as one of the top ten artist video teachers in America. He is also a regular contributor to the *Leisure Painter* magazine.

Alwyn organizes his own successful and very popular painting courses and holidays. In 1992 he co-founded the Society of Amateur Artists, of which he is President.

Fine art prints of Alwyn's well-known paintings are in demand worldwide. His paintings are sold in British and overseas galleries and can be found in private collections throughout the world. Painted mainly from nature and still life, Alwyn's work has been favourably reviewed by the critics. The *Telegraph Weekend Magazine* reported him to be 'a landscape painter of considerable expertise' and the *Artists and Illustrators* magazine described him as 'outspoken about the importance of maintaining traditional values in the teaching of art'.

SKETCHING

ABOUT SKETCHING

The sketch is the beginning. Almost all work that has been created on paper or canvas, in clay, stone, metal, or indeed any artists' medium, started as a sketch. An idea can be stimulated by a thousand things, but a sketch can hold it for all time and be used as a foundation for other work, even though the idea may represent only a fleeting moment of inspiration. Sketching is a means of recording something forever. Therefore I feel strongly that you should never throw a sketch away, no matter how small or insignificant you think it is. You have created something that is unique and original from which you can always learn, even years later.

If we accept that the sketch is the beginning, then we can also accept that sketching can be one way of learning to draw and paint finished pictures. I want to teach you how to sketch out of doors and how to use your sketches either as works in their own right or as training exercises for drawing

and painting. This will enable you to build on the knowledge you already have, or if you are a beginner, will open your eyes to new sights that can be experienced only when you look around you with sympathetic and observant eyes. You will 'see' things in a new light. You could look at a telegraph pole and wonder at its beauty!

It is interesting the way we always tend to think of ourselves as the normal ones, whatever profession, sport or pastime we indulge in. On one occasion when I went sketching to gather material for this book, I ended up at Exmouth. My wife, June, was with me and it was very cold. We walked along the banks of the river Exe estuary and around a small headland looking for a sketching spot. The sea was very shallow in this area and covered with windsurfers skimming across the water. They were falling in, getting up, and falling in, over and over again. Although they had wet suits on, they looked extremely cold – we thought they were mad. Further along we saw two bundles of clothing on the stony beach with what looked like long antennae sticking out. When we were closer, a head peeped out and said: 'Good afternoon.' They were anglers, fishing quite merrily on such a bleak day. We acknowledged them and went on.

Eventually I found a suitable spot to put my chair down and started to sketch the scene in front of me (see fig. 2). The wind was so biting that I was only able to keep it up for about 20 minutes. June had gone for a walk to try to keep warm. When I had almost finished, one of the fishermen came over to me and looked at my right hand blue with cold, and my left hand with a glove on, and said: 'You must be mad sitting out here drawing a picture.' The strange thing is that I had assumed I was the normal one and that the anglers and windsurfers were the odd ones.

I am not suggesting you go out and find the coldest spot and stick it out for 20 minutes. What I want you to be able to do after reading this book is go out with confidence and enjoy sketching. I enjoy sketching just as much or even more sometimes than sitting in my studio painting a 'masterpiece' (my interpretation!). One of the greatest advantages of sketching is that it provides a reason to go out and enjoy your surroundings, even if it is simply to your own garden. The photograph opposite shows me in my garden sketching two new additions to the family – the ducks.

All the sketches in this book, except for the exercises, are reproduced from my sketchbooks. They were *all* done on location, some especially for the book, others from my work over the past few years. This should give a broad 'picture' of sketching techniques and a variety of subjects.

Fig. 1 *Venn Ottery Church, 255 x 180mm (10 x 7 in)*

WHAT IS A SKETCH?

Now let's go back to the drawing board. We know that a sketch is the beginning, but what is meant by the word sketch? Artists use it in so many different ways. A quick sketch can mean anything from something carefully observed and created with only a dozen lines, to a picture that hasn't made the grade in the artist's eyes, and he suggests: 'It's just a quick sketch!' One person can have simply a

Fig. 2 *Exmouth – a cold day, 225 x 280mm (9 x 11in)*

Fig. 3 *Twin Elms, Cambridge,* 280 x 215mm (11 x 8½ in)

Fig. 4 *Me in bed,* 215 x 280mm (8½ x 11in)

VERY CROSS!!
in bed with disc! 16 June 78

pencil and small sketching pad, and inform us that he is going sketching, while another could take everything he can think of: easel, canvases, paints, seat, small table, umbrella, etc., and yet still use the phrase: 'I am going out sketching.'

I have found that usually this simply means, to go out and draw or paint a picture. In fact, I often use the same expression myself, and I might end up with a finished watercolour painting instead of a watercolour sketch. All sketches, whether they are drawings or paintings, can be used as 'finished' works. But, as we are interested in sketching with its 'real' meaning, I have defined the word, from the artist's point of view, to help you through the book. After a lot of careful thought I have broken down my definition of the sketch into four distinct and practical types:

Enjoyment sketch A drawing or painting worked on location, done simply to enjoy the experience.

Information sketch A drawing or painting done solely to collect information or detail, which can be used later at home or in the studio.

Atmosphere sketch A drawing or painting worked in a way that puts atmosphere and mood into the finished result. It can then be used later for information, or as inspiration for a painting done indoors.

Specific sketch A drawing or painting of a specific subject made in order to gather as much information of detail and atmosphere as possible, which also conveys the mood of the occasion. The sketch is used as the basis for a finished studio painting. The specific sketch is really a combination of the information and atmosphere sketches, but the difference is that the object is to go to a specific place to record what you see and feel, and then use all the information for a larger studio painting.

ENJOYMENT

Before you go out you may have a preconceived idea of what type of sketch you are going to do. If you haven't, then go out and do an enjoyment sketch. Get together your sketching equipment and set off, looking at your surroundings with your sketchbook in hand. You have the perfect excuse to wander around and soak in the atmosphere or the visual beauty of things around you, whether you are in an industrial town, a village, on a beach or in the countryside. Your subconscious, too, will retain information on what you see.

An enjoyment sketch contains information even if it is only to show how good your technique was – or how bad. In such cases it can be used to improve it next time, or it may simply serve as a reminder of how much you enjoyed the day out, therefore it doesn't matter how poor the technique was. If you have been out sketching before and had some marvellous times, ask yourself if you would have had them, or even gone out on those occasions, if you hadn't had sketching as an excuse.

To me the self-portrait sketch oppposite (fig. 4) is a typical enjoyment sketch. A few years ago I was in bed suffering from a slipped disc. It had never happened to me before and I was furious. On the second day of lying in bed, I couldn't settle to do any work due to the pain, but I felt like drawing for the sheer delight of it. So with the aid of a mirror propped up on the bed for me, I sketched myself (I was not aware of the scowl on my face as I drew it). If you have a pencil and sketchbook with you all the time you can enjoy yourself anywhere, even with such simple equipment.

INFORMATION

The information sketch speaks for itself. It is a way of sketching aimed at gathering information, to be used later in the studio, usually to work a larger picture from. Naturally you will have your own ideas on what information you need from a sketch, so I leave you to decide. However, it is no good going home and leaving your subject without enough information, because you may never see it again.

Here are some of the points to remember to put on your sketch: the position of the sun, the position of shadows, the sizes and locations of important features, such as a boat, building, tree, lamp-post, person, etc., and their positions in relation to each other. This is very important and I have written a section on how to 'measure from life' and transfer your measurements to paper (see page 40).

Make sure you put something in your sketch to give an idea of scale. In fig. 3, the drawing of the two elm trees, the scale was shown by the sheep and figure. The information I was after was of the trees, not the sheep or the figure, or I would have drawn them larger and in greater detail.

If you are working in black and white prior to working in colour, then you will need to make colour notes. You can make yourself a code, for instance, D.G. = dark green, P.F. = ploughed field, L.R. = light red, and so on. This is very important. A week later when you look at your sketch, it is easy to forget whether a roof was red or blue slate.

However, when you do a watercolour sketch don't put any comments or coding on it. A watercolour sketch, because of the relaxed manner in which it is approached, can often turn out to be a perfect watercolour painting, fit to grace any gallery or home. If you need notes put them lightly on the back in pencil.

ATMOSPHERE

The atmosphere sketch also speaks for itself. The important element to capture is the feel of the subject in its environment. If you were sketching a town scene, the type of day, whether warm, windy, rainy, cold and so on, is not the only component of atmosphere. You would have to capture such things as the mood of the streets, whether busy or quiet, crowded or tree-lined pavements, wind-blown leaves. The atmosphere sketch provides 'the feel of the place', but in general the detail is not there – that may be left to the imagination or put into another sketch.

Fig. 5 *Chichester Cathedral, Sussex*, 290 x 420mm (11½ x 16½in)

THE SPECIFIC SKETCH

I have left the specific sketch until last because in a way it embodies the other three: you must enjoy it, you can collect information, and record the atmosphere. The main difference is that the place and time are usually dictated to you and this means planning.

Before we discuss the specific sketch, let us think about actually leaving home and going out sketching. The most important item is you. You must have enough clothing to be warm. You can't relax and work outside if you are cold. You can always take clothing off to cool down but you can't put more on if you haven't got it with you. Being comfortable is very important.

In painting the Brittany beach the most important element was the planning. Although I was on holiday with my family I knew that I would be doing a specific sketch for this book. We had a villa very close to the beach, and after looking at the beach I decided that this was to be the scene for my sketch. I didn't attempt to do anything the first day because I wanted to get the feel of it and try to decide on the most inspiring view.

I wasn't surprised that the first view that inspired me was the one I finally decided to paint. The only problem I had was the tide. Did I want it in or out? I decided it would be much more interesting to sketch when the tide was out and there would be interest from the rocks and people. For the first sketch (fig. 8) I used a 2B pencil on a cartridge paper sketchbook. I started on the right-hand page with the cliffs and rocks, and progressed over to the left-hand page.

Fig. 6 The photograph I took of the Brittany beach so you can see what changes I made

I had no problem with this sketch, everything went as planned including the group of people to the right playing *boules*. They gave me enough time to sketch them in as a group and I decided to make them the main group on the beach.

The next day I planned to paint the same scene in watercolour to record the colour, and also to paint when the tide was up in case I changed my mind when I got back home and wanted the finished painting that way. It was very hot but a cool breeze was blowing off the land, so we settled down at the back of the beach in shelter. I had just got set up and organized with a board on my knees when within minutes we were surrounded by people setting up camp on the beach with

Fig. 7 *Brittany Beach*, watercolour, 140lb Not surface, 380 x 510mm (15 x 20in)

Fig. 8 My original pencil sketch for *Brittany Beach*, 230 x 580mm (9 x 23in)

sunshades, folding chairs, cane matting, bags and children. It was to be expected – we had found the spot everyone wanted. I couldn't see the water and low rocks, for the suntanned bodies practically on top of my sketchbook! What a start!

There was only one thing to do. Naturally we weren't pleased to have to pack up again and walk in the heat to the middle of the beach. But, once we were settled everything was perfect. I used a sheet of 140lb Not surface watercolour paper and drew in the picture with an HB pencil. The tide was coming in and I left the water line until I was ready to paint the sea. I started with the sky, then worked down the rocks, leaving the paper white where the people were to go

in. Then I painted in the sea which had come up further since I started to draw it. After that I put in the people, the boat and the beach. I took a photograph of the beach (fig. 6) to help you to see what changes I made in the sketches.

When we got back to England and I painted the finished painting (fig. 9) using acrylic (Cryla colours) on canvas, I felt as if I had known that beach all my life. It was a most enjoyable exercise. Some specific sketches can be more demanding, but if all goes well with good planning, they can be very rewarding. You must try a 'specific-sketching' day out, so why not try a beach when you are on holiday, or a local event? Remember: the event won't wait for you, so plan and be ready.

Fig. 9 *Brittany Beach*, acrylic on canvas, 405 x 610mm (16 x 24in)

ELEMENTARY DRAWING AND PERSPECTIVE

You don't need to know all about perspective to be able to paint or sketch a picture. But I believe that if you know the basics of perspective, your sketching will become easier and the result more convincing. Most people are familiar with the terms horizon, eye level and vanishing point, so let us see how they relate to sketching.

When you look out over a landscape, the horizon will always be at your eye level, whether you are on a hilltop or lying flat on the ground. So the horizon is the eye level (E.L.). Inside a room there is no horizon, but you still have an eye level. To find it hold a pencil horizontally in front of your eyes at arm's length and your eye level is the line the pencil makes against the opposite wall. The vanishing point (V.P.) is a point on the horizon where parallel lines travelling away from you would appear to meet, like the way the edges of a road seem to come together in the distance.

To some people perspective comes naturally and to others it is hard work, but unless you are going to draw complicated buildings or large machinery and want a high degree of detail, don't let perspective worry you. You will find you use it (in the sense of drawing diagrams similar to those on the page opposite) very little when you are out sketching. I draw without using perspective guidelines – unless my drawing looks wrong and I can't get it right. Then I go back to the drawing board and check the perspective. If you know a few simple rules you can correct your sketches easily.

UNDERSTANDING PERSPECTIVE

Let's go through a few basic rules so that you know enough about perspective for everyday sketching. When you look at the opposite page please don't let it put you off, just follow the sequence carefully. I drew the diagrams freehand on tracing paper with a Rotring pen, and a felt-tip pen for the thick lines.

At the top of the page I drew the eye level (E.L.). Then I drew a square (fig. 10A) and put a mark to the left at eye level, and used it as my vanishing point (V.P.). The object is to make the square in fig. 10A into a cube. Draw a line from the V.P. to both left-hand corners of the square (fig. 10B), and then do the same to the right-hand corners (fig. 10C). This gives us our two sides.

Draw a line between the top and bottom guidelines parallel to the left side of the square, see points (a) and (b), and this gives you one side of your box (fig. 10D). Then draw a horizontal line from point (a) to link with the guideline on the other side of the box. Do the same again starting at (b) and draw a horizontal line to the lower guideline. Finally

join up the points opposite (a) and (b) with a perpendicular line (fig. 10D). You now have your cube and have succeeded in representing a three-dimensional object (by giving it depth) on a two-dimensional surface (your paper).

PERSPECTIVE IN OBJECTS

In fig. 10E, I have turned the cube into a house, by adding a roof. To find the centre of a square or cube, whatever its proportions, draw two diagonal lines from corner to corner (fig. 10E) and where they converge is the centre. From this point I drew a guideline up to meet another line drawn from the V.P. to the point of the roof. Where these two lines cross is the apex of the roof.

All this has been done looking at a cube side on (showing only one side). In fig 10F the house on the corner has two vanishing points, one on the left and one on the right. The principle is the same as for the first cube you drew, except the lines on both sides of the cube meet at a vanishing point. I have put more buildings into this to show you how a street is built up – two streets in fact, one going to the left and one to the right. The house on the right with the chimney is seen side on, so the other sides aren't shown.

In fig. 10G I have drawn a 'bird's eye view' of the same scene and this has been done by putting the eye level higher the position you would see, for instance, from a window or a bridge. Fig. 10H is just the opposite – the 'worm's eye view'. The eye level is very low, in fact at ground level. Notice how all parallel lines meet at the V.P. and this includes windows, windowsills, doors, gutters, pavements, the line of lampposts.

My way of putting this into practice out sketching (especially if I am doing buildings and man-made objects) is to find my eye level by holding my pencil horizontally at arm's length in front of my eyes. I then draw it in on my sketch pad, position my centre of interest and work from there.

When you do this, hold your pencil at arm's length and let it run down the length of a building or buildings. Take the line of the eaves, say the first house in fig. 10F, and see roughly where it meets your E.L. Then draw that line on to your paper. Again hold your pencil at arm's length, level with the bottom line of the houses, and where it meets the line of eaves is your vanishing point. Then you have a start and you can work everything from that.

As you practise you will learn to 'see' perspective when you are sketching and this page of complicated-looking lines opposite will be a problem of the past.

Fig. 10

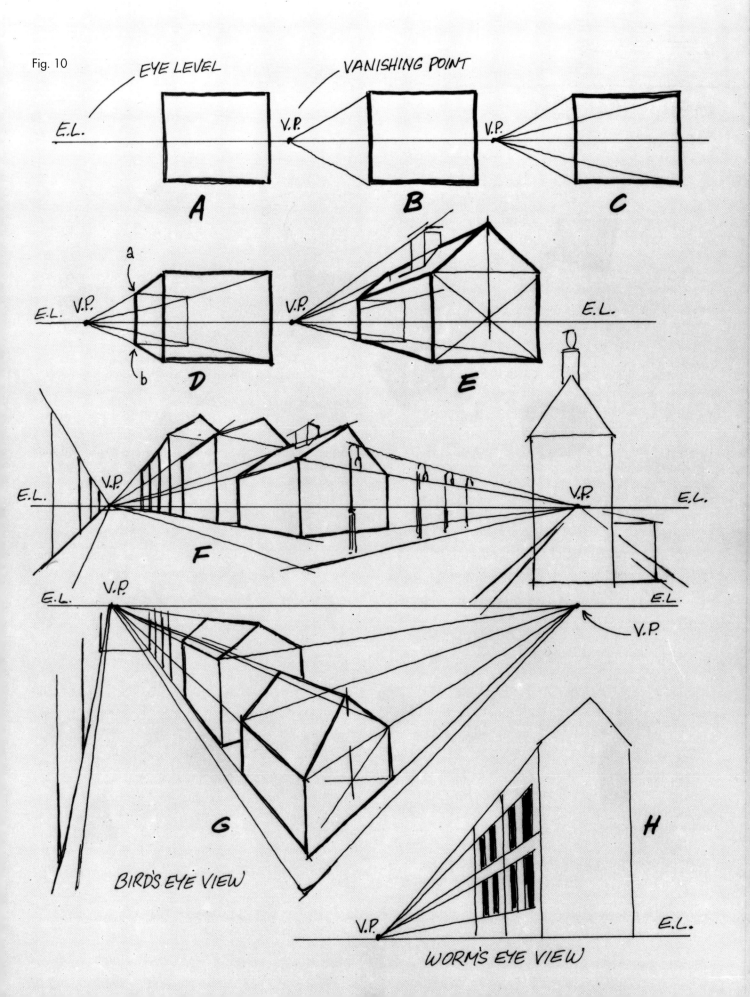

EYE LEVEL

VANISHING POINT

E.L.

V.P.

A

B

V.P.

C

E.L. V.P.

a

b

D

V.P.

E

E.L.

E.L. V.P.

F

V.P.

E.L.

E.L. V.P.

V.P.

E.L.

BIRD'S EYE VIEW

G

H

V.P.

E.L.

WORM'S EYE VIEW

WHAT EQUIPMENT DO YOU NEED?

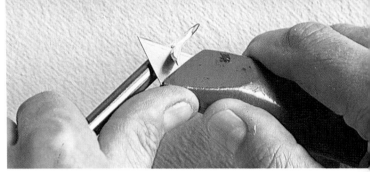

Fig. 11

Sketching equipment can be far less comprehensive than that needed for painting. Some people – and I tend to be one of them – collect a wide variety of different materials, which is all part of being an artist. I have an oil painting palette that I have had since I was at art school, and enough brushes to paint the hull of the QE2. I never seem able to throw away my old equipment, I always think I will find a use for it later. Whatever equipment you get, I suggest you buy the very best you can afford – it makes working easier and you produce better results.

Fig. 12

SKETCHING MATERIALS FOR BLACK AND WHITE

The term black and white usually refers to black as the drawing or painting medium and white as the paper it is worked on. All the materials are listed on this page. On the following pages, I have taken one or two mediums at a time and explained the way to work with them.

The most important piece of equipment is the pencil. We all tend to take the pencil for granted and it is not surprising – we all have one somewhere, and most of us have used one since childhood. A good artist's drawing pencil has 13 different degrees of lead. The middle one, the most common for everyday use, is HB. On the B side the leads become softer and darker as they reach the top of the scale, i.e. B, 2B, 3B, 4B, 5B and 6B (softest); and on the H side the leads become harder and lighter, i.e. H, 2H, 3H, 4H, 5H and 6H (hardest). For general sketching purposes all you need is an HB and 2B. But try out different pencils to see which suit you.

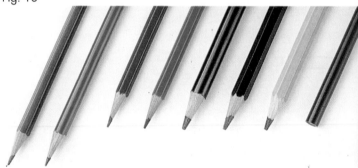

Fig. 13

In fig. 15 you will see the different tones you can produce using HB, 2B and 6B pencils. When you sharpen your pencil (fig. 11), use a sharp knife and cut off controlled positive 'slices', making a long gradual taper to the lead (so you can see the point easily when you are sketching). Fig. 12 shows the first pencil sharpened to a good point and the second pencil sharpened to a flat chisel-shaped end, which is good for shading and making broad strokes. The third pencil is sharpened badly and difficult to draw with – avoid making yours look like this.

Fig. 14

There are two ways of protecting your pencil points when you take them out (see fig. 13). The first is to put them on a piece of thick card or the flat plastic sheet out of a brush holder and secure them with rubber bands; and the other way is to make a cover for the lead out of paper. For

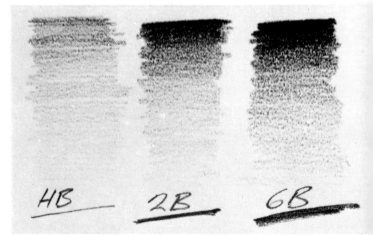

Fig. 15

the illustration I rolled some cartridge paper around the pencil and wound masking tape around it.

Fig. 14 shows a selection of first class Daler-Rowney pencils. I use the No. 804 Victoria. It is an excellent artists' pencil but the choice is as personal as choosing a series of paint brushes. In some pencil ranges, you have a choice of a round or hexagonal shape – some people find hexagonal esier to hold. Series No. 874 Black Beauty (third from right) is an extra thick black pencil (equal to 4B). You can also obtain charcoal pencils (last on right), which are thin sticks of charcoal encased in wood.

CHOOSING YOUR DRAWING MATERIALS

In figs. 16 and 17 are materials you can choose for black-and-white, sketching. If you are just starting don't feel you have to buy everything. You can start – and continue – with only one pencil or pen, and become the best pencil or pen-and-ink artist in the world!

The materials in fig. 16, for our purposes, come under the overall heading of pencils. There are various pencils, charcoal sticks, charcoal pencils, Conté pencils, Conté crayons, a box of pastels with a tonal selection ranging from black through to white, sketchbook, drawing papers, kneadable putty rubber and fixative. Fig. 17 shows materials for sketching in ink: a bottle of black Indian ink, fountain pen ink, pen holder, nibs, palette for diluting ink with water, sable brush, fountain pen, ballpoint pen, Rotring pen, felt-tip pens, sketchbooks and blotting paper.

The size of sketchbook you choose is up to you. I have different sizes for different purposes. If I am going out on a sketching trip or to do a complicated information sketch I take the largest sketchbook I work with, an A3 which is 300 x 420mm ($11^{3}/_{4}$ x $16^{1}/_{2}$ in). I have a smaller one for general use as it's easier to carry and I keep an A5, 145 x 215mm ($5^{3}/_{4}$ x $8^{1}/_{2}$ in) in my car-door pocket, just in case. If there is anything around to inspire me, the sketch pad is always there.

If your pad is too small to rest your hand on, always try to find something to rest the pad on. I have seen students standing up holding a small pad in one hand and drawing with the other, but with nothing to rest their drawing hand on. It is very difficult to draw standing up, but even more so if you can't rest your hand on the drawing surface.

SKETCHING MATERIALS FOR COLOUR WORK

The same principles apply to working in colour as black and white, you can have as many or as few materials as you want.

PASTEL COLOUR

There are over 50 different pastel colours, and each one is available in several tints, making nearly 200 pastels in all. Daler-Rowney pastels are graded from Tint 0 for the palest to Tint 8 for the darkest. The best way to start is to buy a box of 12 or 36 Artists' Soft Pastels for Landscape. I have used the pastels in these two boxes for all the exercises. When you get used to the medium you can buy different tints, colours or refill pastels individually.

Fig. 16 Pencil sketching set

Fig. 17 Ink sketching set

Fig. 18

Fig. 19 shows the basic sketching set for pastel work. The box illustrated contains 12 colours for landscape painting. You will need some paper or a pastel sketch pad with a selection of coloured sheets, plus some fixative, a bristle brush (for rubbing out areas of pastel), a kneadable putty rubber, an HB or 2B pencil and a rag (for cleaning your hands).

WATERCOLOUR

You can buy watercolours in tubes, or in half or whole pans. I do not advise beginners to use tubes because it is difficult to control the amount of paint you get on the brush. You can buy pans individually or in boxed selections. The colours I have used are: Payne's Grey, Burnt Umber,

Hooker's Green No. 1, French Ultramarine, Crimson Alizarin, Yellow Ochre, Coeruleum Blue, Burnt Sienna, Cadmium Red, Raw Umber, Raw Sienna, Cadmium Yellow Pale.

Fig. 20 shows the basic sketching set for watercolour work. You can start with two brushes: a No. 10 and a No. 6 round. Sable hair is the best quality. You need a paintbox to hold 12 whole pans of colour or 12 half pans (the one illustrated holds whole pans), or a small sketching box with its own water container attached (illustrated), which is ideal for putting in your pocket or your handbag. You also need HB and 2B pencils, a kneadable putty rubber (this type will not smudge), a drawing board with watercolour paper or a watercolour sketch pad, blotting paper, a sponge and a

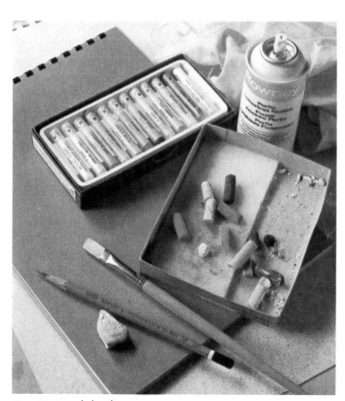

Fig. 19 Pastel sketching set

Fig. 20 Watercolour sketching set

| Bockingford Watercolour | Ingres Pastel | Waterford Rough Surface Watercolour | Waterford Not Surface Watercolour | Waterford Hot Pressed Coloured Pencils |

water jar. I suggest you carry a tube of white paint with your equipment; I use Designers' Gouache.

BRUSHES

In painting, the most important tool that an artist uses is the brush. Like the pencil in a pencil sketch, a brush is used to communicate what you see and will determine how successful you are in conveying it. In the sketching set, I have suggested a No. 10 round and a No. 6 round. Daler-Rowney make various series of brushes suitable for watercolour. Dalon is the brand name for an excellent range of man-made fibre brushes which are less expensive than sable. In fig. 21 there is a selection of brushes to show you the different sizes available. They are all reproduced actual size. All the brushes from size No. 00 to No. 12 are round sable brushes. Some brush series have additional sizes such as Nos. 9, 11 and 14.

Another brush I recommend is the Series 56 Sable and Ox Hair brush, size No. 2, which is ideal for fine line work. Series 270 is a nylon brush and can be used in place of sable if you prefer. The last brush is a Series 63 squirrel hair wash brush, a large flat brush for putting on large watercolour washes.

PAPER

The subject of paper is so broad I cannot give a complete explanation in the limited space available here. To give you

an idea of the basic differences, I have illustrated specific papers in fig. 18 suitable for black and white, and colour work. These are reproduced actual size and I have named the paper and the drawing medium used to help you know what results you can get from different papers.

For pencil work a smooth paper is normally used: cartridge paper which has a slight grain (tooth) is a good all-purpose sketching surface. You can buy all sizes of sketch pads with this paper. A Daler-Rowney sketchbook containing sheets of Ivorex double-sided board with an even smoother surface is ideal for pen, pencils of all kinds, and watercolour washes.

All these papers can be used for colour sketching, but the best watercolour paper is hand made and comes in three distinct surfaces – Rough, Not, and Hot Pressed. The Rough surface paper speaks for itself. The Not surface has a good grain on it (I usually use this one), and Hot Pressed (HP) has a smooth surface. Good watercolour papers are also available in pad form. If you can't get your favourite paper in a pad, buy the paper and cut it to the size you want, then put some sheets on a piece of hardboard and hold them on with clips or rubber bands. Ingres paper is ideal for pastel work and can be bought in various coloured tints in a sketchbook.

Series 63 Squirrel Hair Wash Brush (large flat)
Series 270 Nylon Brush size No. 10
Series 56 Sable and Ox Hair Brush size No. 2

Fig. 21

Round Sable Hair Brushes

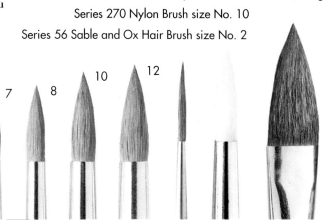

00 0 1 2 3 4 5 6 7 8 10 12

WORKING IN BLACK AND WHITE

PENCIL

Now we can sort out the different mediums available and you will see that your materials can be very simple to carry and don't constitute a tremendous expense. All you need for your basic pencil sketching set are one pencil, a rubber and a sketch pad (fig. 22). This, for me, is the most versatile and pleasing way of sketching. In these photographs I show you how to hold and use your chosen medium. You will see two types of arrow, which are important. The solid black arrow shows the direction of the pencil strokes, and the outline arrow shows the direction in which the pencil is travelling over the paper. I use these arrows throughout the book.

As most of us have used a pencil since childhood, we should have some idea of how to use it! But old habits die hard and all these years we have been holding a pencil for writing. This way of holding it is fine for controlled drawing and careful line work (see the 'short' drawing position shown in fig. 23), but for a more free and flowing movement, especially needed in working the sketch over a large area, you must hold your pencil at least 75mm (3in) from the point and have the pencil at a flatter angle to the paper. This 'long' drawing position will give much more versatility to the pencil strokes (fig. 24).

The 'flat' drawing position shown in fig. 25 is a totally different way of holding your pencil. The pencil is almost flat on the paper, held off by your thumb and first finger, which allows you to touch and move over the surface. This enables you to work in fast broad strokes, using the long edge of the pencil lead to give large shaded areas.

With these three different positions I have described, there are infinite variations. Use them as a base, and learn to work with a pencil all over again. Practise whenever you can, doodle, do anything. Don't worry about drawing, just get used to the pencil and what you can make it create on paper.

On the opposite page are pencil sketches from my sketchbooks that have been put together to form a page of this book. At the bottom of the right-hand side of the page opposite I have doodled to show what the pencil can do. When you practise, try using only three tones – light, medium and dark – with white paper.

Fig. 22 Pencil sketching set

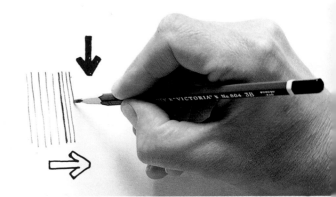

Fig. 23 'Short' drawing position

Fig. 24 'Long' drawing position
Fig. 25 'Flat' drawing position

MIKE

SOVEREIGN MEG

6 MAY SPRING WORKING

DARK
2B pencil

MEDIUM

LIGHT

PRACTICE

Working In Black And White

INK – PEN AND WASH

Pen and ink and pen and wash are two very old and traditional ways of drawing and sketching. Pen and ink simply means using a pen as the drawing instrument. Pen and wash involves using a pen for drawing and a brush for putting on the ink, either undiluted, or diluted with water to enable different tonal values to be applied in wash form over the line pen work. This latter version gives more tonal value to a sketch very quickly. If you use black Indian drawing ink, never put a brush with water into the ink, always use a separate palette (a small round plastic one, for instance). Put a brush full of ink into it and then use your water to thin the ink on the palette. It is really like watercolour painting but using only one colour.

The mapping pen has a nib that gives the finest point and is used universally for fine pen drawing. You can buy various types of drawing nibs, and these are all 'dip-in-ink' pens. This means for sketching you must take with you a bottle of ink, water, and a palette and brush if you intend to work over with wash. You must use waterproof drawing ink if you are applying wash, or the line work you have already done will run when you put watery ink over it.

Experiment with different nibs to start with and get the feel of working with them. Don't be afraid of them, they are more flexible and stronger than you imagine, but if you press hard on an upstroke you could damage the nib. You need a hard-surfaced paper or board for fine nib work. Ivorex board is perfect.

Fountain pens have a less 'scratchy' feel and flow over the board or paper more readily than 'dip-in' pens, and as they have their own ink reservoir, they also have the advantage of not having to be dipped in ink all the time. They can work very well on cartridge paper.

You can buy a type of reservoir pen called Rotring. It is filled with special ink and the nib is a very fine tube, which has a needle valve that controls the flow of ink through the nib. Different grades of nib are available. The only disadvantage is that the pen has to be held upright for it to work properly, but it's worth practising to get used to it.

Fig. 26 shows an ink sketching set, but of course it has variations: 'dip-in-ink' pen, ink and sketchbook; 'dip-in-ink' pen, ink, brush, palette, and water (also take blotting paper and sketchbook); fountain pen and sketchbook; Rotring and sketchbook. The choice is yours.

Fig. 26 Ink sketching set

Fig. 27
Fig. 28

From my Studio Window Feb '82

Seagulls

PARFUMERIE des PORCHES

PEN DARK

MEDIUM

LIGHT

ROTRING

WASH

FROM OTTERY OAK PARK

WORKING IN BLACK AND WHITE

CHARCOAL, CONTÉ PENCIL AND PASTEL

Charcoal is not the medium for the fussy, neat and careful worker. It is for broad adventurous sketching, where one stroke of the charcoal can cover inches of paper to get an effect. It is exciting to use especially for atmosphere sketches of landscape; skies can be put quickly on paper and large masses of landscape can be worked covering your paper rapidly with large tonal areas.

Charcoal can smudge so you will have to practise working with your hand *not* resting on your paper. This is very difficult to get used to, but like all things it is worth trying to get the results you want. You will find that by sketching without resting your hand, your work will become more free and spontaneous, and you can keep detail to a minimum. For some of us this can be one way of getting out of the habit of being too fussy and detail-minded when it isn't required.

Charcoal can be worked on almost any paper, but I suggest you start on cartridge paper. Naturally, work on other surfaces too until you find one that suits you. Charcoal can be bought in different grades, in stick or pencil form. You have more freedom using a stick, because you can use the long edge for broad shading, but a pencil is cleaner and easier to use. Always fix your work with a spray fixative. This will stop it smudging and preserve it for years.

The sketching set in fig. 29 also offers a choice. You can take a charcoal pencil, sketchbook and putty rubber (note: it is not always easy to rub out charcoal), or sticks of charcoal instead of the pencil, or both. Even so, it is a small and easy sketching set to carry. If you have room, take an aerosol can of fixative with you to spray your sketch as soon as it is finished.

Conté pencils also come in sticks and are similar to charcoal but harder, and they can smudge too so be careful. You can buy them in black, white and red. Experiment using white with the black – try a grey paper to work on. You sketching set is simple, pencil or sticks and sketchbook, but as with charcoal, Conté cannot always be rubbed out.

Finally, there is a tonal set of artists' soft pastels on the market ranging from black through five tones to white. Your sketching set is the same as for the coloured pastels, except you don't need coloured paper (page 22 fig. 19).

You can have a lot of fun using these smudgy materials. If you haven't used them before, try them, new worlds may open up to you. But remember – practise.

Fig. 29 Charcoal, Conté pencil and pastel sketching set

Fig. 30
Fig. 31

CHARCOAL

DARK

MEDIUM

LIGHT

CONTÉ

DARK

MEDIUM

LIGHT

Working In Black And White

BALLPOINT AND FELT-TIP PENS

One thing is certain, the old masters didn't use these materials. I wonder what they would have said about them? We shall never know, but they are very good drawing aids for the artist and can be used very well for sketching. The one disadvantage of the ballpoint is that a sketch looks a little mechanical. This is because there is not much variation in the line that is drawn, especially if we compare it with a pencil line. But, look at its advantages. It is inexpensive. You don't have to dip it in ink or fill it. You can get black. You can choose different grades of line (when you buy the pen). If you are miles from anywhere the chances of it not working are remote. You can work with it on almost any surface. You may have one in your pocket anyway, so I like to think of it as a good emergency tool, but not number one.

Felt-tip pens have more character in their lines than the ballpoint and you can get them in all sizes of nib from very fine to very broad. Art supply shops do sell them normally up to approximately 6mm (¼in) wide. These can be used for thin lines as well as thick (figs. 33 and 34), because the nib is usually broad and flat (chisel-shaped).

The normal thin felt-tip pen is used in the same way that a pencil is used and can get good sketching results. I think it should be part of your sketching equipment to be used when the subject or your mood calls for it. Generally you can work with it on any paper that you would with pencil. Remember, there is no rubbing out with a ballpoint or felt-tip pen. This is a good exercise to make you observe the subject well, before drawing any lines on paper. If you draw some lines that are wrong, don't start again; it will give your sketch depth and a feeling of life if you work over them.

A sketching set for this type of work would consist of a ballpoint or felt-tip pen and a sketchbook (fig. 32). My examples are on the opposite page and my doodles are on the bottom right-hand side. Use scrap paper to learn about your drawing tool. Scribble, scratch and scrawl on paper after paper, until you know what you can get from your chosen drawing instrument.

Fig. 32 Ballpoint and felt-tip pens sketching set

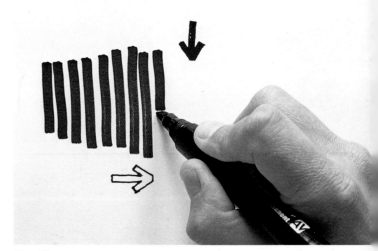

Fig. 33
Fig. 34

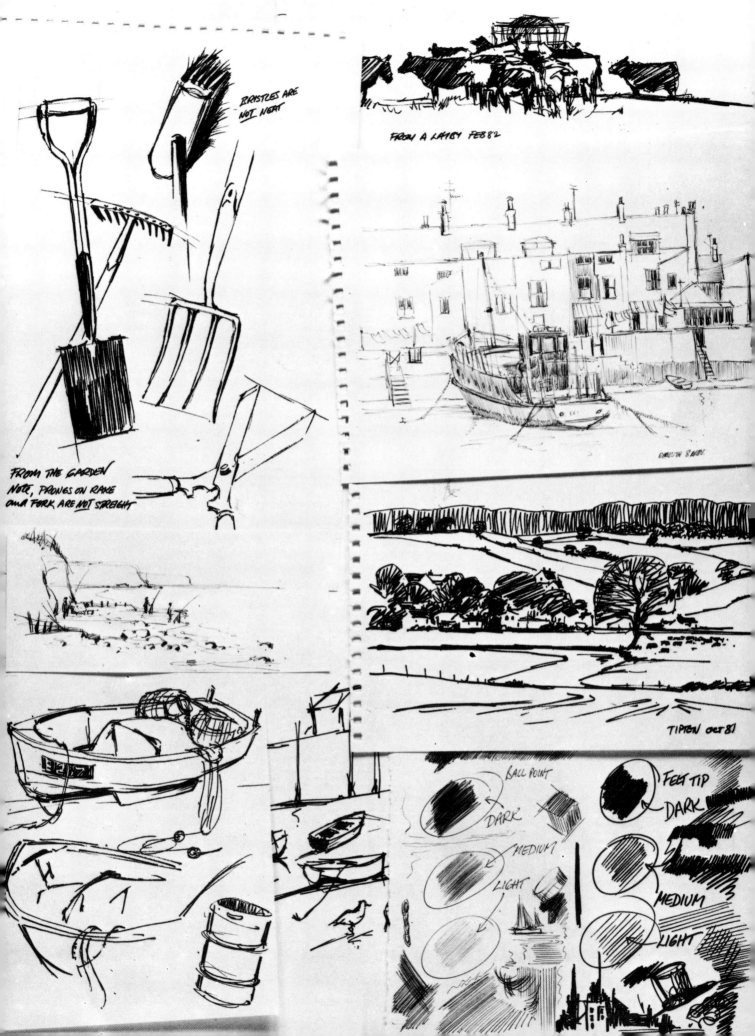

BRISTLES ARE
NOT NEAT

FROM A LAYBY FEB 82

FROM THE GARDEN
NOTE, PRONGS ON RAKE
AND FORK ARE NOT STRAIGHT

TIPTON OCT 81

BALL POINT
DARK
MEDIUM
LIGHT

FELT TIP
DARK
MEDIUM
LIGHT

SIMPLE EXERCISES IN BLACK AND WHITE

Now that you have experimented with black and white sketching materials and are used to them, we can try some very simple exercises. I have done these in stages to show you how I work. The stages are simulated – I have simply drawn them three times from one to three. But in the five exercises starting on page 48 each stage is of the same sketch and was photographed as I drew it, so you can see The exact work that was put into the sketch and how it progressed through to the finish.

The first two exercises here are to help you with broad pencil treatment. Use a 3B pencil held in the 'flat' drawing position to give you broad shading for the tonal work. Start the first exercise by drawing in the line of the field, then put in the buildings (the centre of interest), and follow my stages. Then try the second exercise. Don't labour your pencil work on these exercises, let your pencil work freely, trying for light against dark (strong contrast) with shading. The sketches on these two pages are half as big again as they are reproduced here. Figs. 35 and 36 were done on layout paper.

Fig. 37 I also did on layout paper, but I used a fountain pen to draw with. Let your pen be as free as you like but go through the stages as I did and you will get the 'feel' of how a sketch builds up. You can try any of these sketches with other black and white materials. It will help you to see which subject suits which medium. For instance, it would be difficult to get the atmosphere in the second pencil exercise in fig. 36 if you used a fine-nibbed pen. The sky would be scratchy and difficult to make very black, but with charcoal it would work well.

The last exercise, the hedgerow trees in fig. 38, was done on cartridge paper with a stick of charcoal. As I explained in the section on charcoal, it is for broad adventurous treatment, but this simple sketch shows how it can be used for fine work as well; so it has greater depth than we might at first give it credit for. Work the trees from the bottom upwards and outwards, in the direction of their growth.

These exercises should be useful. They will have made you copy something, which will help you to observe nature when you are out sketching. The more you sketch the more confidence you will have.

Fig. 35

Fig. 36

Fig. 37

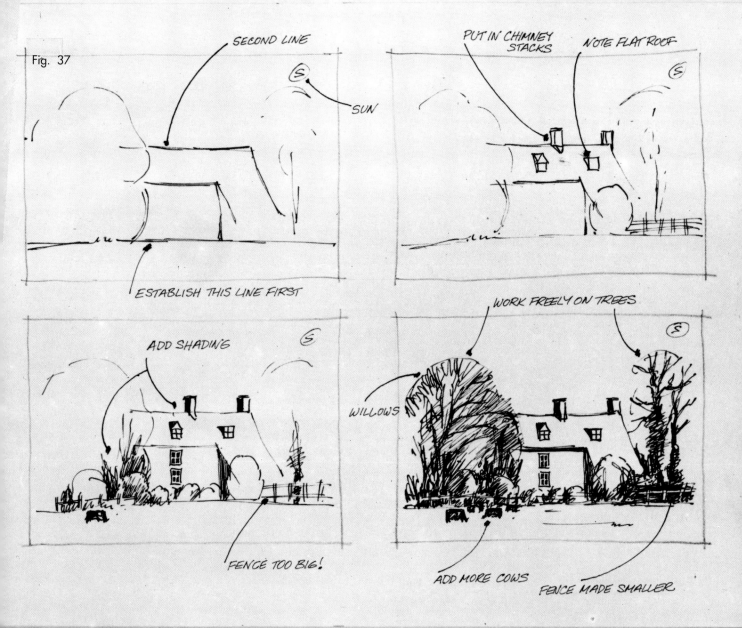

SECOND LINE

PUT IN CHIMNEY STACKS   NOTE FLAT ROOF

SUN

ESTABLISH THIS LINE FIRST

ADD SHADING

WORK FREELY ON TREES

WILLOWS

FENCE TOO BIG!

ADD MORE COWS   FENCE MADE SMALLER

Fig. 38

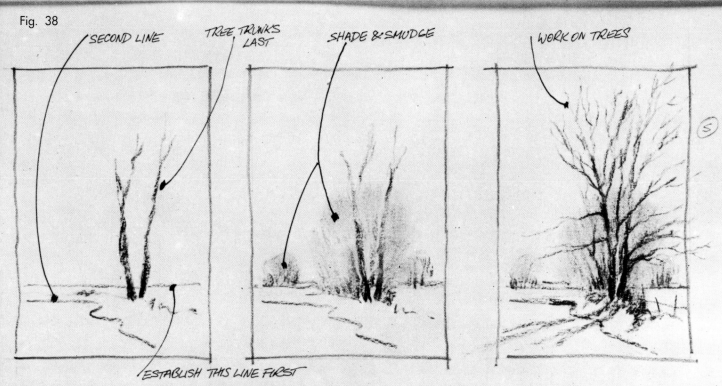

SECOND LINE   TREE TRUNKS LAST   SHADE & SMUDGE   WORK ON TREES

ESTABLISH THIS LINE FIRST

WORKING IN COLOUR

In our sketching we use watercolour and pastel. Over the next few pages I hope to put you on the right road, give you inspiration. Colour is all around us in our daily lives. It can make us happy, it can give the effect of cold, warmth, dark or light, and yet all colours that we paint with can be made up from only three: red, yellow and blue. These are called primary colours. I have two different reds, yellows and blues to give greater scope to our mixing (fig. 40) as they are colours that can't be mixed from others. You will see in fig. 40 that I have mixed primary colours to make other ones.

In watercolour painting you use more water and less paint to make your colours lighter. To make them darker use more paint and less water. I don't use black, only because I was taught not to as it is a dead colour. If you mix a black from primary colours it is much more alive. However many artists do use black, so don't be afraid to use it if you want to, but be careful.

USING WATERCOLOUR

Watercolour is a good medium to learn to paint with. Some students believe oil is better because you can paint over or rub out your 'mistakes'. This is important for the beginner to be able to do, and of course the choice is yours; but I reason that watercolour, although it is difficult to control, is good to start with for two reasons.

First, whether we were artistic or not, most of us were taught to paint with water-based paints at school or even before, usually with poster paint (in jars) or powder paint (in tins, which had to be mixed with water). As both of these types of paint are water-based the materials are cleaned in water too. Many of us will have painted on all kinds of paper, everything from brown wrapping paper to the back of old rolls of wallpaper. So a beginner to painting, at whatever age, does not feel alien to watercolour paints, because at some time he or she will have come into contact with them.

Second, it is a very convenient medium to use indoors to practise with. Getting out a paintbox and working in a corner of a room is relatively easy, and there is no smell. Unfortunately most beginners have never come into contact with oil paint before, so don't know how to apply it to paper or canvas, and it smells of oil and turpentine.

I am asked so many times by potential students, what to start with. My answer is watercolour, if starting from the

Fig. 39

beginning. Once you have got a grounding in colour mixing and brush handling, then try any medium. There is one that will suit your personality and ability more than any other. Try mixing colours to see what you get. The results may surprise you and I think you might find it easier than you thought. The more difficult colours to mix are the subtler ones, and these will only come with practice and observation. At this stage don't worry about shapes, just paint splotches of colour. Doodle as I have done in fig. 39.

When you are out sketching with watercolour, try not to get too involved with subtle colours at first, go for broad areas, using colours that are simple to mix. Time and experience will broaden your colour range. When you are out in the country look into the distance, covering up the foreground fields with your hands. Then look at the foreground fields. The colour in the distance is blue compared to the green of the foreground field. In general, the distance is bluish, and the foreground is warmer and has more real colour. Look at a brick wall or the side of a red-brick house. The colour is there strong and bold. Now look at a brick wall in the distance and the red colour pales to a red-grey.

When you are out look for these colour changes, observe them in your sketches and you will find that the background stays in the distance and the foreground in front; your sketch will have meaning and come to life. In general, to make your colours cooler, add blue, and to make them warmer, add red.

When you practise mixing colours indoors look at the objects around you and try to match the colours. Remember that one colour can look different against another, so if you are painting on white paper and your colour is not quite there (say you were copying the colour of a cushion on a chair) then paint the colour next to the cushion (the chair, for instance) and you will see a difference, and so on.

USING PASTEL

Try working with pastel in the same way, mixing the pastels into each other on paper to get the colours required. As there are so many different shades of pastel you can use, mixing is not so important, but pastels can be mixed on paper to obtain different colours, which makes it a very exciting medium to work with. Fix your pastel paintings when they are finished to stop them smudging.

I suspect most of you haven't tried coloured pencils since you were at school, so why not try them again for sketching? You will find that, to a certain extent, you can mix one colour on top of another to change it. Look at my doodles in fig. 39.

Finally to be able to paint your sketches, you have to train yourself to observe colour, and to be able to mix the colours observed. This can't be done overnight, but with practice (make it enjoyable – don't labour your practice sessions) you will find it will come right and, probably, sooner than you think.

Fig. 40

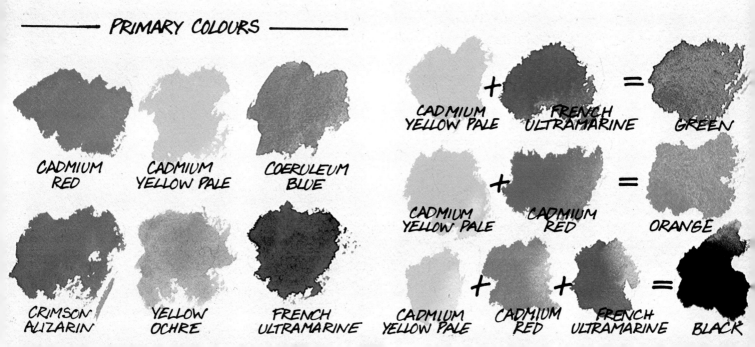

PRIMARY COLOURS

CADMIUM RED   CADMIUM YELLOW PALE   COERULEUM BLUE

CRIMSON ALIZARIN   YELLOW OCHRE   FRENCH ULTRAMARINE

CADMIUM YELLOW PALE + FRENCH ULTRAMARINE = GREEN

CADMIUM YELLOW PALE + CADMIUM RED = ORANGE

CADMIUM YELLOW PALE + CADMIUM RED + FRENCH ULTRAMARINE = BLACK

SIMPLE EXERCISES IN COLOUR

Now that you have practised colour mixing and doodling, you will be ready to try some simple exercises. Don't let the exercises on these two pages worry you because they have shape and form, and seem a far cry from the coloured shapeless doodles you have been working on so far. For instance, if you look at the small rowing boat on the opposite page, the first stage is a shapeless doodle of two colours and the second stage only gets its boat-shape by adding one darker tone in the correct places. This comes from observation of your subject, but you can see how to simplify objects and still make them appear three-dimensional.

Take this a little further and look at the wheelbarrow below the boat. As you gain confidence you will find that you can put the second tone in (the shadow side of the wheelbarrow) as you paint in the first stage. In other words, you would paint in the light area on two sides and then paint in the other two sides with a darker tone. In this way you miss out a stage. When you are painting complicated subjects you will find that this happens throughout the picture. If you find short cuts that enable you to work better, use them. Concentrate on working simply at first. This is especially important when you are out sketching.

ATMOSPHERE AND DETAIL

Look at fig. 41. This is basically an atmosphere sketch. I worked in flat washes from the sky to the foreground. I added the shadows at the end at home to show how they create the illusion of the flatness of the ground. As you can see I used only three colours for mixing in this exercise, but I decided to use a fourth, Cadmium Red, just for the London buses on the bridge. I worked on a sheet of watercolour paper with a Not surface. The sketches on the opposite page were done on cartridge paper and all those in this chapter were painted half as large again as they are reproduced here.

The sketch of the church (fig. 42 on page 38) was done with coloured pencils on tracing paper. Only three colours and black were used; and the black was used only to tone down some of the colours and to add detail giving the sketch depth. I used pastel on layout paper for the sketch in fig. 43. When I painted in the cows I smudged them together with my finger and picked out more detail at the next stage. I added the sky and rubbed gently over the distant fields.

Fig. 41

YELLOW OCHRE
CRIMSON ALIZARIN

FRENCH ULTRAMARINE
CRIMSON ALIZARIN, YELLOW OCHRE

YELLOW OCHRE
FRENCH ULTRAMARINE

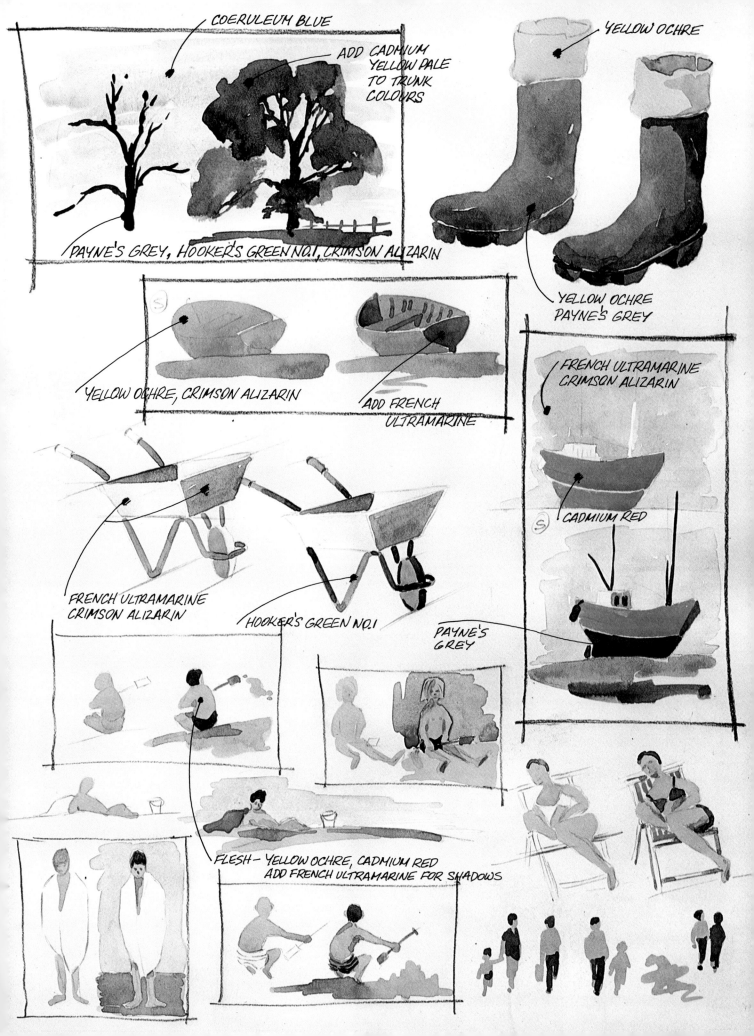

COERULEUM BLUE

ADD CADMIUM
YELLOW PALE
TO TRUNK
COLOURS

YELLOW OCHRE

PAYNE'S GREY, HOOKER'S GREEN NO.1, CRIMSON ALIZARIN

YELLOW OCHRE
PAYNE'S GREY

YELLOW OCHRE, CRIMSON ALIZARIN

ADD FRENCH
ULTRAMARINE

FRENCH ULTRAMARINE
CRIMSON ALIZARIN

CADMIUM RED

FRENCH ULTRAMARINE
CRIMSON ALIZARIN

HOOKER'S GREEN NO.1

PAYNE'S
GREY

FLESH — YELLOW OCHRE, CADMIUM RED
ADD FRENCH ULTRAMARINE FOR SHADOWS

For the sketch in fig. 44, I worked on watercolour paper with a very rough surface and with a pale yellow ochre colour. I used only three watercolours and eventually finished off the sketch with a fountain pen.

In fig. 45 I used cartridge paper again. It is important to get used to working watercolour on cartridge paper, as often you may be in a position to draw a sketch in pencil on cartridge paper and then want to add notes in watercolour.

I have worked very freely with this sketch, but there would be enough information for me to work a larger picture from it in the studio. Never forget that you decide what your needs are for an information or an atmosphere sketch. We all see and feel differently about nature. When you sketch outside, never throw any bad drawings away, they will always tell you something, even if it's how not to do it again. Every artist does some bad sketches.

Fig. 42

Fig. 43

Fig. 44

FRENCH ULTRAMARINE
CRIMSON ALIZARIN
YELLOW OCHRE

CRIMSON ALIZARIN
YELLOW OCHRE

FOUNTAIN PEN LINES

YELLOW OCHRE, FRENCH ULTRAMARINE

YELLOW OCHRE, CRIMSON ALIZARIN

Fig. 45

COERULEUM BLUE
CRIMSON ALIZARIN

ADD YELLOW OCHRE

YELLOW OCHRE
COERULEUM BLUE, CRIMSON ALIZARIN

FRENCH ULTRAMARINE
YELLOW OCHRE, CRIMSON ALIZARIN

SAME COLOURS AS SKY

LET'S START SKETCHING

We have now arrived at what I consider to be the most important section in the book: how to start a sketch. I have discussed already how to find your spot and what materials to take with you, so let us assume you are settled down with your subject in front of you and you are ready to put pencil to paper.

First decide what type of sketch you are going to do. The next step can save a lot of time and frustration. If you were to sketch your own living room, you would be very familiar with it and would understand everything you see because you know it. So, sit on your stool, look at the scene in front of you, and observe. If there are areas that you can't understand, or you can't see properly, move around to different viewpoints until you are familiar with what you are about to draw. This could take up to 15 minutes depending on how complicated the subject is, but that time used correctly is the most important part of your sketch.

MEASURING YOUR SUBJECT

At this point you might understand everything you see, but how do you work out the relative sizes and positions of objects in your scene, and transpose them accurately on to your paper? If you learn how to 'measure' now, and it is the only technique you learn from this book, then that alone will have made both your and my efforts worthwhile. It is a very important skill to acquire. Although to start with you may find measuring tedious, or perhaps feel it is a little mechanical, it will become second nature and is as much a part of sketching as putting pencil to paper. So how do we do it?

The principle is simple. Hold your pencil at arm's length, vertically for vertical measuring and horizontally for horizontal measuring, with your thumb along the near side as your 'measuring' marker (figs. 46 and 47). Always keep your pencil at the same distance from your eye during measuring, or the comparative distances will not be consistent. This is why it is always held at arm's length – it is easy to find the same position.

Now the object of the exercise is to measure the subject and apply it to your paper. Obviously you do not use the same length to measure your actual subject as you do for the subject on your sketch. You are simply trying to get the correct proportions; so let me take you through an example (fig. 49). Draw a part of your sketch, say house no. 3, on to your paper (fig. 49A). Now you want to get the houses from

Fig. 46

Fig. 47

1 to 7 on your sketch as they appear in reality. Hold up your pencil to measure house no. 3 and as you move your hand along, see how many times the pencil goes into the length of the seven houses. It goes nine times. Check your sketch (fig. 49A) and using your pencil on the paper as a ruler, see whether the length of the house no. 3 you have drawn will go along your paper nine times.

In fig. 49A it only goes about five times. So draw a smaller house on the same sketch (fig. 49B) and by simple trial and error you will come to the size of house that will be in proportion to the rest of your picture.

Then holding up the pencil to the real houses, measure how many times house no. 3 goes into houses nos. 1 and 2. You will find they are all the same size. Therefore, on your sketchbook, you can measure from left to right, three houses, the third being no. 3, which is our key measure (fig. 49C).

Looking up at your subject again measure house no. 3 into house no. 4. It goes twice. On your sketch, using your pencil as a ruler, and your thumb as a marker (the same procedure as for measuring your real subject) measure a distance twice as long as house no. 3 to the right of it, and you have the correct size for house no. 4. Carry on in this way until you have your row of houses from 1 to 7 and they will fit your sketchbook exactly (fig. 49D).

Now, to check the height of the houses, measure the width of house no. 3 and turn your pencil vertically, with your thumb still in position, and see how many times the width of the house goes into the height. It fits exactly once, up to the bottom of the eaves. Therefore, on your sketch, using your no. 3 house measure and mark in the height of the houses (fig. 49E). Then check the height of the roofs and so on.

If you take time to do this, you can put as much detail and work into the houses as you want, knowing that your drawing will fit your sketch pad and will be proportionally correct. If you use this method objects can be placed in the right position on your drawing and in the right position in relation to each other.

Let us take a real example (fig. 48). My first key measure would be the stern of the right-hand boat. It goes across the picture approximately six times. You can see the main features that are the same size as the key measure. I also found a half-size key measure (which helps for other measurements), which here is one of the roofs. Put your important subjects into position by measuring and as you draw the rest they should fit into place correctly.

When you are measuring don't be too rigid. If an area of your subject measures a key measure and a bit, then draw it on your sketch the size of a key measure and a bit.

If I were to show you how to do this it would take only five minutes, but to have explained it in writing may make it seem very complicated to you. Please read it over and over again, until you understand the method, and then practise. Try it when you are sitting at home, you will soon get used to it. Frequent practice will train your eye to see the size of objects in relation to each other and to be able to place them on your sketch pad correctly.

Fig. 48 An example of the use of key measures in working out the correct proportions of your sketch

Fig. 49

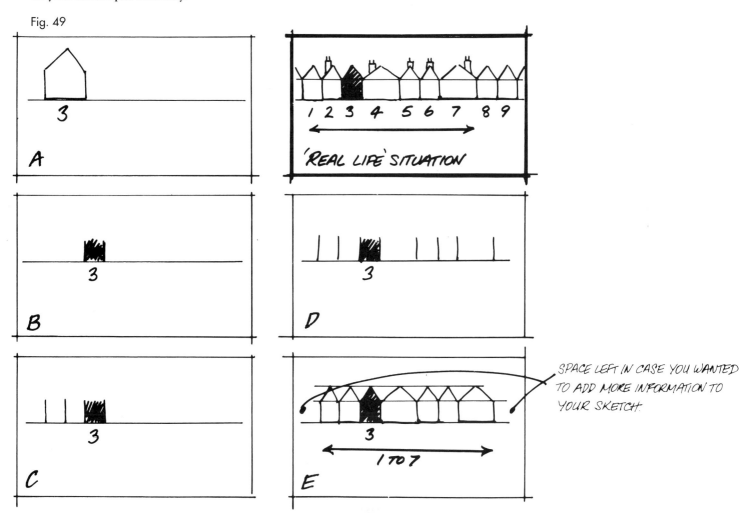

A Sketch Step By Step

Now that you know how to start a sketch, let's go through the development of a simple sketch to see how it works. At this stage you have observed your subject, you are sitting or standing comfortably, you know the type of sketch you are going to do, you can measure, and finally you have decided what your centre of interest is.

First look at stage 9, the completed sketch, to familiarize yourself with the picture. The sketch was taken from nature, but the sequence of stages was done in my studio to explain, simply, the progress of a sketch. I used a fountain pen on layout paper and each sketch is 150 mm (5³⁄₄in) wide.

The first line to draw is the line of the main field. Position this near the centre of the page, then you can add more foreground or sky later. I wanted this picture to be long and thin, as it was the long line of the farm buildings which inspired me.

In stage 2 position your buildings (the centre of interest) and draw them in stage 3. Now in stage 4, complete the buildings, emphasizing the lower part of them so they don't appear to float off the hill, and draw in the new field.

In stage 5, put in the background hills. Draw the tree in stage 6 and if you look at my sketch, I have drawn two more lines across, one above the buildings and one below. This gives you the long shape of the picture dominated by the row of buildings.

It is wise to add more information if you have the time and this I did in stage 7. Stage 8 shows the paths extended and the gate and fence drawn in. This could make a 'happy' well-designed picture with the path leading you to the centre of interest.

The completed sketch in stage 9 has got only a little more work in than the previous stage, but I have shown a different picture shape by cutting the sketch off just above the tree. So this one sketch can make three different picture shapes; stages 6, 8 and 9.

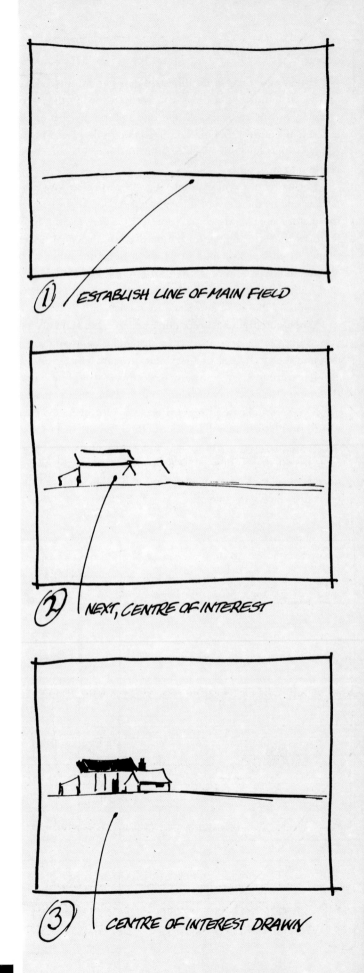

① ESTABLISH LINE OF MAIN FIELD

② NEXT, CENTRE OF INTEREST

③ CENTRE OF INTEREST DRAWN

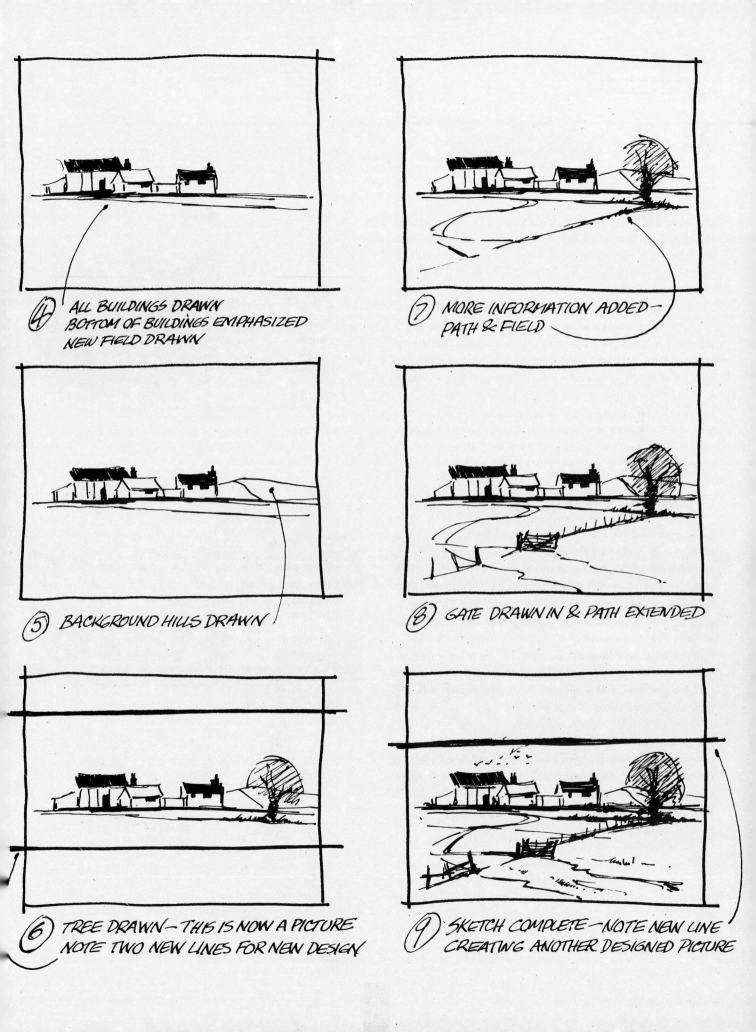

④ ALL BUILDINGS DRAWN
BOTTOM OF BUILDINGS EMPHASIZED
NEW FIELD DRAWN

⑦ MORE INFORMATION ADDED –
PATH & FIELD

⑤ BACKGROUND HILLS DRAWN

⑧ GATE DRAWN IN & PATH EXTENDED

⑥ TREE DRAWN – THIS IS NOW A PICTURE
NOTE TWO NEW LINES FOR NEW DESIGN

⑨ SKETCH COMPLETE – NOTE NEW LINE
CREATING ANOTHER DESIGNED PICTURE

When Is A Sketch Finished?

You stop working on a sketch when you feel you have been drawing long enough, whether it's because you're tired, hungry, cold or just bored with the subject. You are sketching to enjoy yourself (unless it is a sketch that you have to do). If the enjoyment goes, then start another one or go home. This is sound advice if you are tired.

On one occasion I had been sketching for most of the day by a river estuary, I was feeling very tired, a little cold and ready to go home, when a group of boats caught my eye. I thought they would make a perfect group and decided to do a 'quick' sketch – the last one before going home. Well the result was disastrous. You can see it on the opposite page (fig. 53). I still can't make sense of it even now. It went wrong because I had tried to work fast. There is nothing wrong with that, but my brain was tired and didn't observe. I drew it without 'seeing'. Unless you observe, your drawn lines become meaningless.

The two watercolour sketches in figs. 50 and 51 were both done on 140lb Not surface watercolour paper, 380 x 510mm (15 x 20in). The one in fig. 52 was worked on Bockingford paper from a sketch pad, 305 x 405mm (12 x 16in). It was done very freely but I still have enough information to work from. For watercolour, I call fig. 52 a pure sketch, while the other two turned from a sketch into a painting. In the pencil sketch in fig. 54, I have made the distance work for me, but the middle distance and foreground are confusing. This is because I used shading over the drawing. I should have stopped work on that sketch before I shaded the foreground.

The sketch in fig. 55 is ideal. It is open pencil work and I have left the wintery trees unfinished so I could get information onto the sketch of what was going on behind them. I made colour notes on the sketch and would be very happy to work from it in the studio to paint a picture. The sketch in fig. 56 is what I consider to be my normal information sketch, which has line work and tonal shading.

You can see from my examples, on one of them I didn't put enough work (fig. 53); in another (fig. 54) I put too much work (shading); and with the other two pencil sketches, I was very happy. As with the watercolours, two look like pictures, and one like a sketch. You may prefer the less painted one – it is really a matter of personal preference as to how 'finished' you like them. As a rule of thumb, you stop when you have got the information on paper that you are after.

Fig. 50

Fig. 51

Fig. 52

Fig. 53

Fig. 54

Fig. 55

FROM OTTERY CAR PARK. 1982

Fig. 56

NOTES ON SKETCHING MOVEMENT

When you are learning to sketch you must think that there are enough complications sketching something stationary without trying something that moves. So let us take the important stages of drawing a sketch and see how they work for a moving subject. First, you have your subject, you are seated or standing comfortably, and you know the type of information you are looking for. The next stage is to observe and understand your subject.

If anything, this is even more important for capturing movement. Measuring is important, but it can be very frustrating; particularly when, for instance, you measure the length of a horse's head to see how many times it goes into the body length, and then the horse changes position.

I have tried to think whether I have a magic formula that I use when I draw a moving subject, but unfortunately the answer is no. Nevertheless, there are certain ways of approaching your subject that will enable you to master this part of sketching. The most important priorities are practice and self-control, followed by observation and understanding of your subject.

TAKING TIME TO OBSERVE

Assume you are sketching heavy horses. You must look at them and study their most outstanding features. You will find they stand still for minutes at a time. Look for the obvious key positions of their anatomy. Where does a foreleg start, and how long is it compared to the depth of the body, and so on. So you are measuring and positioning through observation, before you start to draw.

Your observation could last anything from half an hour to an hour. It's up to you, but don't 'draw with your eyes' for too long or you will find it much more difficult to actually start sketching. When you do begin, don't try to go faster than you are capable of working. Carry on at your own speed, observing carefully. If your subject moves, stop and start with another. You may find that your subject regains its original position, or that another horse takes up the same attitude so you can carry on your sketch using a different model! Never worry that you don't finish one horse completely. You are learning by observing and when you sketch as well, you record what you see. This combination of activities will quickly give you a good knowledge of your subject.

Naturally the more you do, the more your sketches will flow, particularly as you learn more about your subject. If I were to sketch horses for, say, two hours, I would start by spending half an hour wandering around looking and observing, soaking in the atmosphere. The next 20 minutes I would spend sketching. The chances are it would not be very good, but I would be loosening up, relaxing and getting the 'feel' of the subject. For the next hour I would work very hard, oblivious to my surroundings, completely involved with what I am drawing. It is from this time that the real information would come. If my sketches worked out I would be pleased and then my concentration would start to lapse. The results of the last ten minutes or so sketching would resemble those of the first 20 minutes.

PRACTISING SKETCHING MOVEMENT

If the horses are walking, observe them, and then draw. You will notice the shapes that keep recurring as they move, and your drawn lines will be dictated by what you have observed. This sounds easy, but if you don't practise it will be very difficult. This applies to virtually any moving subject.

One way of training your eye to retain an image long enough to draw its shape reasonably well, is to sketch movement from your television screen. This is difficult, but it can be done. You won't finish anything and your sketchbook may seem to be filled with unsatisfactory work, but these sketches are simply a means to an end. They are a way of training your brain to work and observe faster than normal. You will learn to look for and see things that hadn't occurred to you before, and you will need to see in seconds how to simplify shape and form.

People on the beach are interesting subjects to sketch, and you can usually do it in warmth and comfort! When sketching movement it is useful to remember my rules: be patient, observe, look for simple shapes and forms, work your speed up, and practise, practise and practise!

Opposite are pages from my sketchbooks to show you the type of finish I need for my information. They were not done especially for this book. In fact, the middle pages representing people on the beach were done years ago. The horses at the top were my third page of sketches done at a ploughing match. The chickens were quick information sketches; and the figures at the bottom right-hand side were done on a family holiday in Brittany, when we went picking mussels off the rocks.

18 MARCH 79 · SHACKLEFORD   A3 GUILDFORD

BOURNEMOUTH
BEACH
AUG. 76.

31 JAN 82
OTTERTON MILL

First stage

Second stage

Third stage

EXERCISE ONE
PENCIL

On the following pages I have taken five subjects and worked each one through its progressive stages for you to follow and copy. I have sketched these in my own style and it is the way I work. You may find your own way which is easier for you. I have stressed throughout the book, we are individuals and have our own method of doing things. Initially you need guidance in a certain direction to know whether it suits you or not. But when you have more experience you can find your own natural method.

All these exercises I sketched first outside on location, and then sketched in the studio, stopping at each stage so they could be photographed. Thus, the progression of stages is a true one. It is important for you to know the actual size of the sketch (not of the reproduction) so you understand its relative scale and the type of paper used; these are indicated under the finished stage. In each exercise a detail of the finished sketch is reproduced actual size showing how I drew or painted a particular part.

FIRST STAGE

Establish the main distant field by drawing a line across the paper with a 3B pencil. Put in the line of hills in the distance, and the river. Draw in the rear field line, the path, the willow trees on the left bank, and the dark tree in the middle distance to the right of the willow. Throughout the first and second stages hold your pencil in the 'long' position.

SECOND STAGE

Shade in the distant hills and work from left to right on the trees in the middle distance, starting with the dark tree on the right side of the willows. When you come to the willow on the right-hand side of the river bank, draw in its shape. Let your pencil wander around applying different pressures to form and shape the trees, shading and keeping your lines very free.

THIRD STAGE

Still working with the pencil in the 'long' position, shade the willows in the direction of growth of the leaves and branches, working from the bottom upwards. Keep the shading light where the dark middle distance tree shows against the willow. Darken the trunks with your pencil in the 'short' position, and add the shadow underneath.

Finished stage

Cartridge paper, 290 x 420mm (11½ x 16½ in)

Now work very lightly to suggest the trees left of the willow. With your pencil in the 'long' position again, draw in the willow on the right-hand side of the river and the cows in the middle distant field. (As cows move around, normally I would put in the cows whenever they fit well into my sketch, not necessarily at this particular stage.)

FINISHED STAGE

At this stage put in any detail you want, and give form to certain areas. For instance, draw in some grass on the left-hand bank coming down to the river and darken the far bank where the river bends to the left. Most of this work is done with the pencil in the 'short' position. Now draw in the gate, fence and signpost. Shade in the reflections in the river with downward strokes and then drag your pencil across the river to give the impression of movement. Finally, add grass detail, darken the edge of the river and the path, and shade in the clouds.

EXERCISE TWO
CHARCOAL

First stage

Second stage

Third stage

I have come to like charcoal more and more, but in my experience it is most suitable for landscapes, which is why I have chosen hedgerow trees for this exercise. It makes nature seem undefined, and yet complete. This exercise is very simple and only took about half an hour to sketch, but I hope it will show you the beauty of charcoal drawing. I used a charcoal stick about 50mm (2in) long. Hold your sticks in the 'short' and 'flat' pencil positions. The 'long' position could break the stick.

In the charcoal sketching set, I didn't illustrate a fixative spray as the attraction of charcoal is the simplicity of the equipment. As a compromise I keep one in the car, so that when I have finished sketching I can spray my sketches before setting off home.

FIRST STAGE
First establish the line of the hill, the road and then the background trees. Start the trees from the bottom upwards, drawing the branches in the direction in which they grow.

SECOND STAGE
Now draw in the large foreground tree by scrubbing the stick up and down the trunk to get the density you want; you will find that the cartridge paper grain helps in giving 'bark' texture to the trunk. Work the branches outwards in

the direction of growth, then put shading to the right of the tree to bring in some shadow.

THIRD STAGE
This stage introduces one of the delights of charcoal – smudging. It enables you to get tone over large areas and by working on the area and adding more charcoal, you can build up the tonal work and get plenty of depth into your sketch. Now, for the hedgerow trees, use your first finger to smudge the background trees together and, in places, smudge over the front tree. If you find the tone needs to be darker then draw more charcoal over the trees and blend it in. It only takes seconds to get from stage two to stage three, but notice the depth and atmosphere you have achieved in those few seconds.

FINISHED STAGE
Draw the background trees again, daintily, over the original ones. Try dragging the stick across the paper to get a slightly different branch effect. Then draw in the main tree and add more branches, working some of them over the smudged area. As you do this, you will see how the smudged area recedes and the main tree seems to come forward. Add the shadows across the road, put in some accents on the road edge and, finally, draw in the fence.

Finished stage

Cartridge paper, 225 x 180mm (9 x 7in)

First stage

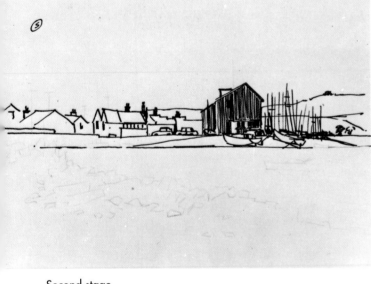

Second stage

Third stage

EXERCISE THREE
PEN

This sketch was done at Exmouth. I like the estuary area very much for painting and I have sketched it quite a few times in many different moods. Variety is one of the great advantages of an estuary; the scene is constantly changing with the tide going in and out and boats changing positions – always plenty of activity.

FIRST STAGE

In this exercise we start from the centre of interest. Locate the water level on your paper and draw it in with your pen. You can draw the main parts of the sketch with your pencil first, but if you feel confident, try using a pen straightaway. Next draw in the top of the quay and the boathouse, and shade it with downstrokes of the pen. Then draw in the boats in front of the boathouse.

SECOND STAGE

Draw in the hills in the background and the water line to the right of the boathouse, then the houses to the left and the cars. Working to the right of the boathouse, create an impression of an untidy group of boats by letting your pen move freely. Draw in the masts, making sure you put them at different angles, some straight, some leaning (see the detail opposite reproduced actual size).

THIRD STAGE

Now draw in the rocks at the edge of the water. Start at the top left-hand side and work down to the bottom right. Shade in the rocks as you work and keep most of them dark against the water. As you work down, put in the three figures when you come to them.

FINISHED STAGE

Draw in the telegraph poles on the quay, the yacht masts, people on the quay and the little boats at the edge. Now shade in the distant hills and draw in the foreground boat. Treat the reflections very freely, working the pen in horizontal strokes, backwards and forwards. For the boathouse reflections, masts and telegraph pole, move the pen line vertically, starting at the top and working in a free wiggly stroke downwards. Add a few horizontal strokes to the left of the boathouse to give the impression of water movement. Finally, put a little more work into the beach and rocks.

Finished stage

Ivorex board, 170 x 245mm (6³/₄ x 9 ³/₄in)

First stage

Second stage

Third stage

EXERCISE FOUR
WATERCOLOUR

It was late afternoon at Widecombe in the Moor, the sun was going down over the hills and that misty half light that seems to merge shapes and create mysterious silhouettes was descending. I was inspired to sketch this scene by the outline of the tree against the church.

FIRST STAGE

First draw the picture with an HB pencil. Wet the sky area down to the roof tops with clean water using a No. 10 sable brush. Mix a wash of French Ultramarine and Crimson Alizarin. Work this into the sky first and as you work down, add a little Yellow Ochre. Then add Cadmium Yellow Pale and paint over the hill and down to the roof tops.

SECOND STAGE

When the sky is dry, use the same brush and a mix of the same colours to paint in the distant fields on the right-hand side and the houses just below. Still using the same colours, only stronger (by mixing more pigment and less water), paint in the church steeple. Start at the top and work down. Change your mix of colours as you paint, to give it some life.

Work left and right of the steeple painting in the houses. Don't paint over the windows, leave the paper showing through. While this is still wet, add some Hooker's Green No. 1 to your colour and paint in the grass in front of the church, allowing it to touch the wet paint and run in places.

THIRD STAGE

With your No. 6 sable brush, mix French Ultramarine, Crimson Alizarin and Yellow Ochre, and paint in the wall. Try to paint the wall stone by stone and leave white areas showing through.

Mix Hooker's Green No. 1 with your colour and paint in the grass verge, and with a little Yellow Ochre and Crimson Alizarin put in the road. Mix French Ultramarine, Crimson Alizarin, Yellow Ochre and Hooker's Green No. 1 to make a strong dark tone and work in the tree at the back. Work from the bottom and keep the paint wet as you move up the trunk and out to the branches. While the paint is still wet, drag a dry brush back into the branches to give the feathery effect of small branches (see the detail opposite). Paint in some additional small branches with the tip of your brush. When the whole tree is nearly dry, start the main tree using the same paint but darker. Repeat the process and work over the tree at the back.

Finished stage

Watercolour paper 140lb Not, 265 x 370mm (10½ x 14½in)

FINISHED STAGE

Mix Hooker's Green No. 1, Yellow Ochre, Crimson Alizarin and a touch of French Ultramarine, and with your No. 6 sable

brush paint in the foreground field, leaving the fence as white paper. Next paint in the windows using the same colours except for Hooker's Green No. 1, and paint little blobs to suggest window panes. Put more work into the wall, by drawing some stones with your brush, using the same colour as for the window panes. Now work on the foreground tree again, making it darker, and put in more small branches. Using dark colour, put shadows on the white fence and signpost and add accents where you need definition. Finally, using French Ultramarine, Crimson Alizarin and Yellow Ochre, paint in the tree's shadow.

55

First stage

Second stage

Third stage

EXERCISE FIVE
PASTEL

When you are out sketching, a scene like this farm on the moors can easily be overlooked. If the sun is out and everywhere is bathed in bright light, the farm can look flat and uninteresting. If it is a dull overcast day, then you could miss the farm altogether as it would merge into the grey background. The best time to see it is when there is sun around with clouds casting large shadows over the moorland, adding drama to the picture. A sunlit scene of this kind does not stay like that for very long – anything from one to 10 minutes. However, the clouds are moving all the time so soon you would see almost the same effect again. Once you have been inspired, start your sketch and catch the effect you want. Try to train yourself to remember the scene, and the more you sketch the easier it will be.

FIRST STAGE

Draw in the main features with a 2B pencil. (If you were outside and working quickly, you might find you could go straight in with pastel, without doing any pencil drawing.) Using Yellow Ochre Tint 2 on its side (the long edge) paint over the sky area in broad strokes from left to right. In the same way paint Cobalt Blue Tint 2 over the top, leaving the area by the road clear, and smudge the colours together with your finger. Now with Green Grey Tint 6 paint in the distant hills and draw in the hedges of the fields and road.

SECOND STAGE

Work Burnt Umber Tint 4 on to the distant hills and rub it in with your finger. Now work in the fields down to the farm, using first a little Yellow Ochre Tint 2 and then Sap Green Tint 3 on the distant fields, applying it more strongly down towards the farm. Rub in the colours to tone down the area. Next paint in the farm roofs with Purple Grey Tint 4, and work over the shadow side (on the right – the sun is left) with Green Grey Tint 6.

THIRD STAGE

Paint in the sunlit walls of the buildings with Yellow Ochre Tint 2, and use Green Grey Tint 6 to shade in the dark wall in front of the buildings. With the same colour, paint in features of the farm such as chimneypots, windows, doors, and the trees on the left-hand side. Then smudge in the trees with your finger.

Finished stage

Ingres paper, 265 x 370mm (10½ x 14½in)

Paint the foreground field using Lizard Green Tint 3 up to the shadow area, then work in some Burnt Umber Tint 4 up to the farm wall and into the green field. Smudge some Green Grey Tint 6 into the farm building here and there, and into the field on the left.

Now with Burnt Umber Tint 4 paint in the field behind the farm on the right-hand side. With Green Grey Tint 6 paint in the hedges, smudging some of the colour across the field. Finally put the telegraph poles in the background.

FINISHED STAGE

Using Yellow Ochre Tint 2 paint in the road, from distance to foreground, and smudge it in to tone it down. With Green Grey Tint 6 create the shadow on the foreground field. Next paint in the shapes of the buildings, telegraph poles and trees in the foreground with Ivory Black and add a little to the shadow area of the field. Use the black in various places on the farm buildings to crispen them up and, finally, paint the sunlit patches on the road with Yellow Ochre Tint 2.

USING YOUR SKETCHES AT HOME

One of the rewards of having sketches that have been drawn outside is that you can use them to work on larger paintings at home. There are many reasons for not being able to go out to sketch. The most obvious is the weather, or more frustrating, the car won't start! Whatever the reason, if your sketchbooks are full you always have information to work from and something to inspire you.

Always sketch when you have the opportunity. It is easy to be lazy and put off doing a sketch. It is usually disastrous to postpone doing it. When you see the subject later, it may look completely different, the light will have changed or the sun will have gone in and you may decide it is no longer worth sketching. There is only one way to fill your sketchbooks: keep one with you all the time and when you see something that inspires you, sketch it.

It is not as easy as it sounds. Even a professional artist can have difficulties. If you have a family, you can't always stop just when you want to. But if you make the effort, that is a good start and you will soon see your sketchbook pages gradually fill up with information.

Fig. 57 This is my original pencil sketch which I drew outside and have used as reference to do three paintings at home in watercolour showing the same scene in different moods

DEVELOPING THE MOOD OF A SKETCH

When searching through my sketchbooks for sketches to reproduce in this book, I was able to relive many happy moments, just by looking at them. After time had gone by I was able to see them in a different context and wanted to paint from them straight away. I love to come across an old sketch and paint from it in watercolour. It gives me an opportunity to try out different techniques and to illustrate nature's changing moods. An advantage in working from the same sketch is you get to know the subject so well that you can concentrate more on the painting, rather than drawing.

The sketch in fig. 57 is one I did after there had been a lot of rain and many fields were flooded. I decided to use this sketch, which I hadn't worked from before, and paint it in watercolour showing the same scene in three different moods. All three were painted on the same size paper: 225 x 290mm (9 x 11½in). The first one (fig. 58) I painted as I remembered it. I worked on Not surface 140lb watercolour paper, as I did for the other two. I kept the painting simple, to create the feeling of freshness one gets after a rainfall. Notice how the water is painted very simply, with the foreground left as white paper.

For the second painting (fig. 59) I imagined it was early morning with a heavy Devon mist. This I achieved by wetting the paper and running the first wash over the whole area, leaving only one or two areas of paper white, to represent the water and the house. When it was dry, I added a second wash of colour, and then worked the dark area under the trees.

The third (fig. 60) is a snow scene. I painted the sky dark with Payne's Grey, Yellow Ochre and Crimson Alizarin. Using the same colours I 'drew' the picture with my No. 6 sable brush. The secret of this effect is in what you don't paint; for instance, I left plenty of white paper showing through to represent snow.

Fig. 58

Fig. 59

Fig. 60

WATERCOLOUR

WHY USE WATERCOLOURS?

Fig. 1

I am constantly asked why I paint in more than one medium. The reasons are varied. An artist sometimes uses a medium because he has been commissioned to do so or because he likes one medium more than another, but more important is the fact that each medium has its own particular quality. There is also the restraint of size. For instance, watercolour paper isn't made large enough for a 760 x 1525mm (30 x 60in) painting and neither is pastel paper so the medium can determine the size of the painting. Finally, the subject matter has to be considered. When I am out looking for possible subjects I see one as a subject for an acrylic painting, another as a perfect watercolour, and so on.

Whatever your reason for choosing watercolour, even if it's the obvious one – you like it! – you have made the choice and we will work together over the next fifty-six pages, from simple beginnings to more serious exercises later.

First, a word of caution. Because your earliest recollection of painting – probably when you were at infant school –

is associated with the use of water-based paint (poster paint, powder colour or watercolour), you may have the impression that it is easy. Well, of course, to enjoy painting and get favourable results is relatively easy. However, to get the desired results through deliberate control of watercolour needs a lot of practice and patience but the more you learn, the more you will enjoy using watercolour.

WHAT ARE WATERCOLOURS?

Watercolours are so called because the adhesive that sticks the pigment powder to the paper is soluble in water. The paint is a finely ground mixture of pigment, gum arabic (the water-soluble gum of the acacia tree), glycerine (to keep the colours moist) and glucose (to make the colours flow freely). You buy the colours either in a half pan, a whole pan or a tube (see fig. 1).

When water is loaded on to a brush and added to the paint on the palette, the paint becomes a coloured, transparent liquid. When this is applied to the white surface of the paper, the paper shows through and the paint assumes a transparent luminosity unequalled by any other medium.

You will find that the paint dries within minutes of its application to the paper as the water evaporates, leaving the dry colour on the surface. This process can be seen when working. While the paint is shiny on the paper, it is still wet and you can move it about or add more colour with the brush, but as soon as the shine goes off the paper (the paint is now in an advanced drying stage) you must leave it alone and let it dry. If you try to work more paint into it, you will get nasty streaks and blotches. Because the paint dries quickly, watercolour painting does not favour faint hearts. If you think you are in that category, don't worry; you will gain confidence as you read and work through the book.

USING WATERCOLOUR

Before you start a painting you need to have a plan of campaign in your mind. Naturally, as you progress, this will become second nature to you. When I was at art school I was taught to look and observe and, ever since, I have always looked at the sky as if it were a painting and considered how it had been done – in which medium, with which brush, which colour was used first, and so on. I see things as shapes and colours, and techniques of painting. The strange thing is that I see most things as watercolour paintings. I think this is because of the very nature of the medium: you have a limited time, you are painting from light to dark (more about that later), a bad mistake can't be overpainted (in true watercolour) and, therefore, it all comes down to observation and planning.

Nevertheless, you will have to accept the fact that not every watercolour painting is a success – not to you, the artist, that is. You will find that you paint a beautiful picture, everyone likes it and it is worthy of being put into an exhibition, but there will be passages of that painting where the watercolour was not completely under your control and it made up its own mind about the final effect. Well, this is an accepted characteristic of watercolour painting – only the artist knows how he made the paint behave or misbehave. But when you paint a good picture with plenty of watercolour effect and it was all under your control, then you will have achieved a small, personal ambition.

Opposite is a list of the available colours (fig. 2). The colours illustrated are those that I use, set out in my palette order, and will be referred to throughout this book. This colour chart is produced within the limitations of printing and is intended as a guide only.

Fig. 2

PAYNE'S GREY

BURNT UMBER

HOOKER'S GREEN No. 1

FRENCH ULTRAMARINE

CRIMSON ALIZARIN

YELLOW OCHRE

COERULEUM BLUE

BURNT SIENNA

CADMIUM RED

RAW UMBER

RAW SIENNA

CADMIUM YELLOW PALE

Additional colours available

Naples Yellow	Crimson Lake	Viridian
Lemon Yellow	Permanent Rose	Terre Verte (Hue)
Permanent Yellow	Purple Lake	Cobalt Green
Cadmium Yellow	Purple Madder	Brown Pink
Aureolin	(Alizarin)	Light Red
Chrome Lemon	Permanent Magenta	Venetian Red
Gamboge (Hue)	Cobalt Violet	Indian Red
Chrome Yellow	Permanent Mauve	Brown Madder
Cadmium Yellow Deep	Violet Alizarin	(Alizarin)
Indian Yellow	Prussian Blue	Vandyke Brown
Chrome Orange (Hue)	Indigo	Warm Sepia
Cadmium Orange	Monestial Blue	Permanent Sepia
Chrome Orange Deep	Cobalt Blue	Davy's Grey
Vermilion (Hue)	Permanent Blue	Neutral Tint
Permanent Red	Alizarin Green	Ivory Black
Rose Dore (Alizarin)	Sap Green	Lamp Black
Scarlet Alizarin	Monestial Green	Chinese White
Scarlet Lake	Olive Green	
Carmine	Hooker's Green No. 2	

WHAT EQUIPMENT DO YOU NEED?

Every professional artist has his favourite brushes, colours, and so on. In the end, the choice must be left to you, to make from your personal experience.

In the last chapter I gave you a list of the colours that I use. I suggest that you, too, use these as you work through this book because I shall refer to them to describe different colour mixes. You may find that you prefer to drop a couple of colours or change some once you have made some progress – this will be fine and, of course, it also applies to other materials used in the exercises.

CHOOSING YOUR PAINTS

To get the best results, you should use the best materials you can afford. The two main distinctions between different watercolour paints are cost and quality. The best quality watercolours are called Artists' Quality and those a grade lower are called Students', some of which are manufactured under brand names such as Georgian. Watercolour paints can be bought in a box, or in separate pans which you can use to fill an empty box with your own choice of colours.

Other boxes carry tubes of paint – you have to squeeze the colour on to the palette (the open lid of the box) and use the paint as if you were working from pans. Colours in tubes are ideal for quickly saturating a brush in strong colour, using less water, but I do not advise beginners to use tubes because it is difficult to control the amount of paint on the brush.

BRUSHES

The best quality watercolour brushes are made from Kolinsky sable. They are hand-made and are the most expensive brushes on the market but they give you perfect control over your brush strokes and, if properly cared for, will last a long time. Also in the fine-quality range of water-colour brushes, but less expensive, are those made with squirrel hair, ox-ear hair and ringcat hair. Man-made fibres are also used in the manufacture of artists' brushes, they are less expensive than sable and an excellent range is available.

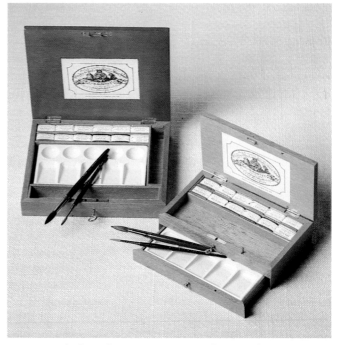

Fig. 3 Both these boxes are copies of original Artists' Water Colour Boxes first sold by Thomas and Richard Rowney between 1795 and 1810

Remember, brushes are the tools with which you express yourself on paper. It is only your use of the brush that reveals your skill to the onlooker and this applies to watercolour more than any other medium. One brush stroke can express a field, a lake, the side of a boat, and so on; therefore, you must know your brushes and what to expect from them.

There are two basic types: a round brush and a flat brush. If you look at fig. 4 you will see brushes of different shapes, made from different hairs. Usually, the handles of watercolour brushes are short but where the brush can also be used for oil or acrylic painting, the handle may be longer.

The round brush is a general purpose one: both a wash and a thin line can be obtained with this shape. The flat brush is used mainly for putting washes over large areas or where a broad brush stroke is called for. Naturally, the width of these strokes is determined by the size of the flat brush. Usually, round brushes are graded from size No. 00 to size No. 12 and some manufacturers make a No. 14 size. This scale can be seen in fig. 4 and the brushes are reproduced actual size. Flat brushes and very large brushes, such as the squirrel-hair wash brush, have a name or size of their own.

Fig. 4   Round Brushes

OTHER EQUIPMENT

Other items you need are pencils – start by getting an HB and 2B (the other grades up to 6B, the softest, I will leave to your own choice); a good-quality, natural sponge for wetting the paper or sponging off areas you want to repaint; blotting paper for absorbing wet colour from the surface of the paper in order to lighten a passage that is too dark; and a brush case (see fig. 5), very necessary when you are painting outside to avoid damaging your brushes.

You need a drawing board on which to pin your paper. You can make one from a smooth piece of plywood or you can buy one from your local art shop. A container to hold your painting water can be anything from a jam jar to a plastic cup; but make sure that it is big enough to hold plenty of water, and keep changing the water so that it is always clean.

A kneadable putty rubber is the best type to use for erasing as it can be used gently on delicate paper without causing too much damage to the surface. When you are using a pen and wash technique in the exercises, you will require a mapping pen and black Indian ink.

A watercolour is never painted right up to the edge of the paper so it is a good idea to have some mounts for offering up to a finished watercolour. You will then be able to see where the painting will be masked when it is framed. Cut mounts of various sizes from cartridge paper or thin card and when you have finished a painting, put a mount around it to see what you think. This will help you decide whether you think your picture looks finished or not.

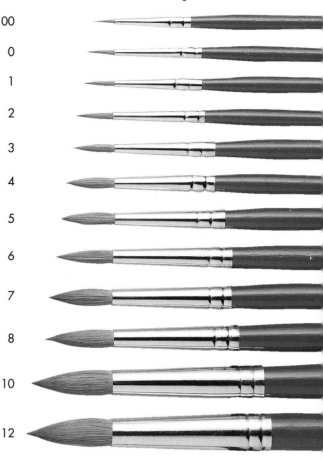

00
0
1
2
3
4
5
6
7
8
10
12

Series 40 Kolinsky Sable Hair Round Brush No.10

Series 66 Squirrel & Goat Hair Mop Brush (extra large round)

Series 63 Squirrel & Goat Hair Mop Brush (large flat)

Dalon Series D88 Wash and One Stroke Brush

Dalon Series D77 Round Brush No. 6

Dalon Series D99 'Rigger' Brush No. 2

ESSENTIAL EQUIPMENT

You will see what you need to start work as a watercolour painter in fig. 6. You can start with only three brushes: a No. 10 round brush (the quality you get will depend on the price), a No. 6 round brush for general detail work and a Dalon Series D99 'Rigger' No. 2 brush for fine line work. You need a paint box to hold 12 colours in half pans or whole pans, HB and 2B pencils, a kneadable putty rubber, a drawing board, paper, blotting paper, a sponge and a water jar.

This short list represents the advantages of watercolour: its equipment, its approach and its execution are simple. However, although you can have a lot of fun with it, you can achieve complete control over watercolour only after a great deal of experience.

I haven't included an easel because it is not an essential piece of watercolour equipment; when you are working outside, your painting is usually small enough to manage on a drawing board resting on your knees. You can work very comfortably at a table, with the top edge of your drawing board supported by a book or piece of wood so that the board is tilted and the washes can run down correctly. If you want to work on an easel, choose one from the variety on the market.

Opposite you can see a picture of a studio area with a range of equipment on display. This has been overcrowded intentionally to show all the different materials you may require as you progress.

Fig. 5 Brush case

Fig. 6 Beginners' basic equipment

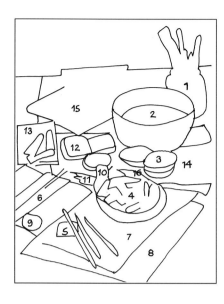

1 A selection of brushes
2 Water container
3 Mixing palettes
4 Tubes, whole pans and half pans of paint
5 Putty eraser, brush and pencils
6 Watercolour box with whole pan
7 Tinted watercolour paper
8 Watercolour paper
9 Sponge
10 Black ink
11 Pens
12 Small watercolour box with half pans
13 Mixing palette and tubes
14 Blotting paper
15 Watercolour pad
16 Knife

WHICH PAPER?

You can paint with watercolour on almost any type of paper. You can work on drawing paper, on the inside of a cardboard carton, or even on the back of a roll of wallpaper. Naturally, there are problems in using any old paper. Firstly, if the paper is too absorbent, the liquid will be sucked into the surface like ink on blotting paper and secondly, if the surface is non-absorbent, the paint will run completely out of control.

The answer, then, is to use paper that has been specially made for the watercolour artist. The finest quality papers are made by hand, by craftsmen whose skills have been handed down over the centuries. Up to the beginning of the nineteenth century, even the cheapest wrapping paper was made by hand but then machinery took over a great proportion of the production. Because the best quality watercolour paper is still made by hand it is very expensive. However, in comparison with a ready-stretched canvas of equivalent size, top quality paper is far cheaper.

SURFACE AND WEIGHT

Watercolour papers have a unique surface texture that is sympathetic to the brush – artists usually refer to it as a 'tooth'. It is this tooth that responds to the brush and helps create the unique watercolour effect. The paper also has just the right amount of absorbency to hold the liquid colour under manageable control.

There are many types of paper on the market but they all have two things in common: they are all finished with one of three kinds of surface texture and they are all graded by weight (this tells us the thickness of the paper). The surfaces are: Rough, Not (called Cold Pressed in the USA) and Hot Pressed (HP). Paper with a Rough surface has a very pronounced texture (tooth) and is usually used for large paintings where bold, vigorous brush work is required. The Not surface has less tooth and this is the one most commonly used by artists; it is also ideal for the beginner. The Hot Pressed surface is very smooth, with very little tooth, and before you try this paper you need to know how to handle your watercolour: if you use the paint very wet, it can easily run.

Usually, you buy watercolour paper in an Imperial size, approximately 760 x 560mm (31 x 22in), but hand-made paper sizes can vary by a few inches. The weight of the paper is arrived at by calculating how much a ream (480 sheets) weighs. For instance, if a ream weighs 300lb (which is about the heaviest paper you can use) then the paper is called (with its surface title) 300lb Not. You will find that a good weight to work on is a 140lb paper. On the opposite page are pieces of watercolour paper, reproduced their actual size. I have put some paint on each one and I have also given its full description.

If this sounds complicated, don't worry. To start with, get used to two or three types of paper. You will learn how the paper reacts to the paint and what you can and can't do. This is as important as getting used to your brushes and colours. When you first buy sheets of paper, pencil the name, size and weight in each corner for future reference. You can also buy watercolour papers in pads of various sizes.

When you have practised and have become confident in handling your colours without spoiling too much paper, buy the best paper you can afford and stick to that one until you know it like the back of your hand. The better you know your brushes, your paints and your paper, the more you will enjoy painting – and the better your results will be.

STRETCHING PAPER

Paper tends to cockle when you put wet paint on it and the thinner the paper the more it will cockle. You can get over this problem by stretching the paper. (Heavy and thick papers do not need stretching.)

Cut a sheet of paper the size you need but smaller than your drawing board, submerge it in a sink full of water or hold it under a running tap and completely soak both sides. Hold it up by one end, let the surface water drain off, then lay it on a wooden drawing board. Use a roll of brown gummed paper tape to stick the four sides down, allowing the gummed paper to lie half over the paper and half over the board.

Now leave it to dry naturally, overnight. In the morning, it will be as tight as a drum and as flat as a pancake, and it will stay flat while you work. The finished result is shown in the photograph at the top of the page. It is heaven to work on.

Paper can also be bought in sheets stuck together on the edges of all four sides to prevent cockling. These are called watercolour blocks, they come in various sizes and are excellent for use out-of-doors. When the painting is finished, you simply tear off the sheet and work on the next one.

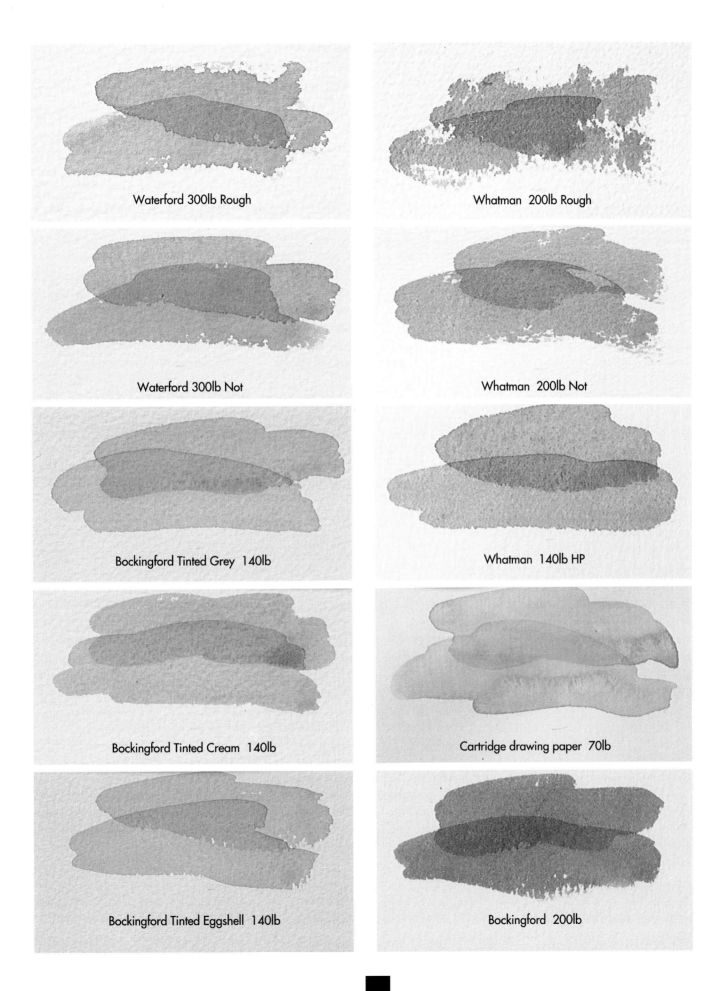

Waterford 300lb Rough

Whatman 200lb Rough

Waterford 300lb Not

Whatman 200lb Not

Bockingford Tinted Grey 140lb

Whatman 140lb HP

Bockingford Tinted Cream 140lb

Cartridge drawing paper 70lb

Bockingford Tinted Eggshell 140lb

Bockingford 200lb

LET'S START PAINTING

At last you can start painting. A lot of people who have not painted before find this the most difficult bridge to cross – to actually put some paint on paper. Unfortunately, we are all self-conscious when doing things we have never tried before and our families don't help either! I have often come across the case of a member of the family who sees someone's first efforts at painting. Remarks such as What's that! and Oh well, never mind, are never meant to hurt or be unkind, but, unfortunately, they can put off a sensitive beginner – sometimes for ever. Well, this is how we will get over that problem, if it arises. It's human nature for us all to strive to do better and if we try to run before we can walk, then this is when disaster will strike and cause those humorous comments from the rest of the family. So we will start at the very beginning and take things in a steady, progressive order.

PLAYING WITH PAINT

Before you start mixing colours, get yourself a piece of watercolour paper or cartridge paper and play with the paint on this. See what it feels like, try different brushes, add more water, less water, mix colours together. You will end up with a funny-looking coloured piece of paper. Incidentally, if the family laugh at this one, laugh with them, show them my doodles on paper and laugh at that!

What you have done is to experience the feel of watercolour paint. You will have noticed that if you add more water, you make the colour lighter. This is the correct method for making watercolours lighter, not by adding white paint. The paint isn't a stranger to you any more, nor are your brushes or paper. You have now broken the ice and will feel much more confident in tackling the next section. Good luck.

MIXING COLOURS

As we progress through the exercises, I will help you as much as I can but you must first spend some time practising mixing different colours. A beginner may find the hundreds of colours that exist somewhat overwhelming. But the choice can be simplified: there are only three basic colours,

red, yellow and blue, which are called primary colours. All other colours, and shades of colour, are formed by a combination of these three. In painting, there are different reds, yellows and blues which we can use to help recreate nature's colours. Look at the illustration opposite and you will see that there are two of each primary colour. These colours, plus another six, are the ones I use, for all my watercolour painting.

I have taken the primary colours and mixed them to show you the results. In the first row, Cadmium Yellow Pale mixed with French Ultramarine makes green. In the second row, Cadmium Yellow Pale mixed with Cadmium Red makes orange. To make the orange look more yellow, add more yellow than red and to make it more red, add more red than yellow. Add more water to make the orange paler.

You may have noticed that my selection of colours does not include black. Some artists use black and others don't. I am one of the don'ts. I don't use black because I believe it is a dead colour, too flat. Therefore, I mix my blacks from the primary colours and I suggest that you do the same. Remember that, in general, if you want a colour to be cooler, add blue and if it is to be warmer, then add red.

Practise mixing different colours on white cartridge paper. Mix the colours on your palette with a brush and paint daubs on to your white paper. Don't worry about shapes at this stage, it's the colours you're trying for. Experiment and practise – that is the only real advice I can give you here. When you're next sitting down, look around you, pick a colour that you can see and try to imagine what colours you would use to mix it.

One last, important point: when there are only three basic colours it is the amount of each colour that plays the biggest part. You can easily mix a green as in the second line opposite, but if it is to be a yellowy green, you have to experiment on your palette; you have to mix and work in more yellow until you have the colour you want. This lesson of mixing colours is one that you will be practising and improving upon all your life – I am, still.

PRIMARY COLOURS

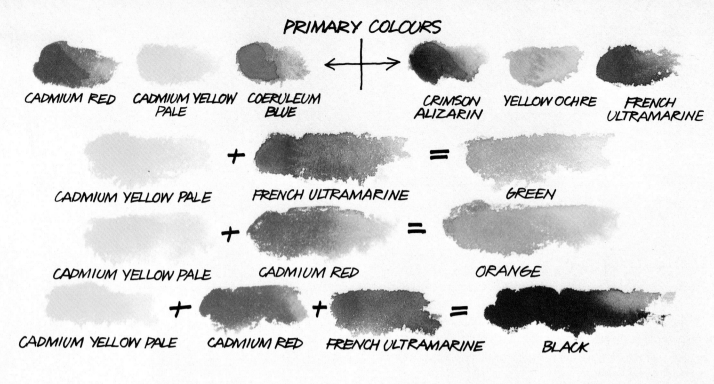

CADMIUM RED CADMIUM YELLOW PALE COERULEUM BLUE ←|→ CRIMSON ALIZARIN YELLOW OCHRE FRENCH ULTRAMARINE

CADMIUM YELLOW PALE + FRENCH ULTRAMARINE = GREEN

CADMIUM YELLOW PALE + CADMIUM RED = ORANGE

CADMIUM YELLOW PALE + CADMIUM RED + FRENCH ULTRAMARINE = BLACK

DOODLE!

BRUSH CONTROL

Now you must learn to control the paint brush. Like all things, when you know how, it is much easier than you had thought. For example, a lot of control is required when painting edges of areas that have to be filled in with paint.

Take a pair of scissors, or anything handy that has round shapes, and draw around it with an HB pencil. You can do this on cartridge paper or watercolour paper. Use your round sable brush with plenty of water. When you start to fill in the curved shapes, start at the top and work down the left side to the bottom (fig. 7). Let the bristles follow the brush, i.e. pull the brush down. Try to do this in two or three movements. When you paint the right side of the handle, your brush will cover some of the pencil lines and you will feel slightly awkward. The answer is to accept that it feels a bit awkward but the more you use your brush like that, the more natural it will feel – practise!

Now, let's go on to straight lines. Here is a very important rule to remember: when you draw straight lines (unless you are drawing very short ones), always move your wrist and arm – not your fingers. Try this with a pencil. First, draw a straight line downwards, moving only your fingers. You will find that you can draw only a couple of inches before your fingers make the line bend. Now do the same exercise but keep your fingers firm and move only your hand, bending your arm at the elbow. The result will be a long, straight line.

This time, draw a square, like the side of a box. Try this one freehand, don't draw around anything. You can paint the edges of the box with the round sable brush again. Use this same brush for filling in the square with the rest of the paint (see fig. 8).

Draw another two squares and paint around both up to the outside edges. Then, paint another box inside the bottom box, without drawing it first (fig. 9). Also, change the colour as you paint, working from the top box to the bottom one. This one will keep you busy!

Now draw your own shapes and fill then in, mixing your own colours. Look around and choose a colour, perhaps the colour of your carpet or a cushion, then try to mix a colour like it to use for painting in your shapes. You are practising all you have learned so far, in one exercise: well done – but keep at it, enjoy it and keep practising.

Fig. 7 CRIMSON ALIZARIN & FRENCH ULTRAMARINE

Fig. 8 BURNT UMBER

FROM CRIMSON ALIZARIN TO CADMIUM YELLOW PALE

Fig. 9

SIMPLE PERSPECTIVE

Drawing, or the knowledge of drawing, comes before painting, so we will take a little time to practise simple perspective. If you believe you can't draw, don't let this worry you. Some artists can paint a picture but would have difficulty in drawing it as a drawing in its own right. It is the colours, the tones and the shapes of the masses that make a painting. Over the centuries, artists have always invented and used drawing aids. Today, there are drawing aids on the market that can help sort out the perspective for you. But it is not too difficult to do this yourself.

When you look out to sea, the horizon will always be at your eye level, even if you climb a cliff or lie flat on the sand. So the horizon is the eye level (E.L.). If you are in a room, naturally there is no horizon but you still have an eye level. To find this, hold your pencil horizontally in front of your eyes at arm's length: your eye level is where the pencil hits the opposite wall. If two parallel lines were marked out on the ground and extended from you towards the horizon, they would appear to come together at what is called the vanishing point (V.P.). This is the effect you see with railway lines that seem to meet in the distance.

DRAWING A PERSPECTIVE BOX

Look at fig. 10A. I have taken our box, the square you drew in the previous section, and put it on paper. Then I drew a line above to represent the eye level. Then, to the right-hand end of the E.L., I made a mark, the V.P. With a ruler I drew a line from each of the four corners of the box, all converging at the V.P. This gave me the two sides, the bottom and the top of the box.

To create the other end of the box, I drew a square parallel with the front of the box and kept it within the V.P. guidelines. The effect is that of a transparent box drawn in perspective. Incidentally, we are looking down on this box because the eye level is high. In fig. 10B I have shaded the box with pencil to show the light direction.

Figs. 10C, D and E show the same box. The first one was painted all over with a wash of Hooker's Green No. 1; the second box was painted with a second wash over two sides when the first wash had dried; the third one was painted with an additional wash on the darkest side, which made the box appear solid. The last one (fig. 10F) shows the same drawing painted to represent a hollow box.

This is a simple exercise but it is the most important exercise you will ever do. You are creating on a flat surface the illusion of depth, dimension and perspective; in other words, a three-dimensional object.

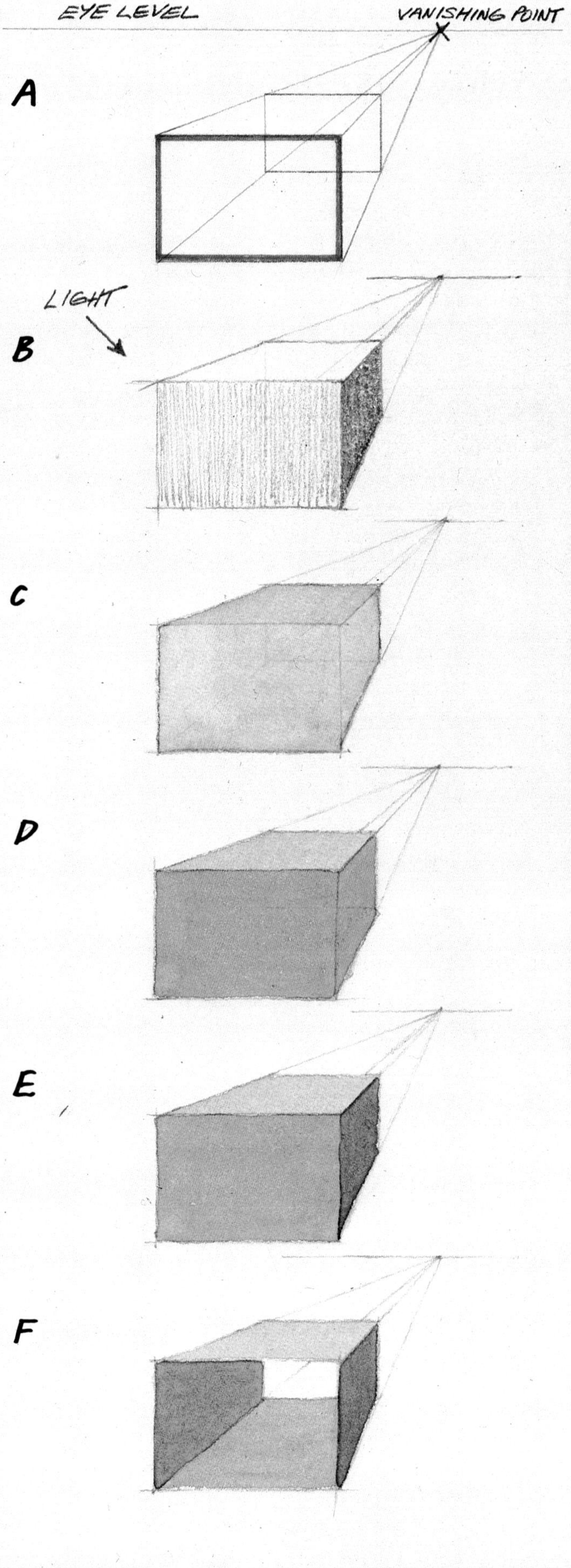

Fig. 10

73

BASIC WATERCOLOUR TECHNIQUES

Before you start the basic techniques, read these paragraphs carefully. When you put the first wash on the box (fig. 10C) did you notice that, although the box was drawn in perspective, it looked flat? This is because there was no light or shade (light against dark). It is this that enables us to see objects and understand their form. If we were to paint our box red, on a background coloured the same red, without adding light or shade, we would not be able to see it. If light and shade were added, it could then be seen.

You must always be conscious of light against dark whenever you are painting. When you are painting a still life or outdoor view, it will help you to see shapes if you look at the scene through half-closed eyes. The lights and darks will be exaggerated and the middle tones will tend to disappear: this will enable you to see simple, contrasting shapes that you can follow.

You will see that while your colour is wet, it appears dark and rich; but when it is dry, it is slightly lighter. You will learn from experience how to adjust the density of your colours in order to achieve the desired effect. In the meantime, don't worry – it won't spoil your paintings. Keep your colours in the same position in your paint box and always use the box the same way round. You will have enough to think about, without wondering where your colours are, when you are in the middle of painting a wash.

WATERCOLOUR WASH
Now, we can study the most basic technique of watercolour painting – the flat wash. In all instructive illustrations I have used arrows to help you understand the movement of the brush. The solid black arrow shows the direction of the brush stroke and the outline arrow shows the direction in which the brush is travelling over the paper. For example, fig. 11 shows the brush stroke moving horizontally, from left to right, and the brush moving down the paper after the completion of each horizontal stroke.

Fig. 11

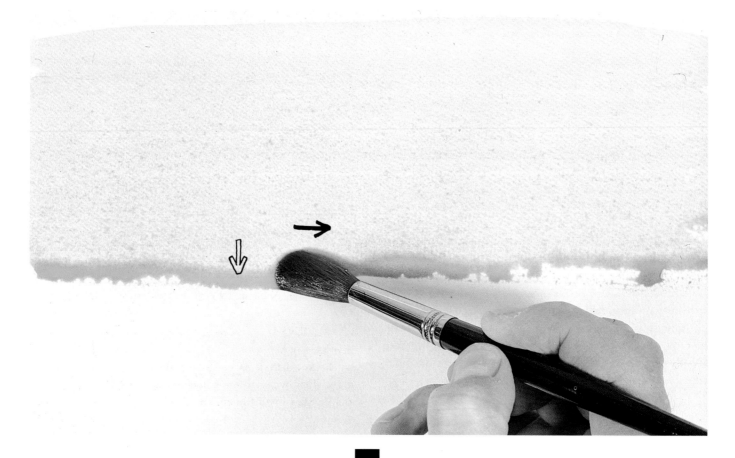

Fig. 13

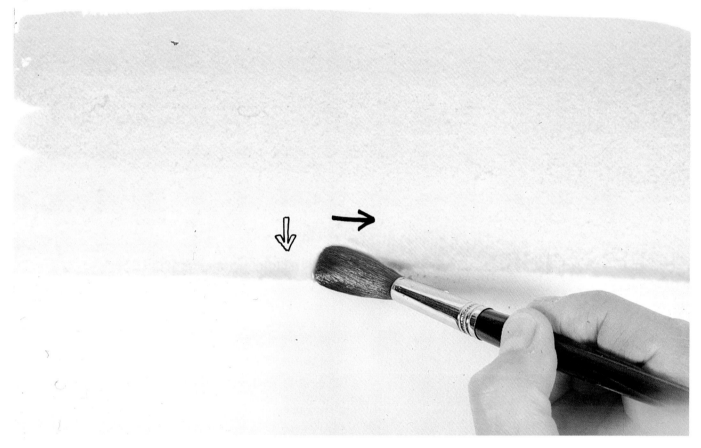

For a flat wash you need plenty of watery paint in your palette. Load your largest brush and start at the top left-hand side of the paper, taking the brush along in a definite movement. Don't rush. When you get to the end, bring the brush back, run it slightly into the first wet stroke and make another brush stroke like the first.

You will, of course, add more paint to your brush when you need it. Because the colour was mixed before you started the wash and you have added no more water, the colour density of the wash should be the same all the way down. Let this wash dry, then paint another one over it, using the same colour but leaving about 12mm (¹/₂in) at the top of the original wash. If you repeat this process at least six times, you will begin to get the knack of putting on a wash. You will practise the watercolour technique of applying transparent colour over and over again, and you will see that the more washes you apply, the darker the colour becomes (see fig. 12).

GRADED WASH

A graded wash is produced in exactly the same way as a flat wash except that, as you travel down the paper, you add more clean water to the colour in your palette. This weakens the density of the colour, with the result that the wash gets progressively paler from top to bottom (see fig. 13).

Fig. 12

Fig. 14

WET ON WET

The term wet on wet is common to all painting mediums and means that wet paint is applied over existing wet paint. It is one of the most intriguing watercolour techniques. It is impossible to predict exactly what will happen when you put wet paint on top of a wet wash (see figs. 14 and 15). You will create some fantastic effects – some of them dramatic, others subtle.

You can see one of my experiments in fig. 14. I painted Coeruleum Blue first, very wet. Then, I added a mix of Payne's Grey and Burnt Umber, very wet, in the middle. When this was dry, I lightly sponged it with clean water, then attacked the middle again with a mix of Payne's Grey, French Ultramarine and Burnt Umber – this is a very strong colour. Immediately, I added more water to the mix and put a daub on each side of the centre.

You can get good skies, using the wet on wet technique, by sponging your paper first with clean water, then painting your sky colours and letting them run together.

You need to experiment with this technique and keep practising control. The overall effect is planned – it's the unpredictable wanderings of the paint that add interest and beauty. If you wait until the first wash is drying, you will have more control over the paint and you will also achieve a slightly different effect. When it is all dry you might see an area that, by happy accident, needs only a brush stroke to make it read better: if the brush stroke is applied correctly, this passage could be a little gem in the painting.

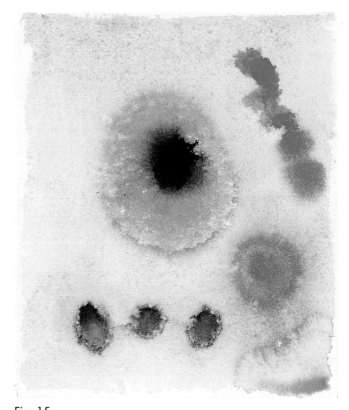

Fig. 15

Fig. 17

DRY BRUSH

Dry brush is another technique that is used in most types of painting. It simply means that a brush is damp-dried before being dipped into the paint or else a wet brush is loaded with paint, blotted out to a damp consistency on a piece of blotting paper and then applied to the watercolour paper.

The technique is used to achieve a hit-and-miss effect. If you try this on rough watercolour paper, it is relatively easy but on a smooth-surfaced paper it needs a little more practice. The chances are that you accidentally produced a dry brush effect when you were doodling or painting the boxes earlier on – because you were running out of paint – but it was unintentional and, therefore, uncontrolled.

The best way to get used to the dry brush technique is to use long brush strokes, from left to right, with only a little paint (see fig. 16). You will find that your brush runs out of paint and finishes the stroke with a dry brush effect. Try to control the amount of wet paint you load on to your brush and take it over, say, 305mm (12in), so that the stroke is finished dry. When you can do this, you have gone a long way towards controlling your watercolour brush work. In fig. 17 I used a no. 6 flat brush for the strokes.

Fig. 16

DIFFERENT WAYS TO PAINT

Watercolour is a very versatile medium. It can be used in different ways by different artists. For instance, six artists could paint the same subject, using the same technique, but each painting would be different. In other words, each artist would have his or her own style. But my wet-on-wet water-colour opposite is painted in a completely different style to my pen and wash watercolour on page 81. Therefore, an artist's style is, to some extent, altered by the technique. To avoid confusion, in this chapter the word style refers to the individual artist's way of painting and the word technique refers to the method of using the paint.

On the following pages are six pictures I have painted of the same subject, using a different technique each time, to show you the versatility and beauty of watercolour. My purpose is to enable you to compare several versions of the same subject so that you can see the difference between each technique. The actual size of each painting is 340 x 225mm (13½ x 9in) and the type of paper I used is indicated below each one.

Some subjects do not necessarily lend themselves to a particular technique but, on the other hand, some subjects cry out for just one technique. Therefore, you must choose your subject and technique carefully. Naturally, a pencil-and-wash or pen-and-wash drawing can be tackled only if you have a reasonable knowledge of drawing, because your control of the pencil or pen plays a large part in these two watercolour techniques.

Whatever the technique, the basis for the painting is still the wash – whether it be flat, graded or wet on wet. I mention this at this stage because you just can't practise washes enough – the wash is watercolour. When you can master it on all scales, small and large, you will be much more relaxed when you work and you will find that fewer disasters come off the brush. Keep practising.

Fig. 18 The pencil sketch on which these painting exercises are based

Flat wash and graded wash   300lb Not

FLAT WASH AND GRADED WASH

I regard the flat wash and graded wash as basic, traditional ways of using watercolour. Having thought out the moves very carefully beforehand, you work up the effect with washes. Remember to use the lightest colours first and work gradually to the darker tones.

The old buildings that I chose to paint have plenty of character and are a perfect subject for the painter. Even the TV aerials add to their character and charm.

WET ON WET

The wet-on-wet technique is a very exciting way of using watercolour but it can be also very nerve-racking. The freedom, the apparent ease and the sheer audacity of letting colours make their own way around the paper excites artist and onlooker alike. But although the finished result looks natural and unlaboured, you have to put in many hours of patient practice.

Wet on wet   300lb Not

Body colour
Grey 72lb Not

BODY COLOUR

You can strengthen your colours by using the body colour technique. Simply add White to the paint and this will immediately take away the transparency of the colour. Generally speaking, White is used instead of water in this technique to make the colours lighter. I painted the picture above on a grey watercolour paper. I made the sky dark for a dramatic effect and I used pure White where the sun catches the window frame.

When you are next painting a watercolour, if you find you have lost it, try using White with your colours and turn it into a body colour painting. Remember that light can be added over dark.

OPEN WASH

The painting below looks a little flat when compared with the others, but it demonstrates a crisp, clean watercolour technique. I have called the technique open wash because white paper is left between different-coloured washes. Apart from its own charm, open wash has a very valuable application. When you are painting outside, it is often impractical to wait for each wash to dry before applying the adjacent one. If you use this method, you can carry on almost without stopping.

Open wash
281lb Not

Pencil and wash   72lb Not

PENCIL AND WASH

Pencil and wash is one of the most delicate ways of using watercolour. It can be very sensitive and detailed. First, I did the pencil drawing – as though it were to be a drawing in its own right. Naturally, the amount of detail you put in depends upon your drawing ability. All the shading was done with a pencil. Washes of colour were applied after the drawing was completed. Incidentally, this fixes the pencil and stops any smudging.

PEN AND WASH

A very popular technique, pen and wash is used at some time or another by many watercolour artists. The addition of the pen line gives a crispness to the painting. I painted the picture first, then added the pen work, but you can work the other way round – pen first – if you find it suits you better.

Like body colour, the use of the pen is another method of saving a watercolour. Next time you want to put a bit more sparkle into a painting, try using a pen – you could transform a mediocre painting into a masterpiece.

Pen and wash   300lb HP

SIMPLE EXERCISES

No doubt you have had a few funny experiences with the paint. At times, you may have lost control or found that runs of paint have broken away from the main wash and run down the paper on to the table or the floor. However, you will have learned a lot, and now you can use this knowledge to do some real painting.

If you have been using cartridge paper or thin watercolour paper and have not yet tried stretching any paper, now is the time to do so. It makes an incredible difference, especially to cartridge paper. You will need to refer to the instructions on page 68.

Before you start a watercolour painting, you must always have clean water in your container. Remember, the paint stains the water to make the colour. If the water is dirty, obviously you will not get a true, clear colour.

To avoid breaking my rhythm when I am painting in the studio, I sometimes speed up the drying time of a wash by using my wife's hair-dryer to blow dry my wash. If you do this, don't hold the dryer too close – what you are trying to achieve is a quicker natural way of drying your wash.

PAINTING A SIMPLE OBJECT

I have chosen a potato for the first exercise. The drawing is not too difficult and if you put a bump in the wrong place, it will not look wrong. Also, although the colour isn't bright or exciting, it can be easily matched. The colour of potatoes varies, so if you don't match it exactly, your painting will still look right.

You may now have the impression that if an object isn't represented correctly, it doesn't matter. Of course, this is not true. What I am trying to do is to make sure that your first painting of an object looks correct to your family and friends; this will boost your confidence which, in turn, will improve your work. Now you can understand why I chose a potato for you – because it has no specific shape or colour.

First, draw the potato with your HB pencil. Using your large round brush, paint the background as a wash. When this is dry, paint the potato and add more colour on the shadow side as you paint down. Before this paint is dry,

Fig. 19

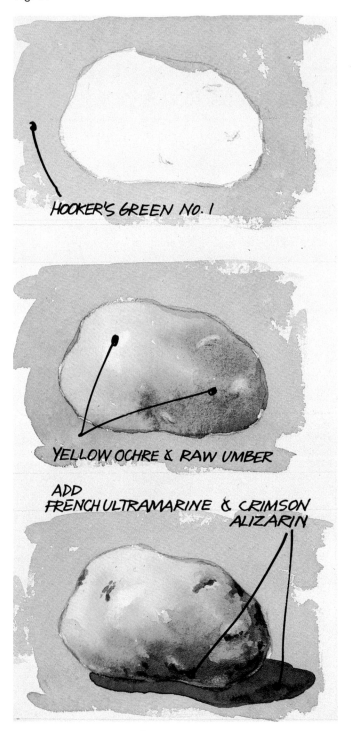

HOOKER'S GREEN NO. 1

YELLOW OCHRE & RAW UMBER

ADD
FRENCH ULTRAMARINE & CRIMSON
ALIZARIN

use the same brush and darker colour to work the dark blemishes. Because the paint is still slightly wet, these marks will run a little and the edges will be soft.

While the paint is still wet on the potato, dry out your brush and wipe out some highlights. These are only subtle effects but they help to give the object form. Finally, put in the shadow. Don't be fussy with the detail and, if it doesn't work out the first time, keep trying. When you can paint that potato, you will have come a long, long way.

SIMPLIFYING YOUR SUBJECT

Below is a complicated pencil sketch I made of the River Hamble in Hampshire. I put quite a lot of drawing into this but, if you preferred just to paint it, you could manage by sketching only the key positions – the horizon, the wooden quay and a couple of the main boats – the brush could do the rest. I used a rough surface for this, and a lot of dry brush, and I scratched out the light on the middle-distance water with a blade.

Fig. 20 Complicated subject

Fig. 21 Simplified painting

Fig. 22

USE THESE COLOURS   CADMIUM YELLOW PALE
BURNT UMBER
CRIMSON ALIZARIN
FRENCH ULTRAMARINE

WASH

PEN & WASH

PENCIL & WASH

BODY COLOUR

WET ON WET

Fig. 23

TRY A BANANA

This time, try a very simple approach to five of the techniques I described earlier. First, draw five bananas on the same sheet of paper with your HB pencil.

Now, paint the banana shapes, using the same colours for all five (fig. 22). Paint the first one using your large round brush and the colours shown. Let the brush strokes follow the shape of the banana. When the paint is almost dry, put on a darker wash and add some darker marks on top of this. Then, paint a dark shadow wash to show up the banana (light against dark). Put in a few dark accents with your No. 6 brush to crispen it up.

Paint the pen-and-wash banana in the same way. Put on the washes first and, when they are dry, use a mapping pen and black Indian ink to draw the banana. Experiment to find your natural style. You can try drawing the banana with pen and ink first, before putting coloured washes over the top.

The next one is pencil and wash. Draw and shade the banana with your HB and 2B pencils as if you were doing a pencil drawing. If you want darker shading on your drawing, use a softer pencil. Next, paint the banana in the same way as the first one but, this time, over your pencil shading.

Now, use the wet-on-wet technique. Use your sponge or large brush to wet the paper then, while it is still quite wet, paint the banana with the same brush. The colours will run over the edges of your pencil drawing. Paint the darker side and add some dark blemishes. When this is nearly dry, use the same brush to paint your background. Start at the left, above the banana, follow its top shape in one brush stroke, then work underneath it.

Finally, use the body colour technique, i.e. adding White to make the paint lighter and opaque. Paint your banana using the same colours as before but adding White to them – don't use a lot of water. You will find that the paint does not flow so easily and you have to work it more than usual. Don't try to put transparent washes over body colour, or the White will run into them and ruin your work.

NOW TRY A ROSE

Use your No. 6 brush to put a wash of Crimson Alizarin and Cadmium Red on the flower. While this is still wet, wipe out some of the paint with a damp brush for highlights. Paint the stem and leaves and, while the leaves are still wet, add some Cadmium Red with the point of the brush. Paint the petals with stronger colour and, when dry, scratch out some highlights.

With the same brush, paint the background – very wet. Be definite when painting up to the leaves – let the brush stroke make the shape. Add some shadow on the stem and leaves under the flower.

CADMIUM RED & CRIMSON ALIZARIN

HOOKER'S GREEN NO. 1
CADMIUM RED &
CRIMSON ALIZARIN

BURNT UMBER &
HOOKER'S GREEN NO. 1

Fig. 24

PAYNE'S GREY & BURNT UMBER

BURNT SIENNA & PAYNE'S GREY

CADMIUM RED & CADMIUM YELLOW PALE

CRIMSON ALIZARIN & FRENCH ULTRAMARINE

YELLOW OCHRE & PAYNE'S GREY

A DRINKING GLASS

I find that most students fight shy of painting this subject and I am often asked how to make it look like glass. The answer, as always, is by observation. Look right through the glass and analyse the shapes behind it. Then, draw the glass and simplify these shapes. If you look at my drawing, you will see that definite shapes are formed in the glass.

Use a large brush to paint the top left, dark area first – leave the rim of the glass and paint into the glass. Then paint the orange areas. Next, use a very pale wash for the white areas, leaving some unpainted white paper in the glass for highlights. Now, using downward strokes, put a dark wash down the left-hand side of the glass, leaving some areas untouched.

When this is dry, go over the area again with even darker colour and add a few dark accents with your small sable brush. Use a sharp blade to scratch out some highlights on the glass.

Set up your own glass and study the background shapes. I am sure you will soon learn the secret of making it look glassy.

AIM FOR THE SKY

I have already said that the wash is the basis of all watercolour painting and if you have been practising your basic techniques, you should now be able to handle a wash quite confidently. The last two quite detailed exercises needed a lot of hard thinking and careful brush work, but you can be a little more relaxed when painting skies. After all, if you get the overall shape of a cloud correct, it doesn't matter if you have an extra bump here and there. Skies are one of the best subjects on which to practise washes and large brush work. Although this is an exercise, you can produce a very rewarding painting.

Tackle this exercise for the sheer joy of painting and enjoy the freedom that the paint and the subject matter allow. You can try all kinds of paper surfaces, weights, colours and so on. I worked these studies exactly twice the size they are reproduced here, i.e. 180mm (7in) wide – a handy size on which to practise free washes because you can have more control over the paint on a small area.

Fig. 25

A

B

C

D

E

A This was a clear, windy day and the clouds were moving across the sky quite fast. I used dry paper and a No. 10 brush. First, I painted a wash of Coeruleum Blue and a little Crimson Alizarin for the blue sky; then, while it was wet, I added Yellow Ochre to the mix and used it for the shadow of the clouds

B Here, I applied a wash of Payne's Grey, French Ultramarine and Crimson Alizarin to dry paper with a No. 10 brush, leaving white areas for clouds. While this was wet, I painted their darker sides. Then I added a touch of Yellow Ochre to the shadows

C This evening sky has a graded wash worked from the top to the horizon, and below the land. The paper was dry and I used Coeruleum Blue, Crimson Alizarin and Cadmium Yellow Pale for the wash, worked with a No. 10 brush

D These big, full clouds were painted first with a mixture of Yellow Ochre, Crimson Alizarin and French Ultramarine. Before they dried, I painted French Ultramarine mixed with Crimson Alizarin (blue sky) between them, leaving white edges – a silver lining to help merge the clouds. Notice the little silhouette of a cottage at the bottom left – this gives the scale of the clouds

E A very wet, drizzly day. The paper was soaked with a sponge except at the bottom, right-hand corner. A mix of French Ultramarine, Crimson Alizarin, Payne's Grey and Yellow Ochre was worked on to the wet paper. Where the paper was dry at the bottom right, I let the brush form the cottage – again, to give atmosphere and dimension

F For this evening sky I applied a normal wash of Crimson Alizarin and Cadmium Yellow Pale over the paper. When the wash was dry I painted the clouds, using a No. 6 brush, and with French Ultramarine added to the colour. Before these clouds were dry, I worked a darker wash over them to form the dark clouds just above the horizon

F

EXERCISE ONE
STILL LIFE

On the following pages I have taken nine subjects and worked them in stages for you to follow, and copy if you wish. I have explained how to do the work and I have shown the same painting from the first stage to the last (the finished stage). This is important because you see the same painting through its stages and you can look back to see what was done earlier. It is also important for you to know the size of the finished painting (not the reproduction) because this gives you a relative scale to adjust to. The actual size is indicated under the finished stage.

The close-up illustrations for each exercise are reproduced the same size as I painted them so that you can see the actual brush strokes and details. Finally, I have used insets to illustrate the method of painting passages that I think you need to see more closely.

When mixing your colours, follow the order I have given and mix into the first colour, adding the following colours to it. The colour named first usually represents the main colour in the mix.

SETTING UP A STILL LIFE

For your first exercise I have purposely chosen a still life subject because the objects are easy to find but, above all, they can be painted under your own conditions. This is the beauty of still life: you can control the lighting, size, shape and colour of your subject. If you use inorganic objects, you can paint the same ones for years. To avoid your spending that long on your still life, I have added some fruit.

Before we start, here are one or two important notes on still-life painting. Don't be too ambitious to start with. Set up just a few objects that have simple shapes and colours, and put them on a contrasting background. The best light source is an adjustable desk lamp which can be directed on to your subject to give maximum light and shade (light against dark). Before you set up a still life, make sure that none of the objects you use will be needed in the near future.

FIRST STAGE

Draw the picture with an HB pencil. Using your large brush, mix Hooker's Green No. 1, Crimson Alizarin and French Ultramarine, and paint a wash down the paper, working around the fruit but painting over the left-hand side of the glass jar. Now, work a wash down the right-hand side of the picture, using French Ultramarine, Crimson Alizarin and Yellow Ochre – again, paint over the jar but leave some white paper for highlights. Paint the table top with the same colour.

SECOND STAGE

Paint the sultanas in the jar, using Crimson Alizarin, French Ultramarine and Cadmium Yellow Pale. While the paint is still wet, dry your brush and wipe out the two highlights on the jar. Then start putting in the fruit. Load your brush with watery paint and start with the orange – use Cadmium Yellow Pale, Cadmium Red and a touch of French Ultramarine in the shadow area. Next, paint the apple with Hooker's Green No. 1 and Cadmium Yellow Pale. Add the red lines of the apples while the paint is still wet so that they will merge and look softer.

Paint the two pears with a wash of Cadmium Yellow Pale and Hooker's Green No. 1. When they are nearly dry, paint the darker, browny-green areas with Hooker's Green No. 1, Crimson Alizarin and Yellow Ochre. The onion is next: use Cadmium Yellow Pale and Crimson Alizarin. With a wash of Yellow Ochre and Burnt Umber, paint all the nuts inside and outside the bowl, except the kernel inside the broken walnut.

When these are dry, add Crimson Alizarin to your wash to give more tone to the chestnuts. Dry out the highlights with your brush. Paint the blue dish, using French Ultramarine and a little Hooker's Green No. 1; add more pigment to the wash so that it gets darker to the right of the bowl – make sure you leave a white rim to the bowl.

THIRD STAGE

By now, all the areas have a wash over them but no detail or depth is apparent. At this stage, darker washes are applied to the painting. Start with the green background, using the same colours but adding more pigment. Paint over the jar again but do leave some areas of original wash showing. As you work on the fruit, use a little more brush work to achieve moulding and shape.

First stage

Second stage

Third stage

Fourth stage

FOURTH STAGE

Now your work on the nuts begins in earnest. Use your No. 6 brush and start with the walnuts. Let the brush do the drawing of the gnarled shells, as if it were a pencil. If you find the line too harsh or too strong, dry your brush and soften the line with it.

Work the brazil nuts and the chestnuts in the same way. Whatever you do, keep the highlights on the chestnuts – they are an essential feature of these particular nuts. Now paint the shadows with a wash of Crimson Alizarin, French Ultramarine and Yellow Ochre; when these are dry, add another wash to the bowl. Finally, use one stroke to put a wash down the right-hand side of the jar and over the sultanas.

FINISHED STAGE

The picture is almost finished at this stage but it lacks that final crispness and a little detail. This work is done with a No. 6 brush. Start with the jar, adding dark line work to give it better definition. Wipe some colour off the left-hand side of the apple to accentuate its shape and to separate it from the orange. Then, add the stalk. Paint some thin lines on the onion and work the sultanas in the jar in more detail. Give all the nuts stronger treatment and paint the shadows cast from the apple and pear on the nuts in the bowl. Put some stippling on the orange for an orange-skin look – use darker paint and work from the dark area into the light, leaving light areas showing through (see below). Finally, paint all the shadows again with a stronger wash.

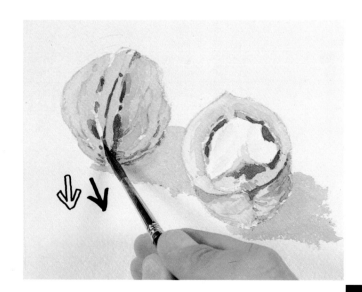

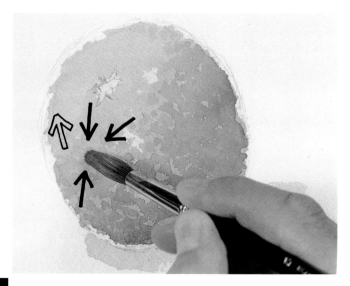

Finished stage

255 x 370mm (10 x 14½in)

EXERCISE TWO
FLOWERS

This exercise is also one that can be controlled to a large degree by the artist. The main point to remember is that flowers change over a short period and eventually die. Therefore, any flowers that you use as a subject must be capable of outstaying your painting time. If you don't manage to finish in time, change the flowers for fresh ones; your painting should have progressed far enough for you to improvise.

Remember, you are expressing an impression of a flower, not a specific one. A vase of different blooms with exciting shapes and colours can be a tremendous inspiration and make a fine painting. It can also be a daunting prospect for the beginner and if attempted at an early stage, can lead to disaster and disappointment. Remember, you must walk before you can run.

At first, study one species and only one bloom at a time. Put one flower against a plain, contrasting background so that you can see it clearly. Observe its characteristics: study how the petals are formed, their shape, how they grow from the stem and, just as important, study the leaves. When you have mastered a certain flower, put some in a vase and paint away.

You will find it helpful, at times, to use other colours in addition to those in your watercolour box, because the colours of flowers are infinite. For this exercise I have chosen flowers that can be painted with the colours I normally use and which have been used throughout this book.

FIRST STAGE

I have painted these flowers in a much looser style than the still life. I have used a much broader treatment and have not worried as much about detail. The vase, in particular, I worked with deliberate brush strokes, allowing the brush to do the drawing and shadowing at the same time (see below). You must get yourself into the right frame of mind to start this painting. It is not one to be worked on for days; it should be very direct and unlaboured.

The same colours are used for the flowers throughout the five stages. They are: for the yellow chrysanthemum, Cadmium Yellow Pale, not quite pure – add just a touch of Crimson Alizarin; for the red and orange flowers, Crimson Alizarin and a touch of Cadmium Yellow Pale; for the shadows of the white flowers, Coeruleum Blue and Crimson Alizarin.

Draw the flowers and the vase with an HB pencil. Next, soak the paper with your sponge and prepare plenty of watery paint in your palette. First, use your large round brush to paint the yellow flower in the centre, then go on to the top yellow flower, the two left-hand ones, the shadow areas of the white flowers and, finally, the orange and red ones. You will find that the colours run and merge; this is intentional – we are really starting with a wet-on-wet technique.

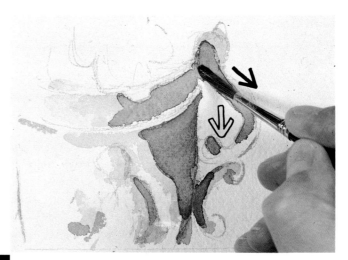

First stage

Second stage

SECOND STAGE

Mix plenty of watery paint in your palette, using Hooker's Green No. 1, Payne's Grey and Crimson Alizarin. Still using your large brush, paint the leaves and stems. As you shape the leaves with your brush you will find that some of them run into each other – again, this is correct. Vary the density and colour of the leaves as you work; this helps to give light and shade to these dark areas. Work freely into the petals of the flowers but make sure that the petals are formed in the right direction.

THIRD STAGE

Work the vase next, using a very wet, loaded brush. Paint the handles and moulding, using French Ultramarine, Crimson Alizarin and Yellow Ochre. If you look at the third stage illustration, you will see how the wet paint formed a natural, long blob at the bottom of the right-hand handle's curve.

Now, add more Yellow Ochre to your mix and paint the background, still using your large brush and working very wet from the top downwards. Go over some of the leaves to give them a little more depth and variation. You can now see the shapes of the white flowers on the right. Put in the shadows cast by the vase on the table top, using the same colours as for the background.

Third stage

93

Fourth stage

FOURTH STAGE

You now need to work over the flowers to add more colour and form. Use the same flower colours that you started with but use more pigment (keep the colour watery but very much stronger). Use your No. 6 brush to draw the petals on the flowers, letting the brush strokes form the petals. Keep the colour of the paint strong, your brush wet, and your brush strokes free – don't get involved with detail. Where you want a little more dark on the red flower, add a little French Ultramarine.

FINISHED STAGE

When using this watercolour technique, if you go too far or put in too much detail at this stage, your picture will lose its charm and freshness. Still using your No. 6 brush, very wet, paint over the inner leaves and main stem, working the dark colour between the petal shapes again to give the final accent (light against dark). You will notice that the two white blooms, top right, appear to be much whiter. This is a typical example of the light against dark principle. Also, the leaf overhanging the vase is much more pronounced, now that it has been painted again. Add some more dark washes to the vase, to give it more definition and to help pull it off the background.

You will find that certain watercolour techniques can only be executed well when the artist is in key with that particular technique. For instance, if you are feeling on top of the world and uninhibited, then this flower exercise or the landscape (see page 98) are the very paintings to work on. On the other hand, if you are feeling cosy, secure and mellow, then you will execute the detailed work in, say, the still life or the pencil-and-wash drawing very much better at that particular time. Remember, the painting comes from your mind, through your arm and hand, into your brush. If you choose the right technique at the right time, you will get the best out of yourself.

Finished stage

445 x 330mm (17½ x 13½in)

EXERCISE THREE
PORTRAIT

First stage

Second stage

Third stage

For the student, portrait painting has many advantages in common with still life and flower painting. You can dictate the lighting, the colour scheme and mood. The painting of a portrait does not depend on the weather but only on your model's availability. But, remember, you always have one model with you – yourself; all you need is a mirror.

Watercolour is not the easiest of mediums to use for portraits but it does have some natural advantages. With watercolour, you can create an impression of the subject that has a very fresh and unlaboured appearance. Also, washes can be used in some very delicate work to give depth to the skin tones. If you find that you start to lose it while working on a portrait, carry on with body colour, or even pen work, and you may find that you have succeeded in painting a good portrait. The likeness can come through as an impression – a feeling. If you want detail, eventually, then you can gradually build up to it through practice and careful observation.

FIRST STAGE

Draw the portrait with an HB pencil. Wet the paper with a sponge and wait until it is nearly dry (when the shine has gone). Then, using your large brush, mix Coeruleum Blue and Crimson Alizarin, and paint the hair, leaving an unpainted area above the forehead. While this is still wet, use Cadmium Red and Yellow Ochre to paint the first wash of the flesh tones, letting this colour mix with the hair.

Use a stronger wash (add Crimson Alizarin and a touch of French Ultramarine to your first wash) to paint the shadow side of the face. This will mix with the wash underneath and keep the edges soft. While it is still wet, paint the beard, using Payne's Grey and Crimson Alizarin.

SECOND STAGE

Now, paint the jacket with a mix of Coeruleum Blue and Crimson Alizarin. While it is still damp add Payne's Grey to your wash and put in the shadows. Paint the wrist and the shadow of the sketching pad.

THIRD STAGE

More detail is to be added to the face in this stage. Use your No. 6 brush and the same colours as in the first two stages, but mix them stronger. If you get a hard line you can soften

Finished stage   325 x 250mm (12³/₄ x 9 ³/₄ in)

it by stroking it with a damp brush. If it is difficult to move, wet the area with your brush and blot up the surface water with blotting paper. (Always keep blotting paper at your side – it is invaluable for getting you out of trouble.) When the face is really dry, use French Ultramarine and Crimson Alizarin to paint the glasses, leaving some areas unpainted for highlights.

FINISHED STAGE

The last stage involves crispening up your painting and adding the jumper. Draw this with a brush, using French Ultramarine, Crimson Alizarin and Yellow Ochre. Now, use your No. 6 brush and a mix of French Ultramarine, Crimson Alizarin and Yellow Ochre: put the dark accents under the right side of the beard, to the left of the jumper, at the back of the jacket collar, and under the jacket lapel. Draw some detail around the jacket pocket and put the shadow on the pad. Finally put a small accent under the hair and paint the pencil.

EXERCISE FOUR
LANDSCAPE

Landscape painting holds the romantic promise of a day spent in the countryside painting away, enjoying ourselves to the full. This applies to many artists but not to all: some people worry about painting while strangers look on, others can't get out into the countryside as often as they would like to. If you lack confidence, the best way to start is to tuck yourself away behind a tree, make a quick drawing in your sketchbook of a scene you would like to paint and mark the main colours in pencil, then paint it at home. As your confidence grows, take your watercolour box outside with you. Remember that nine out of ten people who take the trouble to come to see you will be full of admiration for you and your work.

Sketching in pencil also applies to the person who can't often get outside. Rather than always painting just one scene when you do go out, instead make a few different pencil sketches. Six of them could be completed in a day. Take your watercolour box and some water with you, and make some colour notes on these sketches. Then, when it's stay-at-home day, you can use this information to produce six different paintings.

A landscape can be painted from a window, if necessary, but you must sketch and paint outside as much as possible. Always carry a sketchbook with you; even if you only have ten minutes to sketch a scene and draw only ten lines, you will have had to observe it. The important factor is observation. The knowledge it provides will be committed to your memory and you will find that, in time, you will be capable of painting from memory indoors. Those memory banks must be kept in good condition – take every opportunity to observe and sketch out of doors.

PAINTING TECHNIQUE

I have chosen this landscape for working the wet-on-wet technique; this gives the real, wet, watercolour look. Remember to thoroughly soak your paper. Incidentally, I should warn you that once you start a painting like this you are committed to continue to the end while it is still wet or damp.

FIRST STAGE

I get a great deal of pleasure from using this watercolour technique, especially when worked to the extreme as it is in this exercise. It has an element of risk – where is the paint going? – and one of great excitement. Although you have planned in your mind what you want to do and you can control it to a great extent, there is the certainty of many a happy accident, and even pure surprise. For you to copy this picture, or even for me to copy it, and achieve the same result would be an impossibility. What you have to do is work towards the same composition and if a happy accident occurs, then use it. I will explain what to do, as I have in the other exercises, but remember, your painting will have its own little gems created purely by this wet-on-wet technique.

Draw the picture with your HB pencil, using a minimum of drawing. Soak the paper thoroughly with water. Use your large brush and put on your palette French Ultramarine, Crimson Alizarin, Payne's Grey and Yellow Ochre – don't mix these colours all together in the palette; apply them to the wet paper and they will mix on the surface, creating some beautiful effects. Run the sky into the land and notice the unpainted area I left for the puddle.

SECOND STAGE

Using a wash of Payne's Grey, Crimson Alizarin and Yellow Ochre, paint the middle-distance trees with your large brush. They will run into the sky and lose a bit of shape but don't worry, the impression you are creating is that of a landscape in an early-morning mist. While these trees are wet, paint the main trees into them. Then, using your No. 6 brush, add some smaller branches. Next, take your large brush on to the now damp sky and drag the

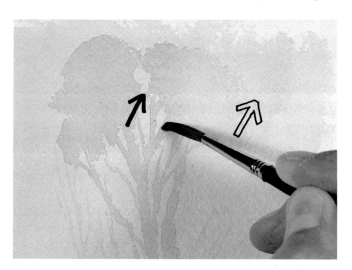

First stage

Second stage

brush down into the wet, small branches (so it all runs together) to form the top of the trees. If at any stage your work dries out too quickly for you, wet the paper again; it may move some of the pigment but if you do it gently, you will get away with it.

THIRD STAGE

With your large brush and plenty of watery paint – Payne's Grey, Burnt Umber, Hooker's Green No. 1 and Crimson Alizarin – paint the foreground. You will notice that the puddle is more obvious, now that a darker tone has been added.

Third stage

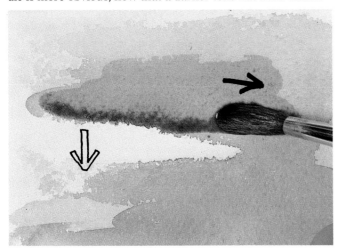

Fourth stage

FOURTH STAGE

Work over the main tree again while it is still damp. Use your No. 6 brush to put in some more branches but keep them light in tone at the top. Also, paint the tree in the left middle distance. Add the little bit of fence to the right of the main tree.

FINISHED STAGE

Put another wash of darker colour over the foreground and add any darker accents you feel necessary for your picture. Don't overdo the detail when using this technique. I will give you some idea of timing on this type of picture: I took about 45 minutes to complete it. The effect cannot be achieved if you work slowly, the very essence of this technique is speed. Some artists use it to start a painting and then, when they reach the final stage, they spend a lot of time working it up into a highly detailed watercolour – you could try that, next time.

Finished stage

370 x 280mm (14¹/₂ x 11in)

EXERCISE FIVE
BUILDINGS

Buildings can be a tremendous source of pleasure to the artist. You may be inspired by the size and splendour of a building or by the quaint, old-world charm of a village street. Watercolour is a good medium to use for buildings, and buildings are a good subject for the student of watercolour. When you look at buildings with a painting in mind, you will see that the colour areas are broken up into quite definite shapes. In an earlier exercise, you looked through the drinking glass to find the shapes and colours; buildings have already done this for you. The shapes of roofs and walls, windows and doors are quite definite and these shapes give you the areas on which to work your washes. But these are disciplined washes and different to those you used for the sky exercises.

A great deal of my watercolour training was done outside, sitting on the pavement, just off the main flow of people, painting buildings. If you are worried about sitting at the top of your local high street to paint, you can usually find some little corner where you can tuck yourself away, unnoticed. One of the great advantages of using watercolour to paint buildings is that you need only a small amount of equipment: stool, sketch block or some paper on a drawing board, paint box, brushes, water container, pencil and eraser. In fact, you don't always need a stool: sometimes, you can get a very good view of buildings from your car, in a car park. I have an estate car and I have often worked from that.

USING PENCIL AND WASH

The subject of this exercise, I believe, is not too advanced and I have made it a pencil-and-wash drawing for those who can draw. If you feel you would rather stick to painting as a technique, you can do so. After drawing the main building areas, simply work with your washes as you did in the still-life exercise. Use the colours I suggest but mix them much stronger (I want the pencil to show through the wash).

For this exercise I used buff 72lb Not paper. It was not stretched, only pinned to a drawing board. Incidentally, I used a piece of cartridge paper as a backing sheet in order to get a better line with the pencil; if you do not do this, the grain of the drawing board can be felt through the paper and will hinder the pencil lines. Because the paper is not very heavy, don't use very wet washes.

FIRST STAGE

Draw the main area of the composition with an HB pencil, then draw the areas that you want to show through the washes. This means all-detail-work areas of tone and shadow. When shading, it is usually best to start at the top of the drawing to avoid working over finished lower areas and smudging them. Start with the chimney and draw the stones, shading a few of them because some are darker than others. Work down on to the tiled roof, then the lower part of the main building, drawing the stones again as you did on the chimney.

SECOND STAGE

Continue drawing with your HB pencil, next working the houses at the end of the street – note that no stonework is drawn on these because this would make them appear nearer. Then, put in the house on the right, working plenty of shading on it because it is in shadow. Put plenty of pencil work on the lean-to against the main building, being very careful with the tiles and windows, and the railings in front of it. Draw the three figures and the shadow cast by the man in broad pencil shading. Add some dark accents with your 2B or 3B pencil. Now, you should have a drawing capable of standing in its own right as a pencil drawing.

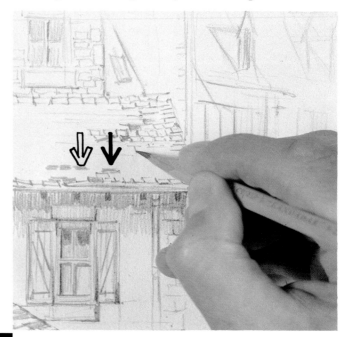

First stage

Second stage

Third stage

THIRD STAGE

Using your large brush, paint the sky with Coeruleum Blue and Crimson Alizarin. Be sure to keep all your washes well diluted so that they do not cover your pencil work. Your pencil must show through in order to achieve the full beauty of this effect. Next, paint the stonework, using Raw Umber, French Ultramarine and Crimson Alizarin.

Fourth stage

FOURTH STAGE

Use a mixture of French Ultramarine, Crimson Alizarin and Raw Umber on the roofs. Paint the red tiles on top of the roofs with Cadmium Red and Cadmium Yellow Pale. Darken the mixture you used on the roofs and use this to work a wash on the windows. Put in the orange-painted wooden beams on the main house and use the same colour for the window frames; put a dark stonework-coloured wash over the buildings on the right and, finally, paint the red canopy at the end of the street with a weak wash of Cadmium Red.

FINISHED STAGE

Paint a wash of Burnt Sienna and Crimson Alizarin over the lean-to extension, then use French Ultramarine and Crimson Alizarin to paint over the windows and the dark wall under the railings. Put a wash on the windows of the left-hand house and add a tone of Yellow Ochre, Crimson Alizarin and French Ultramarine over the front of the house. Put a dark tone on the figure and a broad, dark accent down the right of the two figures against the main house. Apply a wash of French Ultramarine, Crimson Alizarin and Yellow Ochre to the road with your No. 6 brush, using broad strokes. With the same brush, add any dark accents you feel necessary.

Finished stage

370 x 280mm (14½ x 11in)

EXERCISE SIX
WATER

First stage

Second stage

Third stage

A lake or pond (unless discoloured by mud) reflects its immediate surroundings and the sky. In very clear, still water the reflection of a building can be mirror-like; therefore, the water is painted as a building upside-down. This is important: the reflection goes down vertically into the water, not across the surface. It is only the movement of the water that shows as horizontal lines and, remember, any movement breaks up the reflected images. Light on moving water is also seen horizontally. The first, golden rule for painting water is to make sure that all movement lines or shapes are perfectly horizontal. If they are not, you will have painted a sloping river or lake.

The illusion of water can be created quite simply with watercolour. Even leaving white paper to suggest water can be very effective (remember example D on page 87 when you were practising skies – the lake with the silhouette of the cottage at the side is white paper). Painting reflections can be approached in the same way as painting the glass. Observe your subject carefully and decide what the main shapes and colours are. Then go ahead.

A very wet-on-wet technique is usually very descriptive of water. Learn to observe the different moods of water and remember that a reflection immediately creates the illusion of water.

FIRST STAGE

Before you paint water, the surroundings must be painted first because these determine the colours and the shapes on the water. Draw the picture with your HB pencil but don't draw on the water area, these shapes will be created with your brush. Wet the paper with a sponge, then paint a wash of Coeruleum Blue and Crimson Alizarin. Just before it is dry, put in the middle-distance trees with French Ultramarine, Crimson Alizarin and Hooker's Green No. 1. Paint the field underneath, using Cadmium Yellow Pale and a little Crimson Alizarin. Next, paint the roof of the boathouse with Cadmium Red, Cadmium Yellow Pale and Hooker's Green No. 1.

SECOND STAGE

Paint the mooring posts and side of the boathouse, using Payne's Grey and Hooker's Green No. 1. Then paint the tree trunks, working upwards with your large brush and using Payne's Grey, Hooker's Green No. 1 and Burnt Umber. While the trunks are still wet, paint into these with Cadmium Yellow Pale, Hooker's Green No. 1 and Crimson Alizarin to form the leaves. Do this with your No. 6 brush, making diagonal strokes from right to left at a flattish angle to the paper. Paint the boats and bank of the river.

Finished stage   280 x 210mm (11 x 8¼in)

THIRD STAGE

Now wet the paper again over the water area and, while it is still wet, run in the reflected colours. Before you start, decide roughly where they are going to be; for instance, the tree trunks, the red of the roof, and so on. I often have a dummy run over the paper with my brush to get the feel of where the strokes and colours will go. As you can see from this stage illustration, the colours merge and could even be left as finished.

FINISHED STAGE

When the first wash is nearly dry, add more darker-colour washes and more definite reflection shapes to add detail to the water. Finally, scratch out some horizontal highlights with a blade.

EXERCISE SEVEN
SNOW

In some parts of the world snow is never seen. It has a fascination all of its own: the stillness and quietness of a snowy landscape can be unbelievable. The clear rivers of the spring and summer turn to brown and the trees stand out in sharp silhouette.

One of the problems of painting snow is obvious – you can't sit on the ground to paint and, above all, it is usually very cold. If you are going to paint snow out-of-doors, you must prepare yourself for nature's conditions. Always put on more clothing than you think you need – you can always take some off but you cannot go home for more. If you are carrying a sketchbook, put it in a polythene bag so that it will stay dry if it is dropped in the snow. I once dropped mine in a pond – without polythene!

COLOURS IN SNOW

The best advice I can give you, when you are painting snow with watercolour, is to leave as much white paper as possible for snow. Snow is only white in its purest form, when it has just fallen (and even then, it reflects light and colour from all around), but you need the white paper on which to add tone and colour reflections as you build up the painting. Add a little blue to cool the snow colour, or a little red or yellow to warm it up. Never be afraid to make snow dark in shadow areas. In comparison to its surroundings, it can be as dark as a shadow in a non-snow landscape.

FIRST STAGE

Draw the picture with an HB pencil. Then wet the sky thoroughly with a sponge and, while it is still wet, paint it with your large brush and plenty of watery paint, using Payne's Grey, Crimson Alizarin and Yellow Ochre. Before this wash is completely dry, use the same colours, but stronger, to paint the distant trees with very broad, downward brush strokes, leaving the trunks of the main trees untouched.

SECOND STAGE

Now, put in the three dark trees with your large, round brush, using French Ultramarine, Burnt Umber and Crimson Alizarin; work upwards to the top of the tree with a wet, loaded brush. Change to your No. 6 brush while the paint is still wet and work on the small branches. Again, while these are wet, use your large brush a little drier and drag it over the small branches – this gives the shape of the top of the trees. You will find that the paint runs into the branches in some areas and this is what you want. Paint the nearest tree darker.

THIRD STAGE

Start with the farthest trees on the left, using the same colours as before. Paint these very freely and very wet. As you work towards the centre, add Cadmium Yellow Pale, Yellow Ochre, and Hooker's Green No. 1 to warm up the trees that still have some autumn leaves on them. Work these with your No. 6 brush; keep the paint very wet all the time, allowing your small branches to run into each other and merge. When these are nearly dry, add some more distinct branches to bring these trees into focus and to pull the nearer ones away from the middle distance. Also, paint the end of the hut to the right of the main tree, using Cadmium Red and Yellow Ochre.

First stage

Second stage

Third stage

Fourth stage

FOURTH STAGE

Next, work on the buildings. Paint the top edge of the two buildings with Cadmium Red mixed with Cadmium Yellow Pale, using your No. 6 brush. With the same colours put in the front wall of the nearest building, then add some French Ultramarine to your colour and paint the front of the main building (with the door). When this is dry, use the same colour, but darker, to suggest the door; paint the shadow under the gable and the building behind, to the right. Using the same colour, put in the shadow side of the main building (under the guttering). With the same brush and colour, draw the fence at the side of the building.

Now you must put some moulding into the snow and path. Start by working on the ground that is not covered by snow; this is shown as ruts in the earth. Mix Crimson Alizarin, Yellow Ochre and Burnt Umber and use your No. 6 brush to draw these shapes. Remember, the paper you leave unpainted will be snow.

Paint the curve of the canal bank and, adding French Ultramarine to your colour, put in the reflections of the distant trees. With a very wet brush mix Hooker's Green No. 1, Crimson Alizarin and French Ultramarine, work upwards with very free brush strokes and put in the grass and bramble at the bottom right of the picture. You will find that all the colours run together – this is intentional. Mix French Ultramarine and Crimson Alizarin, and paint the shadows on the snow-clad roofs of the buildings, also on the distant field.

FINISHED STAGE

This is the stage that brings the picture to life. Using your large brush, mix French Ultramarine and Crimson Alizarin, and put in the shadows on the snow; keep the edges free and continue the main shadow from the large tree up the side of the wall and over the roof. Keep your colours wet and your brush strokes loose when you paint these shadows; look at the paper first, decide where you are going to paint them, then go ahead. Remember, if you cover up too much white paper, your snow will start to disappear or, at best, the sun will appear to have gone in.

Now, put some more detail work into the large tree and the one to its left. Paint some more small branches and dark accents where needed.

Finished stage   255 x 370mm (10 x 14¹/₂in)

EXERCISE EIGHT
HARBOUR

Usually, artists who like painting the sea also enjoy painting harbours and boats. We feel very similar emotions when we are painting these three subjects but boats make one important difference – they make us feel more intimate with the sea, secure in the knowledge that life is around, especially in a harbour. In this painting of a harbour in Brittany, your next exercise, we can feel the intimacy of the scene: boats are everywhere, creating a feeling of activity, and the sun is dancing on the boats and water.

You need more knowledge of drawing to paint boats than to paint a landscape. For instance, if you paint a branch of a tree lower than the real one, it will still look right in your painting; but if you paint the mast of a boat at the wrong angle, then the painting will look obviously wrong. If possible, spend a few days sketching all the bric-a-brac, natural and unnatural, of a small harbour – from an old wreck sticking out of the mud like the backbone of a great fish, to an old piece of chain, all rusty and abandoned. You will acquire a tremendous amount of knowledge and an invaluable familiarity with the subject.

This harbour scene was taken from a sketch, so I had plenty of time to correct the drawing and make a careful study on the paper in the studio. If I had painted this outside, the drawing would have been looser and the painting would have been more impressionistic. Because of all the activity and the amount of drawing in the harbour, I decided to let you work this as a pen-and-wash drawing. Remember, this is a very sunny, summer afternoon – don't be afraid to use your colours.

FIRST STAGE

Use your HB pencil to draw the picture and make sure that the bottom edge of the harbour wall (i.e. the water level) is horizontal. Now use your large brush to paint a wash of Coeruleum Blue and Crimson Alizarin on the sky, adding more Crimson Alizarin and water as you near the roof tops. With your No. 6 brush and a wash of French Ultramarine and Crimson Alizarin, paint the roof tops; add Cadmium Yellow Pale to the wash and paint the buildings. Let some darker tones work as shadows on the buildings. Add some Hooker's Green No. 1 to this colour and paint the trees. Finally, adding more French Ultramarine to the same wash, paint the near side of the harbour wall, watering down the wash for the distant part.

SECOND STAGE

Start working from the left-hand side of the houses with your No. 6 brush to finish off the houses and little boats; use darker tones and suggest windows with just one brush stroke. Don't worry about too much neatness with your washes because the pen and ink will clean everything up and hold the picture together.

As you work to the right of the buildings, make sure you put in the distinct shadows on the two square, white buildings. Then, let your brush wander along the quay and distant houses, making shapes and suggesting buildings. Work on the middle-distance boats with the colours shown; where you have a white boat use French Ultramarine and Crimson Alizarin for the shadow areas. Work these boats freely – do not get too involved in detail, this will be done by the pen; you are really going for form, expressed by colour and light and shade. For the woodwork on the boats use Burnt Sienna and French Ultramarine, working from the farthest boats to the nearest ones.

THIRD STAGE

At this stage we are ready to paint the water. When you did this in the water exercise, you worked on wet paper. In this harbour scene don't wet the paper first – work on dry paper. Use your large brush, mix a wash of Coeruleum Blue and a little Crimson Alizarin - to reflect the sky colour - and be ready with the local colours of the boats.

Now, start at the harbour wall and work down the painting. It is very important in this technique to leave plenty of white paper showing. Work the brush freely, in horizontal strokes, and add your boat-coloured reflections as you come to them. If the paint runs into another part of the water, let it; this helps to give more feeling to the area. Paint the flat stones on the edge of the harbour wall with French Ultramarine, Crimson Alizarin and Yellow Ochre; use your large brush and keep the strokes horizontal.

FOURTH STAGE

We have now arrived at the pen work. This can be done with various types of pen and using various treatments, but I chose to use a mapping pen. The advantage of using a mapping pen is that you can draw a much finer line than you can with other pens. If you use a felt-tip pen, you can make the stroke down or up the paper equally well, but if

INGENIOUS COMPROMISE: The award-winning NCM headquarters in Cardiff Bay

R OF WALES

Flexible options creep in for EMU

MICHAEL SETTLE
Political Editor

THE temperature in the Cabinet Room at 10 Downing Street is likely to rise by a few degrees this morning as John Major reads the Riot Act to his senior ministers over Government policy on European Monetary Union.

He will undoubtedly tell them – post-Nicholas Bonser – that they must keep their juniors in line to avoid a bloodbath over Europe at the party

Monetary union – the criteria

THE criteria for monetary union are:
● National debts must not exceed 60 per cent of GDP.
● Inflation rates must not exceed 1.5 per cent above the average of the three lowest rates in the EU.
● Interest rates must not exceed two per cent above the average of those of the member states with the three lowest in-

---

ur

erick

ook

er Pontypool the headlines.
hed the then
ested his first
go he became
efore a High
he personally
t to reach the
this century.
is not in the
till able to ex-
t his book at-
ur emerges as
ares to gather
ool perfectly
city.
tion of old
e, next week
st yet of the
w its worries

First stage

Second stage

Third stage

Fourth stage

you try this with a mapping pen and you use too much pressure or the paper has too much tooth, on the up stroke it will bite into the paper and splatter your work with ink, and sometimes bend your nib. So, remember, the down stroke can be heavy but the up stroke must be lighter. Practise on some paper before going on to a painting and, as with your brushes, get used to your pens. Use black Indian waterproof ink.

Now, start on the left of your picture, drawing the houses, windows, shutters, shadows under the eaves, and so on. Work into the distant houses and then use your pen very lightly to get thinner lines because these houses have to stay on the other side of the harbour. Work on the farthest boats in the harbour, giving them shape, and let the pen doodle a little here and there to give a complicated, crowded look in

the middle distance. Remember, you are aiming for suggestion in this area. Work forward, towards the nearest boats, putting in more detail as you near the quay wall. Draw the masts of the larger boats and some rigging. Suggest some stonework on the harbour wall on the right; your pen lines can now be stronger.

FINISHED STAGE

The water is the last stage. Use your pen at a much flatter angle than for the boats and general work (see below). The pen is held very low and makes horizontal strokes. These become thicker and looser than the other pen work. Still leave plenty of white paper. Finally, add any more accents or harbour paraphernalia with the pen.

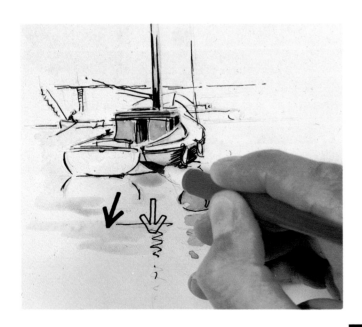

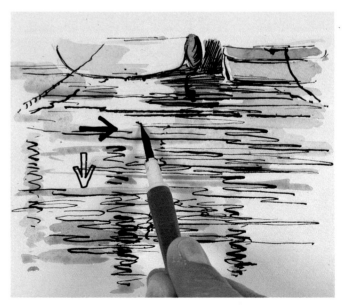

Finished stage

255 x 370mm (10 x 14¹/₂ in)

First stage

Second stage

Third stage

EXERCISE NINE
SEASCAPE

The sea has always fascinated artists. It has extremes of mood, from blissfully romantic to simply terrifying. Like the sky, the sea changes colour and, of course, it is always moving. This must be observed from life: sit on the beach and watch wave after wave coming in to learn how a wave is formed and how it breaks. Then, try sketching with a 3B pencil, concentrating on the overall form of the wave. Of course, you can't draw the same wave but there's another, and another, and another. You have to get a retained image to carry on to the next wave, carry that image on to the next, and so on. Then, you can try painting from life.

Remember that the horizon line must always be horizontal, otherwise the sea will appear to be falling off the paper; if necessary, draw it with a ruler. The sky must match the sea in colour and tone; in general, use the same colours for both. To give a seascape more interest we have cliffs, beaches, rocks and boats. Cliffs and headland give distance and perspective; beaches and rocks give us the opportunity to paint crashing waves and flying spray.

FIRST STAGE

I have taken this painting up to and including the third stage as a pure watercolour. In the final stage, I have continued and finished it in body colour. Basically, this is to demonstrate how, if you find you have lost the quality of a watercolour, you can add White to your colours and, perhaps, save your painting. Also this is another method of working a body colour painting. Now, wet your sky area thoroughly with water, except by the headland, and paint the sky with your large brush, using Payne's Grey, French Ultramarine, Crimson Alizarin and Yellow Ochre. Use the same colours with a touch of Cadmium Yellow Pale to paint the far headland.

SECOND STAGE

Paint the sea with Payne's Grey, French Ultramarine, Hooker's Green No. 1 and Crimson Alizarin, leaving white areas where the waves are breaking and using dry brush to get a sparkle on the water.

THIRD STAGE

Paint the rocks, using Burnt Umber, French Ultramarine and Hooker's Green No. 1. Then, use your large brush to

Finished stage   255 x 340mm (10 x 13 ³/₈ in)

wet the beach and paint it in broad strokes, using the same colours as for the sea but adding Yellow Ochre. You will find the paint runs (wet on wet) to give some lovely, soft, watery effects.

FINISHED STAGE

Before you add White to your colours, put another dark wash over the sky and sea. For the middle distance sea, use White with French Ultramarine and your No. 6 brush; paint the waves (see left) and put the shadow cast by the heavy clouds on the headland. Use almost pure White (add just a little Crimson Alizarin and Cadmium Yellow Pale) to form the large waves and darken them underneath to give shape and form. Darken the beach and, with dry brush technique, add White in horizontal strokes for the foam running up to the rocks.

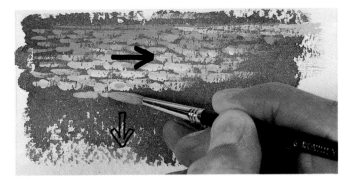

Add more rocks in the distance and let the brush draw some flotsam and jetsam on the beach. Add some white lines on the beach to create ripples of water and some lighter tones on the rocks to show sunlight. Remember, White is added to all the colours in this stage. This is a very popular technique but, like learning how to apply a wash for pure watercolour, you have to practise to get good results.

ACRYLICS

WHY USE ACRYLICS?

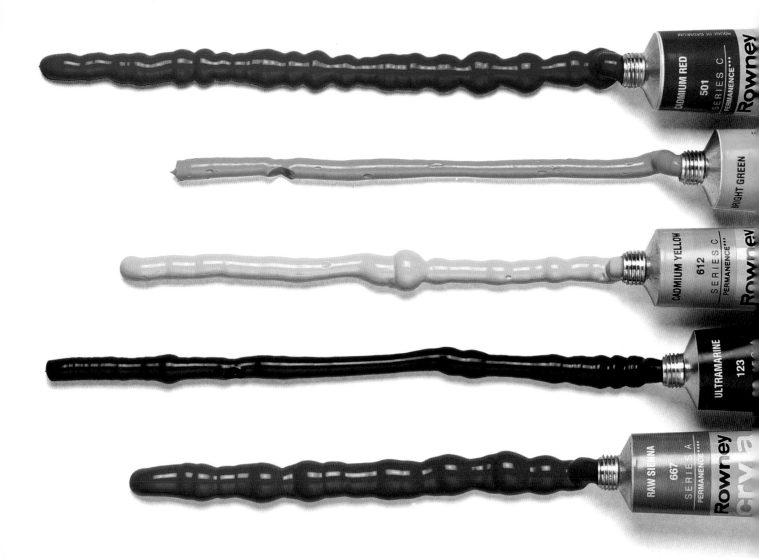

Why do I use acrylic colours? I am constantly asked this question. The quick answer is that I like using them and they suit my personality. I will explain that in more detail and then finish this chapter with a brief technical description of the medium. Acrylic colours first arrived on the market in this country in 1963. Daler-Rowney produce two ranges of acrylic colour which I use, Cryla Colour and Cryla Flow Colour. Cryla Colour is very thick and has a buttery consistency similar to oil colour. Because of its consistency it is highly suitable for palette knife work. A painting can be built up to achieve a tremendous amount of

relief work (impasto). The immediate advantage of acrylic over oil colours used in this way is that oils take months to dry but acrylics take only hours, even when put on really thickly.

Besides artists working with palette knives, there are also artists like myself who use brushes with this medium. This is where the other type of acrylic colour, Cryla Flow Colour, comes in, as it is better to use with a brush, and it takes a little longer to dry than Cryla Colour. Also on the market is a Gel Retarder which you can add to the paint to slow down the drying time; and a paste called Texture Paste for building up heavy impasto. There are also high quality

Fig. 1

nylon brushes, which I use all the time and find best for acrylic painting, apart from small detail work. A Staywet palette, which keeps the paint wet on the palette almost indefinitely, has proved a tremendous breakthrough. It was specially developed for acrylics and it saves a lot of paint that was once wasted by the paint drying too soon.

Why do acrylic colours suit my personality? I believe that a painting comes from the inner self, this gives it the mood – the atmosphere – the invisible quality that makes a painting look alive. If we make a ridiculous assumption and say you have a tremendous urge to paint a particular landscape from one of your sketches and you could paint it in three minutes while that urge was there, then that painting would express your true, uninterrupted feelings on the canvas.

Now, three minutes to paint a picture is ridiculous. However, because acrylic colours dry so quickly, a certain speed is possible. As one stage of the painting is done, you can overpaint immediately without picking up the paint from underneath; consequently, you can keep working while the inspiration is there. If circumstances permit, you can start a painting in the morning and finish it in the afternoon, as each stage will be dry enough for you to follow on with the next. If you like to put detail in a picture, you can do so as and when you feel it necessary, because the paint will dry quickly enough to allow you to work on top of the previous layer.

Being able to paint in this manner is the nearest thing to being able to maintain that feeling throughout the painting. Even if the whole picture can't be finished at one sitting (which is usually the case), at least certain passages can be worked up to your requirements without being dictated by the long drying time of the paint. It is a direct way of painting and this is one of the reasons why it suits me.

USING ACRYLICS

Naturally, as with all painting whether it be oil, gouache, watercolour or whatever, there are techniques to be learned and certain disciplines to be acquired before you can master the medium. Individual techniques are described later in the book. An interesting exercise is illustrated in fig. 1 to show the versatility of acrylic colours. Starting from the bottom, we have a canvas, then a delicate watercolour treatment, followed by Cryla Flow Colour painted flat, then plenty of Cryla Colour giving texture to the surface, and finally Cryla Colour added to Texture Paste (top) to get the ultimate in relief work.

We will now look at the basic working methods. The colours come in tubes; always remember to put the cap back on or the colour will start to dry in the tube. You mix the colour with water – not white spirit or turpentine – and wash your brushes out in water; there is no smell given off when using acrylic colours.

Fig. 2

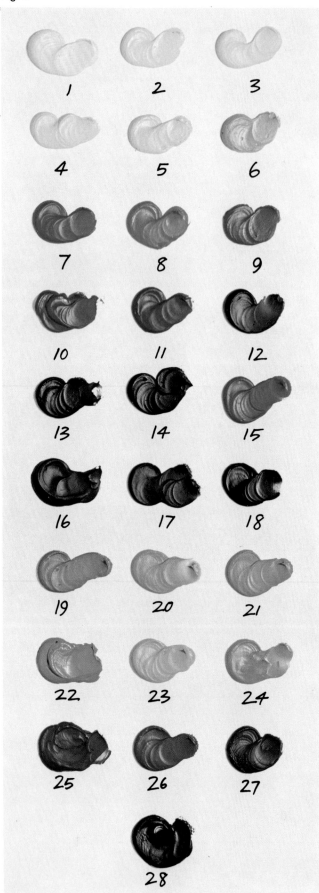

It is advisable to keep your nylon brushes in water all the time – twenty-four hours a day. I have brushes that have lived in water now for seven years. No harm has come to them and since I have been using this method, none has gone hard because of paint drying on it. If you use sable brushes, however, never leave them in water – wash them out immediately after use. If by accident you let a brush get hard, soak it overnight in methylated spirit, then work it between your fingers and wash it out in soap and water.

When you finish using a brush, even if you know you will need it again in a few minutes, put it back in your brush dish; make this one of your first disciplines. When you take it out of the brush dish to use it again, dry it out well on a piece of rag. Keep some clean rag handy at all times for this purpose. Only use a damp brush when working normally, as the acrylic's own consistency is all you need.

When you squeeze your paint out onto the palette, always put the colours in the same position; this is another important discipline. The reason is simple: the way you pick up colours from your palette must become second nature, as you will have enough to worry about without searching for a particular colour. You will see that in fig. 3 I have laid out the colours I use in the order I have them on my palette.

1. Primrose
2. Cadmium Yellow Pale
3. Lemon Yellow
4. Permanent Yellow
5. Cadmium Yellow Deep
6. Cadmium Orange
7. Vermilion (Hue)
8. Cadmium Scarlet
9. Cadmium Red Deep
10. Permanent Rose
11. Red Violet
12. Deep Violet
13. Permanent Violet
14. Indanthrene Blue
15. Cobalt Blue
16. Monestial Blue
17. Monestial Green
18. Hooker's Green
19. Opaque Oxide of Chromium
20. Pale Olive Green
21. Rowney Emerald
22. Turquoise
23. Yellow Ochre
24. Golden Ochre
25. Burnt Sienna
26. Venetian Red
27. Transparent Brown
28. Black

There is no magic about the way these are placed. I started this way at art school and I have stuck with it ever since. Because this colour layout works well I suggest you adopt it. I use these ten colours normally but illustrated on the left, in fig. 2, is the range of additional colours that you can get in both Cryla Flow Colour and Cryla Colour.

If you are not using a Staywet palette, then use either a glass or plastic surface, or even a dinner plate upon which to mix your colours. Remember that the paint will start to dry while you are working. Do not put out more paint than you will be able to use at one sitting unless you are using a Staywet palette.

WHAT ARE ACRYLICS?

I think that's enough to absorb for the time being but, for the technically minded, here is the make-up of acrylics. Artists' acrylic colours are made with the same organic and natural pigments used in the manufacture of oil colours. Instead of being bound in a drying oil, as in the case of oil colours, or a water-soluble gum, as in the case of water-colours, these semi-permanent pigments are bound and dispersed in a transparent, water emulsion of acrylic polymer resin. Acrylic polymer resins are the products of modern chemistry and are familiar to most people in the form of transparent plastics such as Perspex.

Acrylic colours allow a versatility of technique far greater than that of any other medium. The use of additional mediums is covered in the section Basic Techniques (see page 136). The films of paint formed are tough and flexible and not subject to yellowing. Acrylic paintings can be cleaned by gentle sponging with soap and water.

Acrylic colour is today's modern, instant, permanent and multi-purpose artists' medium.

Fig. 3

A   Coeruleum Blue
B   Bright Green
C   Burnt Umber
D   Raw Umber
E   Cadmium Yellow
F   Cadmium Red
G   Crimson
H   Ultramarine Blue
I   Raw Sienna
J   White

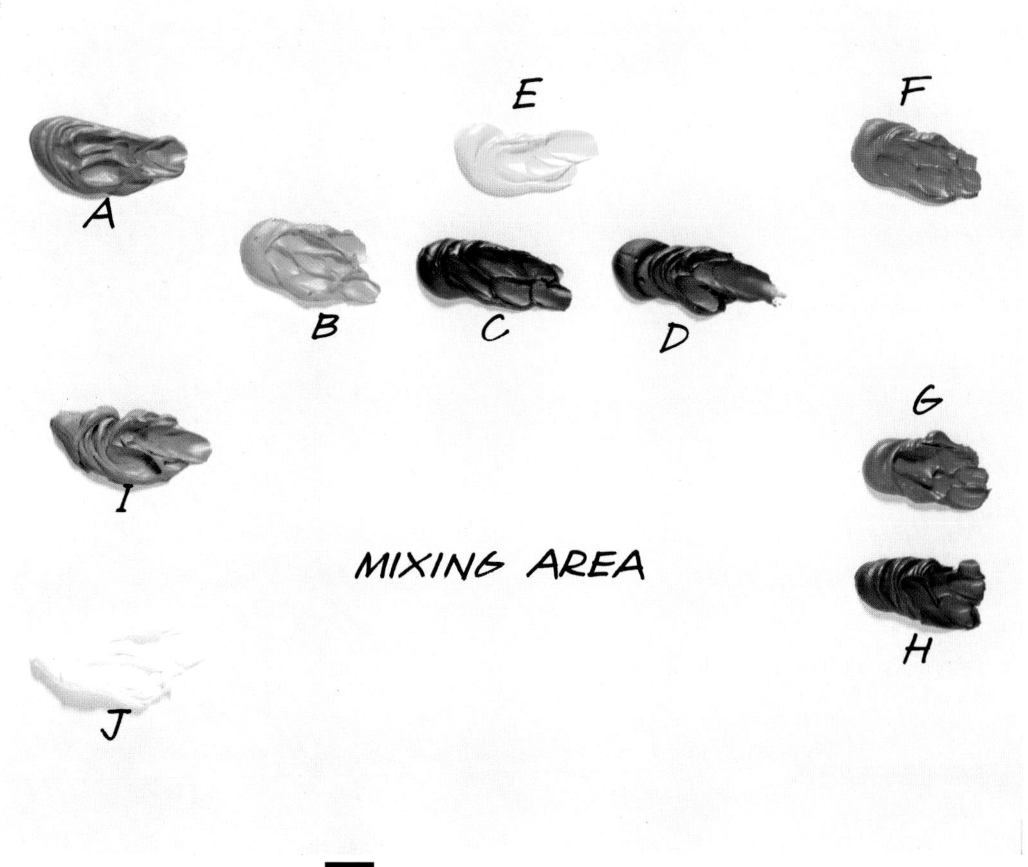

A   B   C   D   E   F   G   H   I   J

MIXING AREA

WHAT EQUIPMENT DO YOU NEED?

Equipment can vary from the basic essentials to a roomful of easels, boards, canvases, a wealth of brushes and so on. Some people collect brushes like some anglers collect fishing floats. There's nothing wrong in this at all – I have far more than I will ever use but I enjoy the feeling that somewhere I have a brush for the job. Anything beyond the basic equipment, I think, must be left to the individual. I will now guide you through the list of basic essentials, bearing in mind that I will recap at the end of this section.

On the facing page is a photograph of a working table in an artist's studio. It is slightly overcrowded intentionally, to show art materials in a working environment and to illustrate how to set up your equipment: the key is below.

BRUSHES

These are the tools of the trade, they are the instruments with which you will create shapes and forms on your canvas and are by far the most important working equipment you will ever buy. I am asked time and time again: What brushes do I need? My answer always is: The best quality; remember, it is the brush that allows your skills to be expressed and seen. Never treat a brush as a showpiece when you are working with it. The brush has to perform different movements and accomplish many different shapes and patterns. If it means that you have to push the brush against the flow of the bristles – then do it. This way, your brushes will gradually become adaptable for certain types of

1   Stretched canvases
2   Staywet palette
3   Easel
4   Water container
5   Brushes, including sable
6   Cryla colours
7   Cryla Flow colours
8   Gloss varnish
9   Paint rag
10 Wooden lay figure
11 Varnish brush
12 Texture paste
13 Gloss medium
14 Painting knives
15 Acrylic primer
16 Matt medium
17 Gel retarder
18 Glaze medium
19 Sketchbook
20 Cryla brushes
21 Water tension breaker
22 Matt varnish
23 Erasers
24 Pencils
25 Drawing board with cartridge paper

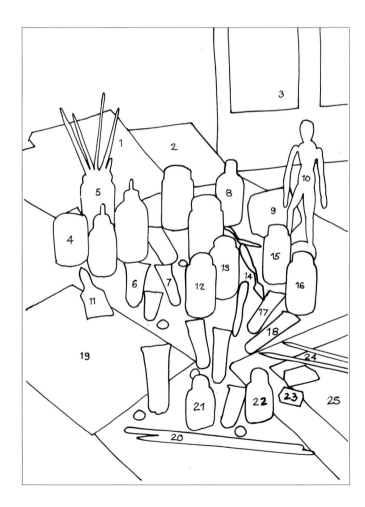

Fig. 4

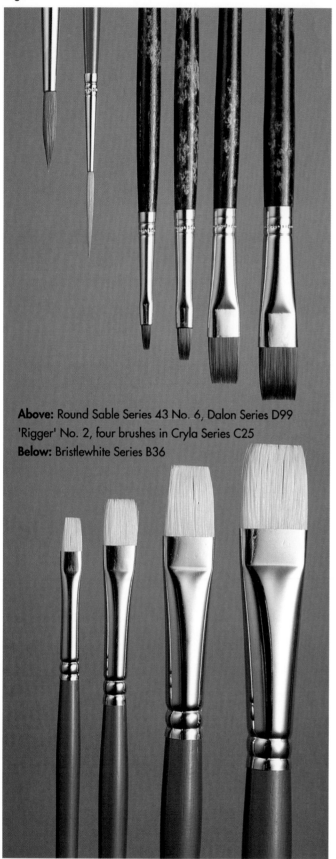

Above: Round Sable Series 43 No. 6, Dalon Series D99 'Rigger' No. 2, four brushes in Cryla Series C25
Below: Bristlewhite Series B36

work; you will get to know them and thus will be able to get the best out of your painting.

For acrylic painting you can use both the traditional stiff hoghair brushes used in oil painting and the soft-haired sable or synthetic brushes usually applied to watercolours. But Daler-Rowney have produced a range of Cryla brushes purpose-made for acrylics (fig.4). These brushes are softer than hoghair and springier than sable, and are available in round, flat and filbert shapes. I recommend Cryla Series C25 flat brushes. However, for dry brush work and applying thick paint with a brush, you may need the extra toughness of hog bristle, and for small detail work you will find a sable or synthetic watercolour brush more delicate. I have listed the brushes you will need with the basic equipment kit on the opposite page.

The tray in which I keep my brushes is an old ice box from the fridge; it is long and flat and has been the permanent home for my brushes for years. When I go out and about demonstrating, I use a tinfoil container, which is just as efficient. There are also special containers on the market for holding brushes in water.

Some artists prefer to use a palette knife instead of a brush. But don't be too rough with the palette knife or you will put a nick in it or catch it in the canvas and flick paint everywhere. Three knives are illustrated (fig. 6) and these could be used as a set to start with.

I have already mentioned palettes and a Staywet palette is illustrated on page 125. This is also the best palette for painting out of doors. You will also need the materials upon which to apply the paint. Canvas, wood, cartridge paper, brown paper, all these can be used as surfaces for acrylic painting. When we start on our first lessons we will be using some of them. You will need a drawing board upon which to rest your paper, to give you a firm support while painting.

Three easels are illustrated (fig. 5). Easels are not essential for small work if you are working on paper pinned to a drawing board, but the small table easel is ideal if you want your board at an angle on the table. The large, radial studio easel is essential for large work, as the support you are using must be held firm. The last easel illustrated is a portable one for use out of doors; it also folds down and turns into a carrying box for your paints and a canvas up to 685 mm (27in) deep. It can also be used indoors as your permanent one.

Gel Retarder is very useful to have as it is used for large areas of painting wet on wet. We will come to this in the section Basic Techniques (page 136). You will need some acrylic primer for surfaces that are porous and Texture Paste for the Basic Techniques exercises. You will need a water jar for washing out your brushes; this can be anything from a jam jar to a Ming vase. Finally, you need HB and 2B pencils and an eraser.

BASIC EQUIPMENT KIT

You will need the set of ten Cryla Flow colours shown on page 123. Your brushes should be from the Bristlewhite Series B36 Nos. 8, 4 and 2, and the Cryla Series C25 Nos. 12, 8, 4 and 2. You can start with fewer than this, but make sure you have a range of small and large sizes. Add to these a Dalon Series D99 'Rigger' brush No. 2 and a round sable No. 6.

Your additional items are a Staywet palette; drawing board and paper – brown paper, white cartridge paper, acrylic-primed paper in a pad (varying sizes); brush tray; acrylic primer; water jar; HB and 2B pencils and an eraser. This basic kit will see you through the first exercises and, as you gain more confidence, you can add to your equipment.

Fig. 6   Fig. 5

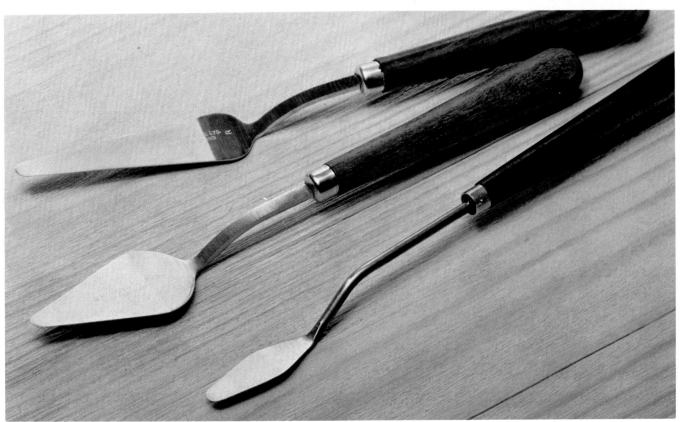

Let's Start Painting

We have now reached the stage where you can start painting. If you have read my comments on this in the watercolour section, you will realize that whatever the medium, the problems are the same. Perhaps there is one advantage, however, when using acrylics as compared to watercolour. If you make a mistake, you can overpaint and change the image, simply because the paint can be used opaquely.

PLAYING WITH PAINT

The best way to start is to find yourself a piece of ordinary brown wrapping paper and play with the paint on it. Feel how the paint comes off the brush on to the paper. Add water to it, try a palette knife, smudge it with your fingers, see how long it takes to dry, use different brushes and don't worry about shapes. All you are doing is doodling (fig. 8), but with a difference. You are being positive with your 'doodles', you are finding out and observing what happens when you do different things. You are experimenting with acrylic colour. You will find this is a very exciting stage of using a new medium, finding out what it can do.

MIXING COLOURS

The main difference to watercolours when you are mixing your colours, is that you add White to make the colours lighter. Remember, you do not use White with watercolours. In fig. 9, I have taken the primary colours and mixed them to show you the results. In the first row, Cadmium Yellow mixed with Ultramarine makes green. If you then add White, you finish up with a light green. In the second row,

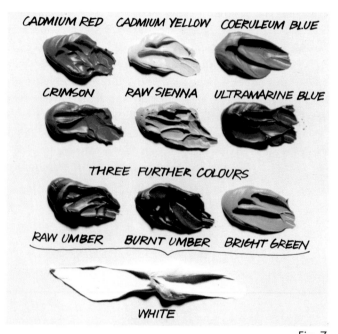

CADMIUM RED   CADMIUM YELLOW   COERULEUM BLUE

CRIMSON   RAW SIENNA   ULTRAMARINE BLUE

THREE FURTHER COLOURS

RAW UMBER   BURNT UMBER   BRIGHT GREEN

WHITE

Fig. 7

Cadmium Yellow is mixed with Cadmium Red and this makes orange. To make orange look more yellow, add more yellow than red, and to make it more red, add more red than yellow. Add White to make the orange paler.

I don't use black paint with any of the mediums I work with. I make my 'black', or dark colours, by mixing the three primary colours together – red, yellow and blue (fig. 7). If you do feel you want to use black, then do, but use it very sparingly. One word of warning – if you use it to darken colours, which is common practice for beginners, it could make your

Fig. 8

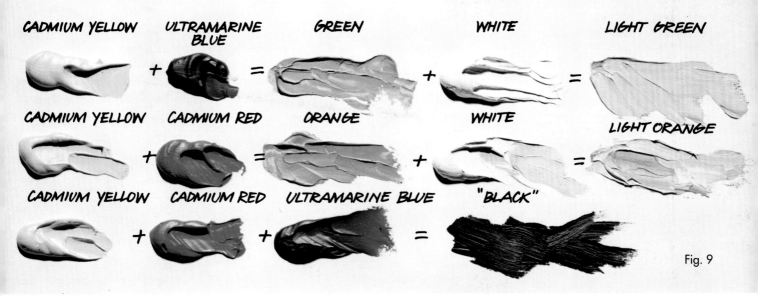

CADMIUM YELLOW		ULTRAMARINE BLUE		GREEN		WHITE		LIGHT GREEN
CADMIUM YELLOW	+	CADMIUM RED	=	ORANGE	+	WHITE	=	LIGHT ORANGE
CADMIUM YELLOW	+	CADMIUM RED	+	ULTRAMARINE BLUE		"BLACK"	=	

Fig. 9

colours look dirty, or dull. It is far better to darken your colours working from the three primaries.

The only advice I can give you for mixing colours is to practise. Some students have a natural ability for this and they adapt to colour mixing very easily, but others find it takes them longer to master it. Practise on some white cartridge paper. It's like doodling, but this time you are doodling with colours. Don't worry about shapes, just go for a colour, mix it on your palette and put a brush stroke on your paper to check the colour. Keep at it, and enjoy this experience.

One last but very important word, which applies to acrylics the same as to other mediums. When there are only three basic colours, it is the amount of each colour that plays the biggest part. You can easily mix a green as in the first line in fig. 9, but if it is to be a yellowy green, then you have to experiment on your palette; you have to work in more yellow until you have the colour you want. The important rule to remember is to put the predominant colour into the palette first, then add the other colours to them.

PAINTING WITH GIVEN SHAPES

Now the time has come to learn to control the paint brush. A lot of control has to be exercised when painting edges of areas that have to be filled in with paint, like the circle in fig. 10. Take a two-pence piece or something similar and draw round it with an HB pencil. You can do this on cartridge paper or brown paper. Use your sable brush with plenty of water. Remember, with Cryla brushes you should just dampen the bristles but with sable brushes you need water mixed with the paint to allow the latter to run out of the brush. Try it now, before you start filling in your circle, and get used to the right mix.

When filling in the circle, start at the top and work down the left side to the bottom. Let the bristles follow the

brush, i.e. pull the brush down. Try to do this in two or three movements. While painting the left side you will notice that you can follow the pencil line but as you start at the top again and paint the right-hand side, your brush will cover some of the pencil line and you will feel slightly awkward. The answer is to accept that it feels a bit awkward but the more you practise the more natural it will feel.

Now let's go on to straight lines. This time, have a go at drawing a square, like the side of a box. Try this one freehand, don't draw round anything. You can paint the edges of the box with a sable brush again or use a small, flat brush as in fig. 11. Experiment with this flat brush, trying out various ways of holding it. You can then use this same brush for filling in the square.

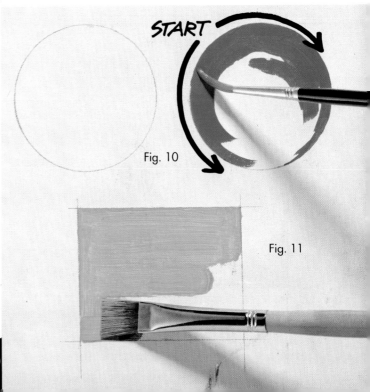

START

Fig. 10

Fig. 11

LOOKING AT TONES

When you are painting, it will help you with shapes if you look at the scene through half-closed eyes. The lights and darks are exaggerated and the middle tones tend to disappear: this gives you simple, contrasting shapes to follow. I made the point earlier that you do not have to be a perfect draughtsman to be able to paint, and if you want to enjoy painting, then you must not let this put you off. If you go round an exhibition by a number of artists, you will see a tremendous range of different types of painting. Some are very detailed, some are almost flat areas of colour.

Look at fig. 12: I have done a pencil drawing of a landscape. In fig. 13, I have simplified it considerably when I painted it. This is what you have to aim for at this stage.

Fig. 12

Fig. 13

PAINTING SIMPLE OBJECTS

We are now ready to paint some simple and familiar objects. The best way to start is to copy my illustrations. This will save your worrying about the drawing problems inherent in copying a real object. However, when you have copied from the book, then get the object, set it up in front of you and have a go from the real thing. You will thus feel more familiar with the object itself, having painted it first from the exercise in the book.

These simple objects must be treated in the broad sense without worrying about detail. Try to paint direct in these exercises; in other words, go for the colour you see and try to get it first time on to the paper. These exercises are not meant to try your skill at details but to give you experience in painting a whole picture, observing shapes and tones, and applying what you see to paper. In this lesson we will use different supports (surfaces) on which to paint.

TRY PAINTING A BRICK

Start by painting on cartridge paper. Our first simple object is a brick; I am sure you can find one somewhere. Paint the brick as a box (you can look at how this works in the water-colour perspective section on page 73), giving each side its own colour to indicate the light and shade.

The background was painted beforehand. The top of the brick was painted first, using the colours shown in fig. 14, then the two sides separately. The recess in the top of the brick was done last by adding shadow to its left-hand side (fig. 14, right) .

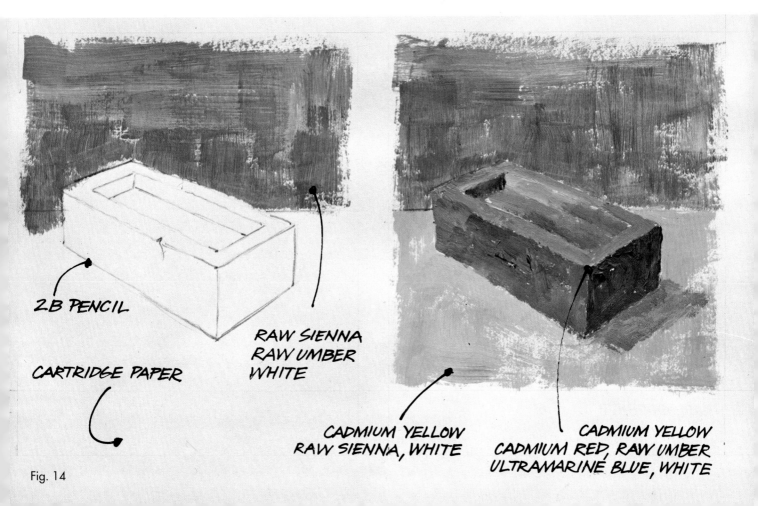

2B PENCIL

CARTRIDGE PAPER

RAW SIENNA
RAW UMBER
WHITE

CADMIUM YELLOW
RAW SIENNA, WHITE

CADMIUM YELLOW
CADMIUM RED, RAW UMBER
ULTRAMARINE BLUE, WHITE

Fig. 14

A STRUGGLE TO DRAW

LGO benefit in transfusion

TABLE TENNIS

Cook getting the other two for Mouchel.

In Division Two the Ae teams started well. Th D 7-3 with their A. Mouchel B 8-4 with the latter match exit John Hodkinson far — other blood in

Nalgo A... a comeback.... John Sterfield....

Newcomers... off to a good start over Old W led by ser... served... over the year... when... match...thel drew... while... Theresa... Brian...

KCETERS NDOORS

art of the ... et com... Leisure ... of which... national... ent in...

surprise ... year's... game... started...

Esher were the vict... run, 66 to 65. Woking and Horsell ... on the wrong side of ... again by the odd run and ... an identical score, 66 to 65. After a bad start, Avorians thrashed Westfield 108 to 53. Keith Bedford pulled them together with a fine knock of 46 after they had lost their first three wickets for 20 runs. Byfleet beat Old Hamptonians 36 to 33 in another well contested game.

and Gordon Aplin all scored one each.

Newly promoted Post Office carried on in Division Three where they left off last season with a 10-0 win over New Haw A, who had ex Division One player Alan Hughes in their ranks.

In Division Four Post Office B were defeated 8-2 by Old Woking C. BAe D beat Byfleet LTC F 7-3. Dave Thomas winning a 1 three. However, BAe E went down 6-4 to Bedseve whose number one, Ian Hunt, won all his games.

Newcomers CUACO drew with Botleys B, their top player, M Derbyshire, winning his three singles. In the same section BAe F won 9-1 over Mouchel D and Hersham B beat Airscrew D 8-2. Both Division Six results were 6-4 wins. New Haw B beat Broadoaks C and BAe G beat Byfleet LTCH.

Division One: Nalgo A 9, 77 D h 1; Byfleet LTC A 5, Mouchel V 5.
Division Two: BAe B 6, Mouchel B 4; BAe A 7, 77 D 3; Old Woking B 3, Premier A 7.
Division Three: Post Office A 10, New Haw A 0.
Division Four: Byfleet LTC F 8, B Office 2; Old Woking C 8, Post Office B 2.
Division Five: Airscrew D 2, Hersham B 8; Mouchel D 1, BAe F 9; CUACO 5, Botleys B 5.
Division Six: New Haw B 6, Broadoaks C 4; BAe G 6, Byfleet LTC H 4.

BEXLEY 1, CHOBHAM ?
(Spartan League)

ALTHOUGH Chobham held the lead for most of the game, they were very lucky to get a point as Bexley posed a very real threat from start to finish. Certainly during the first half a goal to Bexley seemed inevitable as they won the majority of the high balls.

Their attacking moves called for many good saves from an improved Steve Osgood and goalmouth clearances by Mickey Elliott, Pat Folan and Phil Marlow.

Despite this good defence on Chobham's part, Bexley still had more than their share of shots just scraping the cross-bar. An early infringement by Bexley's goalkeeper saw Chobham awarded a free-kick which unfortunately did not pay off. Neither did they benefit from a chance made by Keith Lawrence when, after a fast sprint down the right, his cross was not followed up.

After 25 minutes Norman Rudd got into his stride and ran the ball nicely past Bexley's defence to score for Chobham. Just before the interval Chobham put in a good attack but it was Bexley who at the half-time whistle had a dangerous looking move going, but this was stopped by Elliott putting the ball out of play.

PENALTY

Early in the second half came proof of the over false being adopted by Spartan League officials, when a imprecation on the referee by Bexley's goalkeeper, resulted in his immediate dismissal on the cards, and an indirect free-kick awarded to Chobham.

Despite appeals by Bexley for offside, Peter Hennessy later broke away but his first shot came off the goalkeeper and his second went just over the bar.

With 15 minutes left to play, a good shot by Bexley was headed clear by Elliott. Then to much amazement the referee awarded Bexley a penalty for alleged pushing by a Chobham player. From the spot Peter Raven made no mistake and Bexley were on equal terms.

The home team again came very close to scoring in the closing minutes. Chobham's last chance went to Elliott but his free-kick was superbly pushed over the bar by Bexley substitute goalkeeper.

Nice surprise came after the game. The Bexley players dismantled and stored away the goal posts. It transpires that they also pay for the task's training.

Chobham: Osgood, Marlow, Folan, Elliott, McGonigle, Hennessy, Rudd, Webb, Langley, Lawrence, Finn. Subs: Rocha, Minnett.

Home team in vain bid

RICHMOND VILLA 4, MONUMENT RANGERS 2

VILLA took charge of the match when... VILLA took an early lead when a ball almost... a half almost... their second... near Chamberlain. In the second half play was confused from a midfield... gain had to fight to stay in the game. But the home side scored twice more to end up 4-2 winners.

Monument Rangers: Chamberlain, Lee, Marna, Clarke, Evans, Davies, Crooks, Mandeville. Subs: Hack, Meredith.

Cards loose grip

WOKING RESERVES 0, STAINES RESERVES 4

ONCE again injury prevented Manager John Martin fielding the older heads to steady his younger players in the step up to more senior football.

Staines presented one stronger sides to visit ... but in spite of th... side acquitte... during the int... Un... hal...

Staines' third goal came as a ... had thigh injury. Woking were unlucky when... ... minutes of the... the referee penalise...

Reserve out

FRIMLEY GREEN RES. 1, SHEERWATER...
(Surrey Intermediate Cup)

SHEERWATER travelled to Spartan Leaguers Frimley Green and were unlucky to come away empty handed. The visitors dominated the first half and as early as the first minute a Dave Steel shot was cleared off the line by a defender.

After 20 minutes Frimley took the lead against the run of play, when a ...

long throw-in was headed in by Hickman.

Sheerwater continued to attack and were unfortunate not to equalise before half-time.

After the interval Sheerwater continued to pressurise for the goal they deserved, but it... any with Graham Hancock can... scoring twice... effort go...

Sheerwater Res: ... Annals, Ewing, Dun George, Green, Be... Hancock, Fallon, Steel... Steel. Subs: ...

Flying sta... for ...

WOKING... WEST...

WOKING... flying...

Field still out of luck

MALDEN TOWN 1, WESTFIELD 0
(Home Counties League)

FIELD must be wondering what they must do to change their luck. Playing against an experienced Malden side, they completely outclassed them for long periods of the match.

Town started with a strong wind in their favour, but the dash and control of Channon, Stillwell, and Jones had their defence in a shambles.

Twice in 20 minutes a Malden defender scrambled the ball off the goal line.

Field's centre half had to come off because of a twisted ankle and Dave Robson took his place, with John Rose moving to defence.

Brian Paramore and Ian Barrow were doing well in Field's defence. Good interpassing by Rose and Robson... good space for Stillwell to get the ball to goal, but without result.

Just after half-time a 3 by Jones was cleared... Field had chances to have seen...

... started with Pete Jeffries hit a long pass to Andy Brown who scored easily.

Virginia Water fought hard to get back into the game, but found Daly, Styles and Nick Ford in excellent form.

In the 30th minute Brown beat two defenders to score his second goal. Then a mistake by the Field left-back enabled Virginia Water to score, making it 2-1.

Just before half-time Fore scored the best goal seen at Woking Park this season. Fore started the move deep in half. The ball touched five players before he hit a tremendous 20yd volley into the Virginia Water net: 3-1 to Field.

Westfield: Gould, Unsworth, Barrow, Paramore, Parsons, Legge, Channon; Stillwell, Jones, Rose, Buchan. Sub: Robson D.

WESTFIELD RES. 3 VIRGINIA WATER 1

THE Reserves continued their run of seven games without defeat, with a brilliant win as the Intermediate Cup.

Field quickly settled down to good constructive football chances falling to Dodd and Collett.

In the 15th minute Pete Jeffries hit a long pass to Andy Brown who scored easily.

Westfield: Jeffries, Balchin Daly, Styles, Rowbotham, Fox, Collett, Dodd, P. Baldwin, Brown. Sub: Dodd A.

Replay will decide issue

BISLEY 3, HORSELL 3

IN extra time Bisley went ahead. But on the turn town Peter Eyles scored to give Horsell a draw and a replay in the Surrey Junior Cup.

Horsell: King, Clark, Ken... Durgin, Povey, Eyles, Mintram... Pratt, Mercer, Harper, Inge... Pelham, Richards.

Woking takes command

... 5, HAMBLE OLD BOYS 2

... at a Woking ... domination ... d in this game. ... y against a good side ... from a... igher league.

Woking started well and the goals from Preshaw and Oliver were just rewards for their efforts. The game, however, was...

Continuous pressure brought about a short corner, which resulted in a penalty flick when a solid stick tackle prevented the shot being made. This was coolly converted by Browne, one of several new young players in this year's first team. A misdirected push in from a...

Craig, Wren, Oliver, Preshaw, Corner, Browne.

HAMBLE OB II 5, WOKING II 2

THE teams were well matched. The score could easily have been Hamble 8, Woking 8, but it was not to be, and Hamble ended up winners on the day.

Gaps in the Woking defence allowed the second of the two...

to Woking's first goal. A deceptive shot from Peirce glided past the goalkeeper to make it 3-1.

Hamble failed to convert a penalty flick, the shot being saved by Wareham, but another led to the fourth goal.

A fifth soon followed with the defence very square. However, Woking were still able to reply, Burch scoring a fine goal with...

Rugby
(Saturday, October 14)

A XV: Chobham v. Guildford and Godalming. Ex A XV: Chobham v. Haslemere. B XV: Chobham v. Haslemere. BAe 1st XV v. Wimbledon II (away); BAe 2nd XV v. Wimbledon II (home).

Netball
(Saturday,...)

Han... Division...

PAINTING FRUIT

We will now use newspaper. On the opposite page (fig. 15) is a newspaper with a banana painted directly on to it. The banana was drawn on the newspaper with a 3B pencil and then the background was painted. Don't try to keep to the pencil line as if it were a magnet. If you go over, it doesn't matter because the colour will cover it up.

Now paint the banana using a No. 4 brush and a mix of Cadmium Yellow, Raw Sienna and White, and Burnt Umber for the spots. Use Burnt Umber and Ultramarine for the background. Keep the paint thick rather than wet, as the newspaper is porous and water will make it mushy. Once the paint is dry, it will strengthen the paper because you have put a thin layer of plastic (paint) on the surface.

The next banana (fig. 15, bottom left) was painted on top of primer. The paper was primed first with acrylic primer to counteract the absorbency of the newspaper. When it was dry, I drew the banana with a 3B pencil and painted it using the same colours as before.

The orange (bottom right) was painted direct on to the newspaper without priming. Mix Cadmium Red, Cadmium Yellow, Burnt Umber and White for the fruit, Bright Green and Burnt Umber for the background. This time, try using the paint very thick; use Cryla Colours to create texture. You will also gain experience in using paint that is not quite so easy to handle as Cryla Flow Colour.

PAINT A SAUCEPAN

Now let's turn to brown paper; find some, and we will use that for our next exercise. I have chosen a pan for this one (fig. 16), for a very good reason: you will have to draw a round object instead of a square one. Here the only problem is the ellipse; that is the oval shape you see when you look at the pan. An ellipse is a circle that gradually flattens according to your eye level. Take a two-pence coin and hold it upright in front of you: it is now a circle. Now turn it round, closing one eye; as you turn, the circle flattens and becomes an ellipse. When you draw the ellipse, never give it pointed ends, the line must be continuous as if bent out of a piece of piano wire. If you look closely, you will see there are no sharp corners but just one continuous line all the way round.

Instead of the clean, crisp edges of the box, you now have rounded forms which will enable you to practise moulding and graduating your colour to show a curved surface. On the pan side, you can do this by either working the paint from light to dark or by starting with the dark side and adding lighter colour as you go to the light edge of the pan. You may need to work at this pan more than once to get used to round surfaces.

Fig. 15 (left)   Fig. 16 (right)

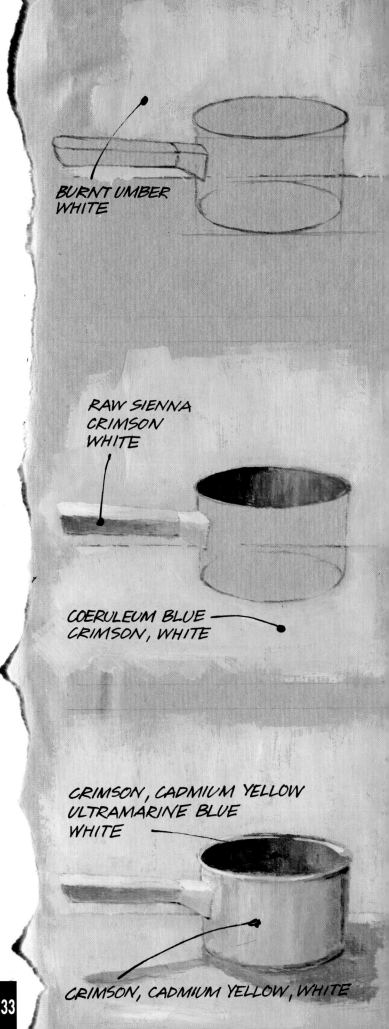

BURNT UMBER WHITE

RAW SIENNA CRIMSON WHITE

COERULEUM BLUE CRIMSON, WHITE

CRIMSON, CADMIUM YELLOW ULTRAMARINE BLUE WHITE

CRIMSON, CADMIUM YELLOW, WHITE

Fig. 17
Fig. 18

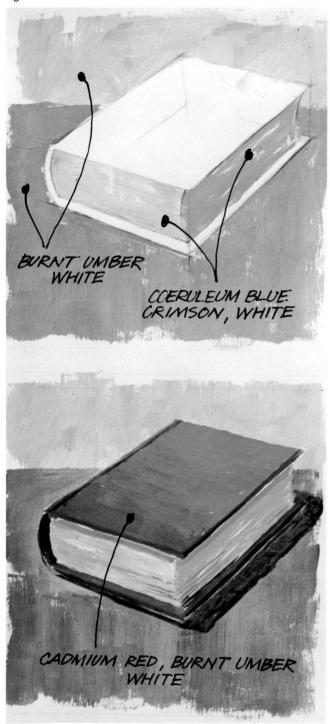

BURNT UMBER
WHITE

CŒRULEUM BLUE,
CRIMSON, WHITE

CADMIUM RED, BURNT UMBER
WHITE

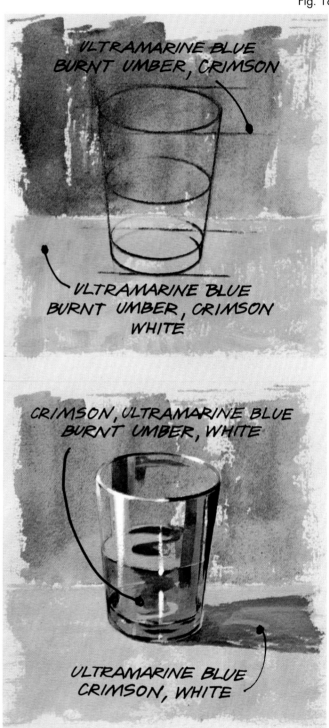

ULTRAMARINE BLUE
BURNT UMBER, CRIMSON

ULTRAMARINE BLUE
BURNT UMBER, CRIMSON
WHITE

CRIMSON, ULTRAMARINE BLUE
BURNT UMBER, WHITE

ULTRAMARINE BLUE
CRIMSON, WHITE

WORK ON A BOOK

Now back to cartridge paper. Find yourself a book, preferably a plain-coloured one, and try this on white cartridge paper. We are back to a simple shape again, but this subject demands the extra skill that you should have now acquired.

Paint as usual but where you come to the pages, half-close your eyes to see how dark the white pages are on the shadow side. I think you will be quite surprised to find how dark they are. Use a broad, flat brush and take it along the pages; you will find that some of the brush strokes look like the edges of the pages.

LOOKING AT GLASS

Now try working on coloured paper. Here is the trickiest object so far, a glass. Use one that is plain and simple in shape; the secret lies in what you leave out, not what you put in. Paint the background thinly, to let the drawing show through. Then, working from top to bottom, put a dark tone on the shadow side of the glass. Remember the ellipse; now draw that on the top and bottom of the glass with a small sable brush. Working again from top to bottom, put in the highlight on the left. If you thought that glass was colourless, you will have to think again!

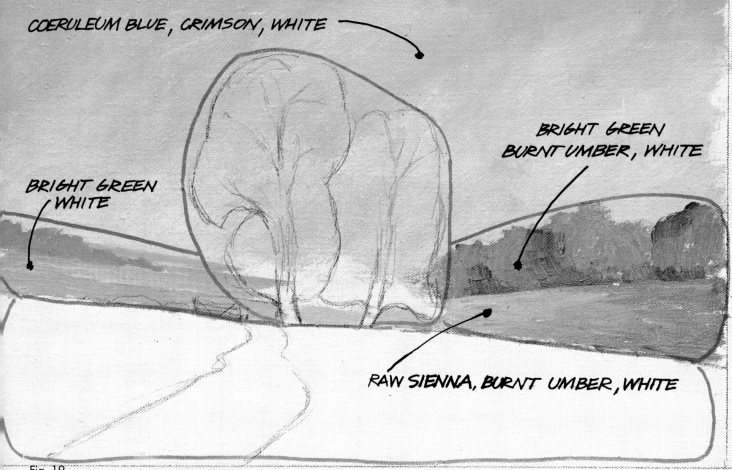

COERULEUM BLUE, CRIMSON, WHITE

BRIGHT GREEN
BURNT UMBER, WHITE

BRIGHT GREEN
WHITE

RAW SIENNA, BURNT UMBER, WHITE

Fig. 19

LANDSCAPE EXERCISE

Now try a canvas. In this exercise I have sketched on canvas a simple landscape with a tree. This is the last exercise you will do before you learn some of the different techniques of acrylic painting. It may be somewhat advanced at the moment but it will add a little spice to the exercises you have been doing. I want you to use the same methods you have been using up to now, avoiding detail and going for the shapes, colours and tones.

Draw the picture with an HB pencil and paint a clear, blue sky, using the colours shown. At a second stage, when the sky is dry, paint the middle distance. Next, using a broad treatment, paint the large tree and foreground. For the lighter greens and for the foreground try using Cryla Colours; they will add texture and will help to bring the foreground near to us, pushing the background further away. Don't try to put detail in this picture, that will come at a later stage.

BRIGHT GREEN, CADMIUM YELLOW
RAW UMBER, WHITE

BRIGHT GREEN, RAW UMBER, WHITE

RAW UMBER
WHITE

Basic Techniques

By now you should be used to handling acrylic colour and know the feel and texture of it. While working on the previous lessons, you will have found different techniques for using the paint. This you could have done consciously or subconsciously. If you have found a way of painting a thin line with a thick brush for instance, don't think this is wrong. Generally speaking, any way you find to achieve a desired result is fine. In this section I will explain some of the techniques I use for acrylic painting.

In all the illustrations I have marked the movement of the brush strokes with black arrows. Also, to indicate the movement of the brush in relation to the canvas, when you are working from top to bottom or bottom to top, I have marked the direction with an outline arrow. For instance, if you look at the first illustration (fig. 20), you'll see that the brush is being moved left to right, and travelling from top to bottom.

Fig. 20

WET ON WET

This is a name given to the method of brushing wet paint onto and into more wet paint on a canvas. This helps to mould colours into one another and graduate them evenly from, say, dark to light. On small areas, this can be done quite easily with acrylic colour, but if a larger area, say 510 x 405 mm (20 x 16in), is to be painted wet on wet, use acrylic Gel Retarder, which will slow the drying process and allow wet on wet painting. Try using one brush of Gel Retarder to one of paint. You will find from experience how much you need for your own requirements. Move the brush from side to side, moulding the colours together and getting soft edges. If you follow my example in fig. 20, work from the light of the cloud, down the canvas to the darker tones.

PAINTING THIN

Painting thin is a way of painting transparently and can be done at any required time. If you paint thinly, it means that the underlying surface will show through your paint. The surface could be the clean canvas or areas of colour. Painting thin is a way of glazing. In this example (fig. 21) the painting-thin technique is being used to paint the sky over the drawing of buildings while still retaining the drawing. To achieve this, brush the colour in more than usual and it will spread, thin out and become less opaque.

Fig. 21

DRY BRUSH

This is a technique that works well in most forms of painting. It is used to achieve a hit-and-miss effect, thus giving sparkle and life to the brush stroke. Although it can be applied to many subjects in order to express certain feelings, one of its most natural areas of application is water. Dry brush can give ripples, sparkles, highlights and movement to water. The illustration (fig. 22) shows water reflections and the dry brush is adding sparkle and movement.

Dry your brush out more than usual, load it with paint, work out the excess paint on your palette, then drag the brush from left to right in straight horizontal strokes across the water. The paint will hit and miss, leaving parts of the background showing through. For some effects you can work thick paint in a dry-brush technique over the same area time and time again. This will give you depth in the area you are painting. With acrylic colour this can be done quickly, as the paint is quick-drying.

Fig. 22

Fig. 23

MISTY EFFECT

A misty effect in a landscape or seascape can give it a lot of atmosphere. Using acrylic colour, I have found that I can add the mist to the painting at any time, rather than having to work it in as the painting is being progressed. Since the paint dries quickly, there is usually no waiting time for this effect to take place.

Dry the brush out and add a small amount of paint, rubbing it backwards and forwards on the palette until it is very dry. This is really a very, very dry brush technique. Scrub the area to be painted with the brush and you will cover areas in mist; by continuous scrubbing you will find that, as the brush uses up most of its paint, the areas of mist now being applied will be more transparent, showing some background through. This, of course, is part of the effect. The mist in fig. 23 was painted in this way.

Try not to have too much thick paint left by earlier brush strokes on the surface where you intend to have your mist patches.

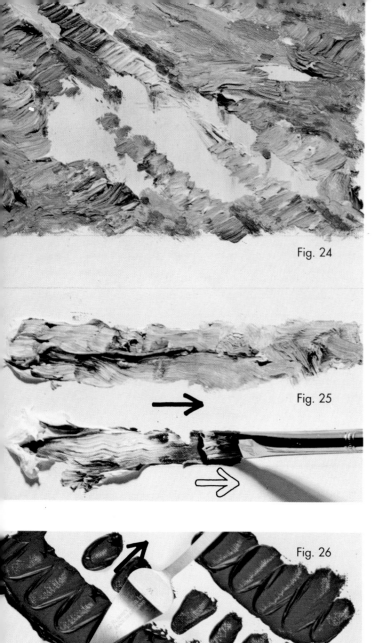

Fig. 24

USING TEXTURE PASTE

Texture Paste is an acrylic polymer extender for building up heavy impasto textures. That is the technical phraseology! It looks and feels like a very thick white paint. It can be put on canvas or any painting surface very thickly, up to 20mm (³/₄in) thick if required. When it sets, it is hard and can be painted over. I use Texture Paste for foreground work where impasto effects help with moulding (see fig. 24).

Put some Texture Paste on your palette as you would do with paint. Lift some off with your brush and put two or three lumps on the painting. Then load your brush with paint, push the brush into the Texture Paste, press and pull away (fig. 25).

The ways of moulding the Texture Paste on the canvas are endless. You will find that the colour of the paint will be weaker where it was mixed with the white of the Texture Paste. If you want darker areas, paint those when the paste is dry.

Fig. 25

Fig. 26

USING A PAINTING KNIFE

Cryla Colours are unsurpassed for thick impasto work. The colour can be used undiluted, with a painting knife, to create many textures and forms. The paint retains its sharp edges and will not crack, even when put on very thickly. Figs. 26, 27 and 28 show a variety of shapes and forms that can be produced by different knives. In fig. 26, the small, pear-shaped knife is shown producing first positive and then negative shapes. The flexibility of the blade allows sensitive control. Fig. 27 shows a medium, pear-shaped knife being used to mould forms and create surface-texture patterns. Fig. 28 shows a narrow, trowel-shaped knife being used to cover an area with paint. Always clean painting knives after use.

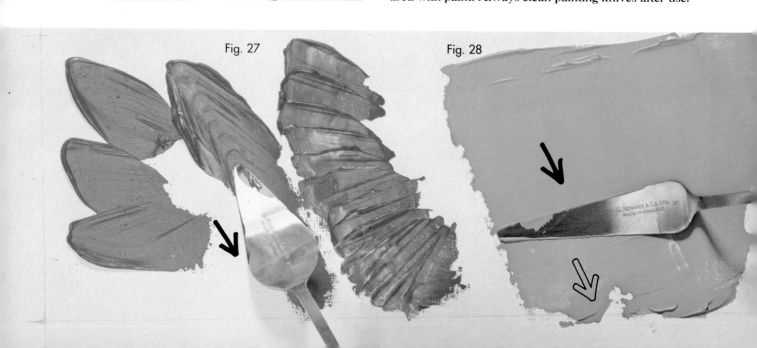

Fig. 27

Fig. 28

Fig. 29

GLAZING

Acrylic colours will produce rich, transparent glazes when mixed with a glaze medium. The more glaze medium you add to your paint, the more transparent your glaze will be. A succession of thin glazes will produce soft colour gradations and the effect of colour fusion.

In fig. 29, the three primary colours were used, starting with yellow, then overpainted with red and finally with blue. This gives secondary colour effects where the primary ones have crossed each other. In this illustration, a mixture of one part colour to ten parts of glaze medium was used.

In fig. 30, a glaze was applied to a conventional painting to achieve the smoke effect. Use the brush as in the misty effect, but this time add glaze medium. This allows the paint to move better on the canvas because it is wet with the medium. It also makes sure that the paint is truly transparent. That part of the painting that has been glazed will look glossy and the rest will be matt. When you varnish your painting, this difference will disappear as the whole picture will be glossy or matt, depending on which varnish you use – a matt finish or gloss finish.

Fig. 30

STAINING

Cryla Flow Colours can be diluted with water and painted into unprimed canvas to get an even, matt surface of colour. An acrylic water tension breaker can be added; this is a medium for helping the flow of paint on to the canvas when very large areas are to be painted or the surface of the support is very, very porous and must stay that way, as in the unprimed canvas in this exercise. Water tension breaker, when added to the water, will give minimum dilution of the colour at the same time as retaining maximum colour intensity. This technique gives the appearance of a stained canvas, rather than a painted one (see fig. 31).

PRIMING

Priming is a method of sealing absorbent surfaces before applying paint. Acrylic primer should always be used. Use a small, household brush to paint on the primer or, for larger areas, a household squeezy painting pad. Try to avoid leaving brush strokes on the surface, brush them well out. Wash your brush out after use. I am often asked if paper should be primed: the answer is no.

Fig. 31

EXERCISE ONE
STILL LIFE

For your first exercise in acrylics I have chosen a still life subject. During your first lesson on painting simple objects, you started with a brick; this was comparatively easy to find but, above all, it could be painted under your own conditions.

When you set up a still life subject, you can control the shapes, sizes and colours in your subject, and also the lighting to create a contrast of light and shade. Make sure that you will not need to use any of the objects in the near future. If you have your subject on a board and it has to be moved, fix the objects with Plasticine, drawing pins, Blu-Tack or staples.

In this exercise and all the others to follow, it is important to know that when mixing colours, the first colour to mix into is the one I have named first: add the other colours (smaller amounts) to this one. The first colour is usually the

one representing the main colour. White is last unless, of course, White is the main colour.

FIRST STAGE

The light source is coming from the left and above. To start, draw the line that divides the background from the flat surface, put in the vase, the line of the cloth, the marrow and then the onion, lemon and orange. Now, using a mixture of Raw Sienna, Crimson, Ultramarine and plenty of White, paint the background using your No. 12 Cryla brush. For the table surface use the same colours but add much more White, as this area is getting direct light from the light source. Paint thinly over the drawing so as not to lose it.

SECOND STAGE

The colours to use for the vase are Raw Sienna, Burnt Umber, Crimson and White. Study carefully the delicate tones, highlights and shadows; use your No. 4 Cryla brush for the rim and inside. Paint from the light side to the dark side inside the neck, adding the shadow while the paint is still wet (use a little Ultramarine to darken the shadow). Now, with a No. 8 brush paint down the vase, letting the brush follow the ellipses. This will give the vase that hand-made feeling as the brush strokes follow the natural way the vase was turned. Paint the vase as though its dark brown pattern didn't exist. Now paint the dark pattern over the vase, using Burnt Umber mixed with a little White and your No. 4 brush.

Mix Bright Green, Cadmium Yellow, Burnt Umber, Ultramarine, Crimson and White for the cloth. Five colours and White seem quite a lot for painting a single colour; the basic colour is green made from Bright Green, Cadmium Yellow and Burnt Umber. The other colours are there to help to give it light and shade, to stop it looking flat.

Start painting from the left of the vase and work down, adding dark and light and painting the folds and shadows. Use a dry brush technique to recreate the texture of the material. Next, add the shadows of the vase and marrow: use a No. 4 brush with Ultramarine, Crimson, Cadmium Yellow and White. Note how the shadow is lighter towards the back.

VASE –
RAW SIENNA
BURNT UMBER
CRIMSON
WHITE

MATERIAL –
BRIGHT GREEN
CADMIUM YELLOW
BURNT UMBER
WHITE

ORANGE –
CADMIUM RED
CADMIUM YELLOW
WHITE

LEMON –
CADMIUM YELLOW
BRIGHT GREEN
CRIMSON
WHITE

MARROW –
BRIGHT GREEN
ULTRAMARINE BLUE
CADMIUM YELLOW
CRIMSON, WHITE

First stage

Second stage

THIRD STAGE

Using your No. 8 brush, mix Bright Green, Cadmium Yellow, Crimson and White, and paint the light green of the marrow, letting your pencil lines show through. Now the onion: mix Cadmium Yellow, Crimson and White and use your No. 4 brush. Start at the top of the onion and let your brush strokes form the veins of its skin. The darker area is a piece of skin coming off: add a little Ultramarine to paint this.

Now the lemon: use the same brush and mix Cadmium Yellow, Bright Green, Crimson and White. Start with the highlight near the top left and work down into the shadow areas. Work the ends of the lemon very carefully and add the dark accents to show their shape. Note the reflected light on the bottom where it meets the shadow; add this highlight. Paint the orange in the same way, using the same brush (after washing it out), but mixing Cadmium Red, Cadmium Yellow, a little Crimson and White. Remember the reflected light at the bottom, as on the lemon.

FINISHED STAGE

Start with the marrow, using your No. 4 brush and mixing Bright Green, Ultramarine, Cadmium Yellow, Crimson and a little White. Paint the dark stripes, letting the brush miss

Third stage

141

the light areas, thus creating the speckled, light shapes. Look carefully and add the shadow cast by the vase. Use Ultramarine, Crimson and Bright Green and paint over the marrow transparently. Using the same colour, paint the right-hand, shadow side of the marrow and the front. It will acquire form and recede into the picture. Paint transparent washes on the onion with your sable brush to give the skin a transparent look, and mark in some veins.

Now darken the shadows on the cloth with your No. 4 nylon brush, using Ultramarine, Crimson and Bright Green. Then, with Cryla Colours Bright Green, Cadmium Yellow and White, and a No. 8 brush, work in the light areas quite freely. With your No. 2 brush and the colours originally used for the lemon, stipple the highlights and shadows on the lemon; then finish off with your small sable brush. Use the same treatment for the orange. Darken the shadows that you have already put on the vase; use the paint thinly. Also, darken the shadow cast by the vase and marrow.

Draw the bull motif in pencil and then paint it with your Rigger brush: first a dark line, then on the highlight edge paint a yellowish-white, broken line and on the opposite edge a middle-tone line, transparently. This will give the illusion of an engraved contour.

Details from finished stage (above and below)
Brush work detail (below right)

ALWYN CRAWSHAW

EXERCISE TWO
FLOWERS

One good reason for painting flowers is that they can be done indoors and therefore you have complete control of the painting conditions. After all, it is a still life subject and all the elements of setting up a still life apply to setting up your flowers. But, one important difference is that flowers are 'alive', they do move. Blooms can close up or open up. They can droop and can alter positions in the vase. Eventually they will lose their lustre and die. Therefore it is essential that you know you can paint them while they are still fresh and full of life. Naturally, if you need longer than the flowers' life, you will by that time have observed them as you painted and have a good idea what they are like, and you could probably finish the painting without the flowers. However, if you have a 'nearly finished' painting and a vase of dead flowers, then get just one fresh bloom and use this as your model for all the blooms in your painting.

You may find that you need more colours than I use normally, as the pigmentation of flowers is unlimited. But for this exercise I have chosen flowers that can be painted with the colours I have used for this book.

FIRST STAGE

The source and angle of the light are the same as in the still life. Draw the line between background and table top first, then the teapot and, finally, the flowers and leaves. The large leaves, incidentally, are rhododendron and will last a long time. Using Raw Sienna, Cadmium Yellow, Crimson and White, paint the background; remember to paint thin where you want your drawing to show through.

SECOND STAGE

For the leaves, mix three tones of dark, medium and light green on the palette, using Bright Green, Ultramarine, Cadmium Yellow and a little White (medium tone); add more White (light tone); add Crimson and more Ultramarine (dark tone). Paint the leaves with your No. 4 brush, wet on wet, working the brush into the centre, then down each side in turn, following the direction of the veins. With a mix of Cadmium Yellow, Crimson and a little White, paint the orange flowers. Start at the centre and work the brush up and down to form petals, going around the centre and spreading out to the extreme edge of the flower. Continue in the same way with the yellow flowers, using Cadmium Yellow, Raw Umber, a little Crimson and White.

THIRD STAGE

Now the table top: I have chosen a non-shining surface, so you only have to contend with shadows and not reflections as well. Mix Raw Umber, Crimson, Raw Sienna and White; using a No. 12 brush, paint from the background down to the bottom of the canvas. Don't try to paint up to the teapot with your brush, let it go over the pencil lines; the excess will be covered when you paint the pot.

Using a No. 8 brush, mix Burnt Umber, Crimson, Ultramarine and a little White, and start on the teapot. Keep your brush flat and move it down the pot. Bow the shape of the stroke as the pot is curved. Work in the lighter areas as you paint and add some orange and yellow for the flower reflections. The shadows on the background are the next stage. Use your No. 4 brush; mix Raw Umber, Crimson, Cadmium Yellow and White. The brush strokes should follow the direction of the cast shadow.

BACKGROUND—
RAW SIENNA
CADMIUM YELLOW
CRIMSON, WHITE

LEAVES—
BRIGHT GREEN
ULTRAMARINE BLUE
CADMIUM YELLOW
WHITE

ORANGE FLOWERS—
CADMIUM YELLOW
CRIMSON, WHITE

YELLOW FLOWERS—
CADMIUM YELLOW
RAW UMBER
CRIMSON, WHITE

VASE—
BURNT UMBER
CRIMSON
ULTRAMARINE BLUE
WHITE

First stage

Second stage

Now the table-top shadows: change to a No. 8 brush, and mix Raw Umber, Ultramarine, Crimson and White. Keep your brush strokes horizontal to make the shadows look flat. Be very careful to meet the background shadows spot on. This helps to give the picture two definite planes, i.e. the vertical background and the horizontal plane of the table. Where the shadows have gone over the teapot, use your sable brush to paint the edge back onto the teapot. You can see where I did this on the bottom left edge of the spout.

FINISHED STAGE

Start by working on the flowers. To achieve the appearance of hundreds of petals while showing only some, you should realize the importance of light against dark. Look at the top right-hand flower. The dark shadow on the leaf underlines the shape of the light flower and the two bright petals against the dark petals beneath stress the bottom edge formation. However, the same flower has lost some of its contour into the background at the top and right-hand side. This has been done to give depth to the flower: if sharp accents were everywhere they would cancel each other out, and no accents at all would give a very flat picture. This secret of knowing what to put in or leave out, especially in painting flowers, will come from observation and practice.

Third stage

You have already painted the light and dark areas; now, using your sable brush, mix Cadmium Yellow, Crimson and White, and add the light areas of the yellow blooms. Follow the shapes you have already painted in the second stage but, this time, be more careful and precise with the petals. Work from the centre outwards; press the brush down, pull it towards you and slowly lift off; practise on some scrap paper. Make sure you make some nice petal shapes against the teapot – light against dark! Do the same exercise with the orange flowers. Finish all flowers by adding some dark accents to help form the petal shapes (sable brush) and add some extra highlights using Cryla Colour. This will stand in relief off the canvas and catch the light, providing those very important light accents.

Now darken some of the leaves to give them form. Paint over the stems in the middle; this will give them tone, enabling them to recede. Paint in the fallen flower on the table – watch for the light petals against dark. Glaze the teapot with a blend of Burnt Umber and Crimson, using your sable brush. When the glaze is dry, paint back the yellow reflection and the highlights and add some dark accents.

It is advisable to leave the picture for twenty-four hours or so and come to it again with a fresh eye. You will then see things that you had not noticed before. You have only to correct them and your painting is finished.

Details from finished stage (above and below)

Brush work detail (below right)

Fig. 32

Fig. 33

Fig. 34

Fig. 35

NOTES ON TREES

For the landscape artist, the tree is nature's most valuable gift to assist with the composition of a picture. For instance, one lone tree can make a picture. Trees can be used to break the horizon line; they can be positioned to stop the eye going forward or to lead the eye into the picture. When you next go out to sketch, instead of drawing a scene, pick out a good tree – one that shows the characteristics of its species – and draw it. Don't sketch it, make a very careful study, trying to draw all the branches you can see.

The best time to do this is when the trees have lost their leaves and you can see their shapes. By drawing carefully and observing the tree, you will get used to the growth pattern. This will help you when you draw trees with leaves on. In the summer, look carefully at a tree in full leaf and see how many large and small branches are showing – if you haven't bothered to take note before, you will be surprised how many can be seen against the foliage. This is important because, in a painting, these branches against leaves help to give the tree depth and interest. Start by drawing one type of tree and really making a study of it. If you then paint from memory or imagination indoors, you will always have a tree that you can paint.

You can get a real feel of the bark on the tree trunk by using Cryla Colours – only use these on foreground trees as the texture you create brings the trees closer; you can't have your distant trees coming to the front of your painting! In fig. 32 you can see how this texture is achieved. Use plenty of Cryla Colour, work the brush up and down the tree (mostly up) and the texture will be formed.

There is a problem with trees – how to make them appear to grow out of the ground. Unless the tree is on a lawn in a park, it will usually have growth of one kind or another at its base (fig. 33). This natural cover enables your tree trunk to grow out of the ground without showing the actual base.

When you are painting trees in the middle distance, you can't neglect them just because they are a long way off. Carefully observe them, pick out the different shapes and think about them (see fig. 34). A tree can form the basis of a composition for a painting, as in fig. 35. I saw this fallen willow with Dedham Church in the background, a different view of the church tower created overnight by nature. Always remember when painting trees, paint them with feeling – they are alive, not just planks of wood.

NOTES ON WATER

The colour of water is normally a reflection of the sky and the immediate surroundings. When you see very clear, still water, because there isn't any surface movement, a reflection will look mirror-like. In fact if you painted, say, the reflections of a tree in still water, it would be like painting a tree upside down. The only difference would be that in general all reflections are a little darker than the real object.

Reflections can vary a lot. I have seen one that reflected a building on a large lake, and the reflection reached the bank I was standing on. I have also seen the same situation, where the reflection only appeared to come halfway across the lake; and at other times there is no reflection at all. I don't know all the reasons for seeing different reflections. My answer to a student is, if it looks right on your picture, then it is fine. Study and observe all types of reflections whenever you see them.

When starting to paint water with acrylics, use the paint like watercolour – very, very watery – and move your flat brush from top to bottom, left to right, as in fig. 36. The colour of this first wash is dependent upon the reflections in the water. It might be necessary to paint more than one wash to get the depth of tone required; this is fine, in fact it can give more feeling to the water, but let each wash dry before applying the next. Using the paint in this way, i.e. very thinly, it can be quite simple to create the illusion of water.

In fig. 37, the water of this puddle was painted as in fig. 36, except that the tone was much lighter. Then dark colour was painted around to represent earth or muddy path, as you will do in the landscape painting. On the left-hand edge some very dark areas were painted with a small sable brush, to express shadows. The third sketch, fig. 38, was done in exactly the same way, except that the water was painted dark and the path light.

When you have movement on the water, i.e. ripples or small waves, paint the water first as in fig. 36. This applies to large lakes or small puddles. Then, with a small brush, paint the different tones over the water. Let the brush strokes create the effect of movement – the more broken the water the more brush strokes you will need. In this case, you may find that seventy-five per cent of your original wash is covered up. But it is this wash that holds it all together and helps to create the illusion of water (see fig. 39). If you are painting water with no distinct reflections and the water needs one to make it read, then put one in: a post, a fence, a fallen branch. A reflection gives the illusion of water immediately. Observe the moods of water at different times. Sit in the bath and wiggle your toes, let the tap drip – a lot can be learned in comfort!

Fig. 36

Fig. 37

Fig. 38

Fig. 39

EXERCISE THREE
LANDSCAPE

Landscape is perhaps the most painted and favoured subject among all artists, professional and amateur. It has a long tradition and many masterpieces from around the world have been painted from landscape subjects. One of the greatest aspects of landscape painting is its versatility. If it was practical, you could stand in one spot in a field and paint a different scene looking from four different directions (the four points of the compass). From those positions you could paint a sunrise or a sunset. Add to that rainy, sunny, misty, cloudy and stormy days, and so on. There are the four seasons, which change the landscape completely. In fact there are hundreds of paintings that could be done just from that one field, and then there is the next field, the next hill, and valley – landscape subjects are almost infinite.

If you live in the country, then your subject is very close at hand. If you live in a town, it means perhaps a long journey to find a painting spot. If this is the case, why not try pencil sketches? They are much quicker to do, and you could do three or four and then work from them in paint at home. But remember to make enough notes and colour notes on the back of your sketches. It is the only reference you have, once you return home.

SKY –
ULTRAMARINE BLUE
CRIMSON
RAW UMBER
WHITE

LIGHT TREE –
RAW UMBER
CADMIUM YELLOW
BRIGHT GREEN
WHITE

DARK TREE –
RAW UMBER
BRIGHT GREEN
CRIMSON
ULTRAMARINE BLUE

GRASS –
BURNT UMBER
BRIGHT GREEN
ULTRAMARINE BLUE
CRIMSON
CADMIUM YELLOW
WHITE

WATER –
ULTRAMARINE BLUE
CRIMSON, WHITE

FIRST STAGE

After drawing the horizon line, draw the two sloping fields left and right of the path, then the path, the two main trees and, finally, the trees in the left middle distance. For the sky, mix Ultramarine with Crimson, Raw Umber and White. Start at the top and work down the canvas, using a No. 12 brush. Then, with the same brush not washed out, darken the colour by adding a little Raw Sienna to give it a bit more body and paint the darker clouds.

Wash the brush and mix Cadmium Yellow, Crimson and White and paint the lighter cloud area down to the horizon. As you get nearer the horizon, add more Crimson and, to the right of the trees, a little more Ultramarine. For this sky use Gel Retarder to help you with the wet on wet technique you will have applied.

SECOND STAGE

Paint the light coloured field in the middle distance, using Raw Sienna mixed with White. Next, add to it a little Ultramarine. Using the dry brush technique, drag it along the top edge of the field to form the distant hedge. Now, using a No. 4 brush, mix Ultramarine, Crimson, Cadmium Yellow and a little White: apply the dry brush technique and paint the trees on the left and right of the path. Don't put any detail in yet and don't worry about the funny shapes the brush makes at the bottom: they will disappear when you paint the field. For this, use Bright Green, Burnt Umber, Crimson and White. Paint a darker area under the trees.

Now use Cryla Colours Raw Umber, Cadmium Yellow, Bright Green and a little White for the left-hand tree (it has caught the sun halfway up the trunk). Start with plenty of paint and a No. 4 Cryla brush, working up the trunk and painting branches until the brush is too big. Change now to your sable brush and continue painting the branches. Always work up and out when painting branches, in the direction in which they grow.

Now paint the right-hand tree, using Raw Umber, Bright Green, Crimson and Ultramarine. When painting the

trees, you will have noticed that you had the background coming through in places. This is correct and if your brush is worked up and down the trunk, it gives the impression of bark. Don't worry about light and shade, this will be added later, but remember: the light is coming from the left. The more Cryla Colour you use on the trunk the more relief you will get – bark, gnarls, lumps and bumps – but only use thick paint on close-up trees.

THIRD STAGE

Begin with a very dry No. 8 brush and paint the feathery branches on the left-hand tree. Use Cadmium Yellow, Crimson and Raw Umber. Move the brush down to form the top shape and as you get into the tree, let the dry brush strokes follow the growth of the branches. For the right-hand tree, which is darker, use Ultramarine, Crimson and Burnt Umber. Using the same dry brush technique, add the hedge. Add Cadmium Yellow to the colours used for the right-hand tree. Push the brush up the canvas in the direction of growth. Now, using Ultramarine and Crimson with a little Raw Umber and White, very watery, paint the water area in downward strokes. Finish this stage by using your No. 4 brush and adding some brush strokes on the foreground field to show its contours; use Raw Umber and Bright Green.

FINISHED STAGE

Start underneath the hedge on the right and paint the field. Use Texture Paste technique with Bright Green, Burnt Umber, Crimson, Cadmium Yellow and Ultramarine. Work your brush in the direction of the contours of the field. Flick the brush up into the hedge occasionally to break straight lines.

Paint the path next, using the same size brush and blending together Raw Sienna, Raw Umber, Burnt Umber, Crimson, Ultramarine and White. Drag the brush loaded with paint into some Texture Paste and then down the edge of the puddle. This will form a very natural edge for the water. While this area is drying, with your Rigger brush paint the small branches of the large trees, starting with the left-hand one. With a dry brush technique, work in the highlights on the trunk and branches, then with your sable brush, using watery paint, apply the shadows.

With dry brush technique, mix Ultramarine, Crimson and White and paint the main trunk and branches of the left-hand, middle-distance tree. Paint the gate and fence, using a sable brush, with Raw Umber, Bright Green and White. Add the shadows at the bottom of the path using watery Ultramarine and Crimson for a transparent effect. Suggest some shadows on the dry Texture Paste and add accents where needed.

Details from finished stage (above and below)
Brush work details (below right)

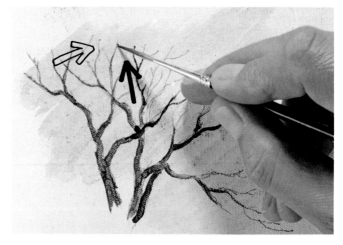

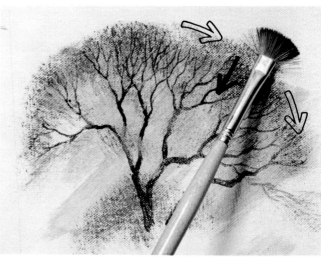

ALWYN CRAWSHAW

EXERCISE FOUR
SEASCAPE

The sea is endlessly fascinating. You will find that most of the stalwart landscape artists have had their fair share of painting the sea. Two of Britain's finest landscape artists, Constable and Turner, couldn't resist the call of the sea, and in the eighteenth and nineteenth centuries, it wasn't just a case of jumping in a car after Saturday lunch and reaching the sea in a couple of hours. I think the sea holds its fascination by seeming endless: you can go around the world by leaving from the shore where you are painting. It is vast and restless; it has extreme moods that range from romantic to terrifying.

Like the sky, the sea changes its colour all the time and, of course, it is never still. This must be observed from life. Sit on the beach and watch the waves coming in and breaking on the shore, studying how they are formed. Try sketching in pencil, recreating the shapes that you see. You can't watch the same wave all the time, of course, but you will have a retained image to carry on to the next.

The sky must belong to the sea in colour and tone. Generally speaking, use the same colours for both. To give more interest in composition and colour to a seascape we have cliffs and headland to give distance and perspective, beaches and rocks enabling us to paint crashing waves with spray and foam flying everywhere. In the picture prepared for this exercise I have painted rocks because they are a good subject for acrylics.

FIRST STAGE

Draw the horizon line with an HB pencil. Use a ruler to get it horizontal on the canvas. Then draw the rocks and waves. The bottom of the rocks is formed by the sea washing around them; therefore, it will follow the movement of the water and in most cases it will be level.

Mix Ultramarine, Crimson and White for the top of the sky, add Cadmium Yellow with Crimson for the lighter clouds. Make this colour stronger (not as much White) on the right of the big rock. Paint this sky with a No. 12 brush and use Gel Retarder to paint wet on wet.

SECOND STAGE

Paint the sea from the horizon to the big wave and rock. Use your No. 4 brush, mixing Ultramarine, Crimson, Bright Green and White. To the right of the rock add some more White with a touch of Cadmium Yellow, as little highlights where the sun is coming through and catching the breaking waves. Under the top of the large breaking wave paint very thin (watery) Ultramarine and Bright Green. This will give the transparent colour of the wave.

Now paint the shadow under the wave; this is the darker colour. The lighter colour is the foam that is running up the wave, and here it is in shadow. The darker areas were achieved with Ultramarine, Crimson, Bright Green and a little White. The light foam was painted leaving dark areas and following the contour of the wave.

Paint the side of the rock with Burnt Umber and Bright Green. Now, add much more White to the same wave colour and paint the rest of the wave – do not add too much White at this stage, leave some brightness up your sleeve. Lastly, paint the water breaking over the big rock. Keep this in shadow. Start at the rock and work your brush up and away. Let the brush – and yourself – feel like spray bouncing off a rock, get excited about it and you will find the result will be worthwhile. Experiment on a piece of paper if you like.

SKY –
ULTRAMARINE BLUE
CRIMSON
WHITE
CADMIUM YELLOW

DISTANT SEA –
ULTRAMARINE BLUE
CRIMSON
BRIGHT GREEN
WHITE

FOAM –
WHITE
ULTRAMARINE BLUE
CRIMSON
CADMIUM YELLOW

ROCKS
BURNT UMBER
BRIGHT GREEN
ULTRAMARINE BLUE
CADMIUM YELLOW
WHITE

THIRD STAGE

All you have to do in this stage is paint the rest of the sea. This is treated as underpainting because finally, it will have foam added over it. The rocks have been left unpainted at this stage, as all the sides except the bottom of the rocks appear in front of the water: it is easier, therefore, to paint them when the majority of the sea is finished so that they will have a clean edge against the sea. Using your No. 8 brush, mix Ultramarine, Crimson, Bright Green and White and paint the sea, starting from underneath the large wave and working across and down the canvas. Keep the brush strokes horizontal to keep the water level. As you come nearer the foreground let your brush strokes loosen up, add lighter and darker tones and your brush will form movement in the water. Don't be too critical of yourself; remember, a lot of this area will be covered in the next stage.

FINISHED STAGE

Now to paint the foam on the water. Use a No. 4 brush with White, Ultramarine, Crimson and Cadmium Yellow. Work the brush horizontally in short strokes, changing the tone and colour (very subtly) all the time. You will be working on this part of the sea until the picture is finished. For the finishing touches on this foam use sable brushes to enable you to paint the finer modelling.

Next, work on the big, breaking wave: use your No. 8 brush loaded with White plus a little Cadmium Yellow and Crimson. Put the brush on the edge of the rock and then push it up and away to get the spray effect. If it doesn't go right first time, paint it dark again and have another go; or

Third stage

155

just practise on a piece of paper as you did in the second stage. Now retouch the big rock, just up to the wave and give it a clean edge. This part of the painting contains the darkest and lightest areas together, which produce a very sharp contrast. With the same brush and colour, paint some flying spume on the top of the large wave. Now dry the brush out and with a dry brush technique, using White and Ultramarine, work over the big rock and the bottom of the large wave by the rock; this will fuzz up the area around the rock and breaking wave, giving a feeling of misty spray.

For the rocks you will need Texture Paste, Burnt Umber, Bright Green, Ultramarine, Cadmium Yellow and White. Use a No. 8 brush, and don't mix the paint too much on the palette, let the mixing occur on the rocks. The Texture Paste and paint will thus make streaks of colour following the direction of your brush strokes and you will find that the rocks' contours are formed reasonably well, as long as your brush is worked in the direction of the rock surfaces.

When this is nearly dry, add shadow to the dark side by dragging darker rock colour on to the rocks. You will find that it will drag up some of the existing paint in places; this again helps to show form and ruggedness. When the rocks are completely dry, with a dry brush add more colour – light and dark – to give even more texture. Finally, with a sable brush, pick out some shapes with dark or light colour. This is where you finish the large sea (foam) area. Work on this again, now that you have the tone of the rocks painted in, and go over all your important highlights with Cryla Colour White.

Details from finished stage (left)
Brush work details (right)

ALWYN CRAWSHAW

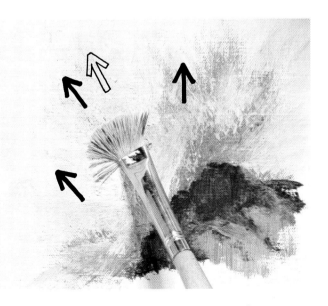

EXERCISE FIVE
SNOW

I really enjoy painting snow. I don't know why, but it fascinates me. I like the quiet of a snow landscape and I like the crunch of hard packed snow under my feet and even melting wet snow on the pavement and roads in a town scene.

When painting snow using acrylic colours, the easiest way for beginners seems to be to paint it with pure white paint. Never use just white paint for any of it. It is only white in its purest form – just fallen – and even then, it reflects light and colour from all around. So even the whitest snow should have some colour. Add a little blue to cool the white paint or a little red or yellow to warm it up. Never be afraid to make snow dark in shadow areas. It can be as dark, in comparison to its surroundings, as a shadow in a non-snow landscape.

The way to paint snow is to paint it in a low key: if we take our darkest shadow as a number ten and our brightest snow as number one (see page 160), with a natural graduation of tone in between, you should paint your snow in the range from eight to three. This will leave enough reserve up your sleeve to add darker shadows and brighter highlights.

FIRST STAGE

Use an HB pencil to draw the landscape, starting with the horizon. Next, draw the edge of the field with the two main trees on it, the other trees and the river banks. For the sky use Coeruleum, Crimson and White mixed with Gel Retarder. Halfway down the sky mix Cadmium Yellow, Crimson and White and paint back up into the wet 'blue' sky. Then paint down to the horizon, adding more Crimson as you go. This will give that lovely, luminous-sky effect.

SECOND STAGE

With Coeruleum, Crimson, Cadmium Yellow and White, using a dry brush technique, paint the distant trees; then, with the same colours but much more White, paint the field underneath with a No. 4 brush. Paint the house with the same brush, the chimneys with your small sable brush. Put the highlight on the left of the house where the sun hits it. As in the landscape exercise, use a dry brush to paint the middle-distance trees and the hedge. Since the time is late afternoon, there is a warm glow in the sky and this should be reflected in the trees where the sun touches them: use more Crimson and Cadmium Yellow.

Next, paint the snow on the lower field in the same way as the first one but make it very dark under the left-hand trees, as this area is in shadow. Next, paint the two main trees with Cryla Colours Raw Umber, Burnt Umber, Bright Green, Ultramarine and Crimson.

THIRD STAGE

Start by painting the feathery branches on both trees, using your No. 8 brush in a dry brush technique. Mix Cadmium Yellow, Crimson, Raw Umber and Ultramarine. Next, paint the hedge, using your No. 4 brush with Cadmium Yellow, Crimson and Ultramarine.

Now the water. This was painted as watercolour, i.e. using your No. 8 brush loaded with water and paint. You will find the paint runs down the canvas, which is how it should be. Use the brush flat on and run it down the canvas, starting each stroke at the top and at the side of the previous one. You will find the brush strokes will merge, giving a watery appearance. Use Burnt Umber, Crimson and Ultramarine.

SKY-
COERULEUM BLUE
CRIMSON
WHITE

BANK-
BURNT UMBER
CADMIUM YELLOW
ULTRAMARINE BLUE

SNOW-
WHITE
COERULEUM BLUE
CRIMSON
RAW SIENNA

SNOW HIGHLIGHTS-
WHITE
CADMIUM YELLOW
CRIMSON

First stage

Second stage

When the wash is absolutely dry, apply another over the top. If you look at the stage three illustration, you will see where my second wash came over the first one, which appears lighter. When the second wash is nearly dry, paint the reflections of the trees and bank. Use your No. 4 brush and start under the bank, bringing the brush down. You will find the paint mixes slightly with the second wash, giving a soft edge. Don't try to put all the branches in. Then, with horizontal strokes, paint the reflections under the river bank; keep your paint very watery.

FINISHED STAGE

Paint the bank on both sides of the river: use your No. 4 brush and mix Burnt Umber, Cadmium Yellow and Ultramarine. The white area now left is going to be snow. Remember: paint from eight to three on your tone chart. Start under the trees, using White, Coeruleum, Crimson and Raw Sienna. Break up the line of snow under the hedge and change the tones and colours of the snow as you go, working down to the river bank. Drag the brush over the bank and into the painted bank areas. Now paint the trunks of the left-hand, middle-distance trees with your Rigger; use the paint thinly, working from the bottom of the trees upwards. With the same brush paint the small branches of the large trees, working downwards; for the left-hand one use warm

Third stage

colours, as the sun is catching it. Notice the two small branches that have broken off and are in the hedge under the tree.

Now you can finish the reflections in the water, using Burnt Umber, Ultramarine and Crimson with you sable brush; paint the reflections watery. You will have to repeat the wash over the area a few times as this will help to express the movement of water over the reflections. When this is dry, paint the highlights with White, Cadmium Yellow and a touch of Coeruleum (slightly watery). Remember to keep your brush strokes horizontal. With your No. 4 brush mix a snow shadow colour from Coeruleum, Crimson, Raw Sienna and White. Paint the shadows on the left bank and run the paint slightly over the bank colour.

You now have to bring the snow to life by highlighting it. Mix Cryla Colours White, Cadmium Yellow and Crimson, use your No. 4 brush (very clean) and drag in a dry brush technique over the sunlit areas. If you have painted the snow in the right low key, you will be surprised how white the highlights appear and how the snow seems to sparkle. Next, paint the gate and the fence, using your sable brush with Raw Umber, Bright Green and White. Finally, paint in the winter grass and plants that show through the snow; they will add depth and perspective.

Details from finished stage (above and below)
Tone chart and brush work detail (below right)

EXERCISE SIX
BOATS

We are back to the pull of the sea again. After all, boats are found on the sea and, therefore, the emotions we feel when painting boats are very similar to those we feel for the sea. I did a small watercolour of the scene in this exercise, when I had a holiday in Brittany. The inspiration came from the shape of the boat, which to me was in a perfect position for painting. I find a three-quarter view of a boat is its best attitude. The red colour of the boat was ideal against the cool greys of the water and buildings.

When I do a sketch of a harbour scene, I usually take a photograph of it as well. Then if there is any detail you can't understand from your sketch, you can check it against the photograph. Remember you must be careful with your detail and be as accurate as you can. But do remember, you are making a painting of a boat, not a maritime architect's working drawing! I am sure that some of the boats I have painted, if put to sea would sink! But they look fine in the painting.

SKY, WATER
ROOF-TOPS—
COERULEUM BLUE
CRIMSON
WHITE

RED BOAT—
CADMIUM RED
CRIMSON
BURNT UMBER
WHITE

BLUE BOAT—
COERULEUM BLUE
CRIMSON
RAW UMBER
WHITE

BEACH—
BURNT UMBER
BRIGHT GREEN
CRIMSON
CADMIUM YELLOW
WHITE

FIRST STAGE

I drew this harbour scene from a sketch and, therefore, had plenty of time to correct the drawing and make a careful study on the canvas in the studio. Had I painted this outside, the drawing would have been looser and I would have corrected it as I painted.

First, draw the harbour wall; make sure the bottom is horizontal on the canvas. Next, draw the hill, a few of the main buildings in the distance and the middle-distance boats that have definite shapes. The other boats, which make this a bustling harbour, will be ad-libbed when you are painting. Finally, draw the main boat and the little one on the beach.

The sky and water are exactly the same colour at this first stage. Using a No. 12 brush, mix Coeruleum, Crimson and White. Paint from the top, well over the hill and buildings, adding more Crimson as the sky disappears behind the hill. Using the same brush and paint, continue over the water to the beach.

SECOND STAGE

Apart from the hill behind the harbour, which had Bright Green added to the previous colours, all the rest of the buildings in this stage were painted in Coeruleum, Crimson and White for the roof tops, adding Raw Sienna, Cadmium Yellow, Raw Umber and White for the walls. It appears that a lot of colours were used but if you look closely, the real colour is Coeruleum for the roof tops and Raw Sienna for the rest. The other colours are there to be added sparingly, but remember it is this variation of colour and tone that gives a painting life.

Use your No. 4 brush, paint in the hill, then the roof tops and then the lower parts. Don't try to make every building just like mine, it would be impossible. It is an impression of buildings you want to achieve. They are in the distance, so paint them in low key. Put no more detail than the windows and shutters (only suggested) with a sable brush. On the right of the picture let the buildings merge even more to give distance. Paint the background inside the cabin windows when painting the buildings.

For the main fishing boat use Cadmium Red, Burnt Umber, Crimson and White. Only add Crimson to the shadow areas and White to the light parts. Start with the cabin, leaving the window frames, then the hull. In my original, a

No. 4 brush was almost plank size, which was ideal because you must paint the hull plank by plank, starting from the top. At the stern of the boat add White where the light catches the wood. Paint over the red with White, Coeruleum and Crimson in the spots where the paint has worn off the boat. Then add Cadmium Yellow to the white in the cabin framework.

THIRD STAGE

Use the colours that you adopted for the buildings and a very wet No. 8 brush to put in the reflections. Start underneath the harbour wall, using the brush flat, and work down, changing the colours slightly as you paint along the canvas. Paint over the drawing of boats. While the paint is still wet, put in the window reflection.

Now paint the boats: the secret is to give an impression of a harbour busy with small craft and to keep them in the distance so as not to overpower our fishing boat in the foreground. For your white paint now use Cryla Colour to mix with the colours for the boats. Use your No. 4 brush and toned-down colours; with light colours paint oblong shapes to represent boats in the distance, then add some dark areas (cabins, ends of boats, etc.). Put in some masts with your sable brush, some light and some dark. If you look closely at the stage three illustration, you will see that the only real boats are the cabin cruiser on the right and the bows of the yacht to the left of the red boat. These you have to paint carefully as it is these that give the eye the impression that

Third stage

all the shapes and masts behind are boats. A little more detail will be put in at the final stage.

Now add the old boat on the right. Use your No. 4 brush and paint it in planks as you did the red boat, using Coeruleum, Crimson, Raw Umber and White. When dry, drag over some darker paint using the dry brush technique to give an ageing look. Finally, paint the front of the bows on the red boat.

FINISHED STAGE

There are a lot of small details to be finished and it would not be possible for me to describe all the necessary passages. The important thing is to paint them with the right brush and in the correct order. Read this section through carefully before continuing and you will get the feel of what there is to do.

Using a No. 4 brush, paint the reflections of the red boat and the old one. Use as watercolour a mix of Coeruleum, Crimson, and Burnt Umber and as you wash this down to the beach, add Cadmium Red. Put at least two washes on, then paint a very dark shadow under the boats with Ultramarine, Crimson and Burnt Umber; spread this up onto the boats to merge boats and water. Next, work the masts with your sable brush; then, with the same brush, line in the red boat – for instance, the edges of planks and the shadow side of the windows; add a bit more dark at the same time to the cabin windows. With your Rigger brush, paint the lobster pot on the cabin with a dark colour, then with the same brush add lighter lines to give it shape – Raw Sienna and White.

Put a wash shadow to the right of the red boat bows: use Ultramarine and Crimson. Put the mast on the yacht and darken the hull next to the red boat. With your sable brush add the mast reflections. With your Rigger, paint the rigging lines: keep the paint watery. Now, with the Cryla No. 4 brush paint the blue boat, using Coeruleum, Crimson, Raw Umber and White, adding Ultramarine for the darkest shadows. Using the same brush, mix Burnt Umber, Bright Green, Crimson, Cadmium Yellow and White, add Texture Paste and paint the beach. When it is dry add some shadows and the bits of old lobster pots on the left with your sable brush. Put a dark shadow under the blue boat and on the beach. Using the paint thin, darken the old boat with Coeruleum, Crimson and Raw Umber. Add some Cryla Colour Cadmium Red and White to the red boat to give some weathering.

As with the other exercises, leave your painting at this stage, come back later with a fresh eye and then make your final statements by adding dark and light accents. This painting will take a long time if you put all the details in. Have patience, it will all come right in the end, although when you are working this seems a long way off.

Details from finished stage (left)
Brush work details (right)

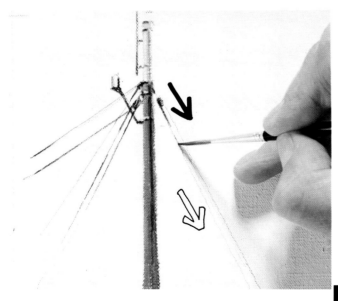

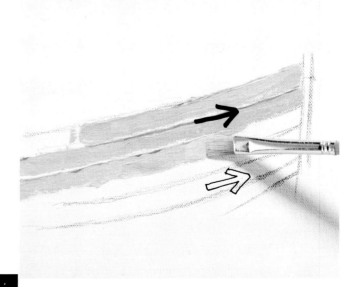

OILS

WHY USE OIL PAINTS?

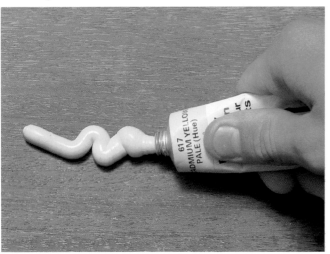

Fig. 1

I think two of the most difficult questions I am asked are: which medium do I prefer to use and which season do I prefer to paint – winter, spring, summer or autumn? The answer to both questions is very similar. When I am, say, working in watercolour, I get so involved that I can't believe I would be as happy working in another medium. But then I put the watercolours to one side and work, say, in oil, and within a short time I have forgotten all the pleasure that watercolour gave me and I feel so involved with oil that I am convinced it is the only medium that can express my painting creativity – until I work with another medium, and so on.

It is the same with the seasons of the year. When I am painting in summer I enjoy it so much that I can't believe the winter will give me the same inspiration; but when winter comes I forget all the other seasons and enjoy it as though there were no other times to paint. I suppose what I am trying to say is that whatever I am doing at the time, I try to enjoy it to the full.

You have chosen to paint in oil. If you are a beginner, perhaps you have chosen oil painting because it is very traditional. You may have been to some of the public galleries and found the majority of pictures are oil paintings, so you are inspired to paint in the same way; or it could be that you have been given a set of oil paints as a present; but whatever the reason, you have been inspired to have a go.

There is one other very obvious reason for choosing any medium in which to work, and that is the single fact that you like it, either because of the way you have to work it or the look of the end result. If you find after working with oil

paint (giving yourself plenty of time to practise and find out) that you cannot get on with it, then perhaps this medium isn't for you. Don't despair – there are many others you can try.

FINDING YOUR SCALE

First, let us take a closer look at oil painting. We all have a 'natural painting size' that we like to work, or we find more comfortable when working. Some artists work very small, say 125 x 75mm (5 x 3in), and others very large, up to 1525 x 1015mm (60 x 40in) or bigger. This is one of the beauties of oil painting – there is no restriction on size, except for space to paint, and your bank account if you work very large! My natural size for a landscape is 510 x 760mm (20 x 30in). I don't paint many larger, and the largest I have painted is 1525 x 760mm (60 x 30in). I find 180 x 125mm (7 x 5in), 255 x 205mm (10 x 8in) and 255 x 305mm (10 x 12in) ideal sizes for sketching outdoors.

For the exercises in this book, I have purposely kept the sizes small. I think this is very important for a beginner. The reason is simple: if a picture for an exercise were too large, say 510 x 760 mm (20 x 30in), then you could become bored or even disenchanted. To you, nothing would appear to be happening with the picture because there was too much canvas to cover and work on. The spreading of the paint and handling of the brushes, and even the mixing of colours, can be done more easily and more confidently on a smaller scale. If you feel strongly about painting large canvases, however, please don't let me stop you; after you have gained some experience you will recognize your natural working size.

When I was sixteen years old and at art school, I was asked by the owner of a local 'olde-worlde' gift shop if I could draw and paint a monk, life-size on a board, to stand outside the shop as an attraction. I was very flattered, especially as I was to be paid what was in those days a lot of money for the work. I accepted my first large painting commission very gratefully and with tremendous enthusiasm. It wasn't long before the enthusiasm turned to despair as I laboured hour after hour working on a board much taller than myself! The areas to cover in paint seemed as large as oceans and my wrist ached with the movement of the brush strokes. But, of course, it is only by doing it that one builds up experience and confidence. I was a better artist for it, and I also learned that very large paintings were not my natural size!

OIL COLOURS

Now let us look at the materials we are going to work with. Oil paint is pigment ground in oil and it is the oil that sticks the paint to the canvas or paper. This explanation is simplified, but it serves our purpose as painters. Oil paint is bought in tubes (fig. 1) and is squeezed out onto a palette for working. Then, with a brush, we add a medium to the paint which helps to thin it down or make it spread more easily over the canvas. You can get mediums with an additive for speeding up the drying of the paint. Finally, there is another medium for washing our brushes out. More about all this a little later.

Some pigments when ground with oil harden very quickly, while others take a long time to dry. For instance, Ivory Black dries much more slowly than other colours, so if you drew your picture with your brush, or underpainted, using Ivory Black, other colours painted over the top would start to crack as they dried. I don't use black for any of my painting, whatever medium I am using. I prefer to mix a livelier dark colour from the three primary colours, red, yellow and blue. But if you decide at a later stage to use black, I suggest you don't get Ivory Black because of its slow drying time.

In general, the slow drying times of oil paints and the tendency for some colours to harden in the tube have been rectified by the artists' colourmen (the manufacturers). When you buy your tubes of paint you will find that the drying time and working life of all these paints will, with some slight variations, behave in the same manner. I have some tubes of colour many years old and they are still usable.

THE COLOUR PALETTE

There are two qualities of oil colours: they are described as artists' professional quality and students' colours. Artists' quality are expensive, but you will find students' colours perfectly adequate. I have used Daler-Rowney Georgian oil colours (a students' quality) for all the exercises in this book, and I would not hesitate in recommending that you use them.

The colours that I use for all my oil painting, including those used throughout this book, are shown in fig. 2 in the position I place them on my palette. This is very important; you must always put your colours on your palette in the same position every time you paint, to enable you to reach your brush into a particular colour without even thinking about it, so that it becomes second nature. Also illustrated in fig. 2, to the right of the palette, are five other useful colours you can try later on when you have gained experience.

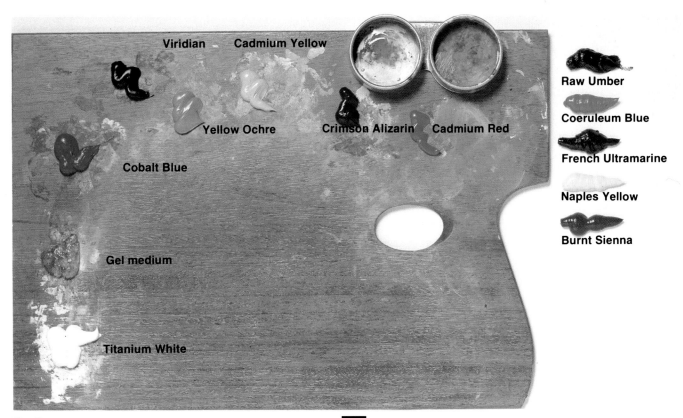

Fig. 2

What Equipment Do You Need?

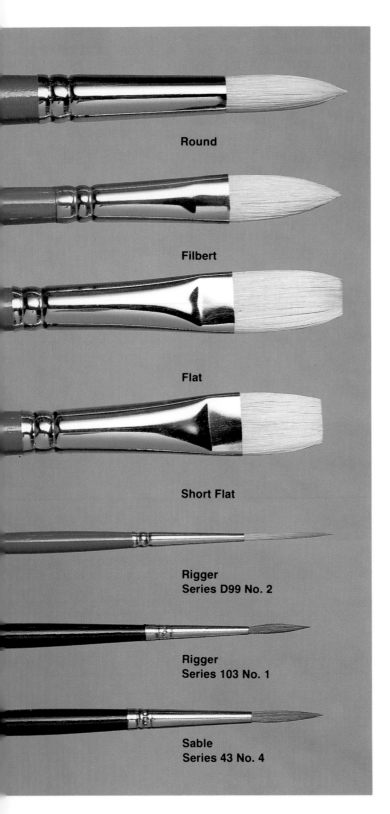

Round

Filbert

Flat

Short Flat

Rigger
Series D99 No. 2

Rigger
Series 103 No. 1

Sable
Series 43 No. 4

Fig. 3

BRUSHES

The brush is the most important item of your equipment. It is the brush that makes the marks on the canvas that eventually join together and create your picture. Always buy good quality brushes, as a good brush (if looked after) will last you for hundreds of painting hours. I have brushes that I have used for many years. In fact, you will find that a brush will get better as you use it, and as time goes on it will become a very familiar part of your painting life.

The choice of brush is very personal. To help you decide what you need to start with, I have listed on page 174 the brushes I used for the exercises in this book. Fig. 3 is a photograph of brushes used in oil painting; they are actual size. Naturally, different shapes of bristles give you different marks. There are three basic shapes of brushes: round, filbert, and flat. I prefer the flat brush, but I use a small round sable or nylon brush for detail work. Series of brushes for oil colours start at No. 1 (the smallest) and continue up to No. 12, in most series, the largest.

Keep your brushes clean by rinsing them in turpentine substitute (white spirit) and then washing with soap. Put some soap on the palm of your hand and rub the brush into it under running cold water. Make sure you rinse out the soap, and dry the brushes before you use them again.

During normal working keep your brushes in turpentine substitute to stop them from drying out. When you pick up a brush for use, wipe it on a piece of rag to remove the turps.

PALETTE KNIVES AND PAINTING KNIVES

Palette knives are often used for mixing up paint on your palette, but unless it is a large quantity I want mixed, I mix the colours with my brush. However, mixing a large amount with the brush can get the bristles too full of paint. If this happens, carefully squash the brush bristles on the palette with a palette knife to squeeze out the excess paint. The same knife is also used to clean paint off the palette.

A palette knife is illustrated in fig. 4. Three painting knives are also illustrated on the same page. The difference between palette and painting knives is that the painting knife has a cranked handle to allow you to apply paint onto the canvas when painting a palette knife picture, and the blade is more delicate. There are many shapes and sizes to choose from and, as with brushes, the choice is personal. However, I have suggested which ones to use in the section on palette knife painting on page 192.

Superior Canvas Board

Painting Knives (actual size)

Canvas Panel

Oil Sketching Paper, Fine Grain

Hardboard with two coats of Hardboard Primer

Double Dipper

Oil Painting Board

Varnish Brush

Canvas

Oil Sketching Paper, Rough Grain

Cartridge Paper with two coats of emulsion paint

Palette Knife

Fig. 4

PAINTING SURFACES

The traditional surface (support) for oil painting is canvas. It is usually bought already primed and stretched. This means that four wooden stretcher pieces have been slotted together to form a frame and the canvas has been professionally stretched over and fastened onto the frame. Two wedges are put into each corner of the frame. When these are knocked in with a small hammer, the canvas tension increases as the frame gets slightly larger, until the canvas is 'drum' tight. Then it is ready to paint on.

Fig. 4 shows brush strokes on different painting supports reproduced actual size. Canvas is the most expensive. However, there are many other less expensive surfaces to work on, but take note: all absorbent surfaces should be primed, or the oil will be sucked into the surface, leaving behind the pigment lying on the top with no adhesion, so it could then be 'brushed' off. Most supports are already primed for working on when you buy them. The most common one that is not primed is hardboard. This is a very popular oil painting surface and usually it is the smooth side that is used. Incidentally, use indoor quality hardboard, not exterior board, as the latter has been treated and could cause problems with the oil pigments.

To prime the board simply means to seal the surface and at the same time allow the paint to be easily applied. You can buy a purpose-made primer for hardboard, which contains a special resin that produces a hard and durable surface. It dries in less than three hours, and I would suggest giving your hardboard two or three coats for the best results. You can also prime hardboard with two coats of emulsion paint or household undercoat paint. If a non-water-based paint is used as primer, it is better to seal the surface first with a size, which you can buy from a hardware shop.

If you want to work on a large piece of hardboard, say over 405 x 510mm (16 x 20in), it is best to glue some wooden battens on the back to stop it from warping. Hardboard has one disadvantage: it doesn't have a grain (tooth) to the surface. It is smooth and some students at first find it a little difficult to paint on. The other side has a very rough mechanical-looking grain and is not recommended: it also takes a lot of paint to cover the surface.

If you have any difficulties with the smooth surfaces, or you don't want to prime, there are plenty of ready-primed canvases or canvas boards on the market. The sizes range from about 180 x 125mm (7 x 5in) up to 915 x 610mm (36 x 24in). They have different surface qualities and are excellent to work on. There is also oil painting paper which is ready primed and can be bought in pads or sheets.

MEDIUMS

As I said earlier, a medium is added to the brush to thin the paint or help it move over the painting surface. There are many different mediums on the market and some artists make their own, sometimes complicated, sometimes secret mixtures. But I recommend that you stick to the manufactured mediums – I do!

The first most important medium is turpentine. This you use to thin down the paint for underpainting, and especially if you want to paint thin lines. It is not to be confused with turpentine substitute (white spirit) which you use for cleaning your brushes and palette. Some people find the smell of turpentine too strong, and some people are also allergic to turpentine. There is an alternative product called 'Low Odour Oil Painting Thinner', which has no smell but naturally has the same properties for oil painting as turpentine. I have used it for all the work in this book.

Because oil paint takes a long time to dry, I find it very helpful to use a medium that speeds up the drying time. I use Alkyd medium. This is a liquid that helps thin the paint and speed up the drying process. I also use Gel medium: this is squeezed out of a tube and helps to spread the paint without thinning it too much; like the Alkyd medium, it has a drying agent added. I am very happy using these mediums for all my work, and I suggest you use them and forget, at the moment, that others exist.

Daler-Rowney market a white paint called Alkyd White. Used in place of oil white, it speeds up the drying process by half and, as white paint is used constantly throughout a painting, it is a great aid for artists who want their paintings to dry more quickly. Try it.

PALETTE

There is nothing mysterious about an artist's palette. It is simply the surface on which the paint is squeezed from the tube and mixed before being applied to the canvas. Palettes are made from either wood or white plastic; some artists use a sheet of glass placed on a table.

The traditional palette shape is called a studio palette, but the oblong shape (fig. 2) is very popular today. Keep your mixing area cleaned when you are not using it. Clean it with painting rag and turpentine substitute (white spirit).

Fig. 5

Fig. 5 is a photograph of my old art school palette. Don't let yours get into a state like this. It lives in my studio today only as a reminder of those happy days, not as a palette for working on. It is almost a piece of creative art in its own right!

EASELS

Your painting surface must be as steady and firm as you can make it, therefore a good strong easel is important. Some easels are illustrated in fig. 6. Table easels are quite adequate if you haven't got the space for a floor-standing easel. Also, you can make do by placing your painting surface on a kitchen chair and leaning it at an angle against the back of the chair. Most oil colour sketching boxes (fig. 7) use the inside of the lid to support canvas boards. You rest the box on your knees when working outside, and on a table when indoors, and the lid becomes the portable easel.

CARRYING BOX

A drawer in which to put all your equipment when you are not working is ideal, but if you are going to work outdoors then you have to carry your equipment. You can use an old small suitcase, a canvas carrying bag or, of course, buy one of the ready-made ones on the market. Fig. 7 is a typical sketching box that carries all your requirements.

Whatever your hobby or pastime, when you need equipment it is so easy to get carried away, money permitting, into buying too much. Don't let me stop your enjoyment of trying out new materials, but until you have gained experience of what you really need, keep them down to a minimum. Then, go out and treat yourself; experience different brushes, colours, supports, and anything that takes your fancy.

Fig. 6

Fig. 7

BEGINNERS' BASIC EQUIPMENT KIT

After reading the last few pages on equipment, you may be getting a little confused as to what you need just to get started. This is why I have listed below the materials that will cope with all the exercises in this book. The following items are what you need for your beginner's basic equipment kit (fig. 8), and I have used these materials to paint the exercises.

COLOURS
Cobalt Blue, Crimson Alizarin, Cadmium Yellow (Hue), Yellow Ochre, Raw Umber, Viridian (Hue), Cadmium Red (Hue) and Titanium White.

BRUSHES
Remember I said earlier that brushes are a very personal choice. The ones I am using may not be the best for you, but try them to get you started. It is best – but not essential – if you get two of each size. This will enable you always to have one to use for dark colours and one for light colours. In this way you can keep a dark colour in your brush and not have to wash it out to use a lighter colour.

The hoghair brush series is Bristlewhite Series B48 brush sizes Nos. 1, 2 and 4. Add to these a Series 43 sable No. 4, a Dalon Series D99 'Rigger' brush No.2 and a Series 103 sable 'Rigger' brush No. 1 for small and detail work.

OTHER EQUIPMENT
You also need a palette knife with a 75mm (3in) blade; oil painting medium or turpentine; a bottle of Alkyd medium or a tube of Gel medium; and a double dipper for your palette to hold the oil painting medium in one and Alkyd medium in the other. Keep an old jam jar for holding your turpentine substitute for washing out your brushes and a paint rag for wiping and cleaning brushes and hands. The other items are a palette; canvas board or oil painting paper; a plastic eraser and an HB pencil.

Naturally there are ways of cutting down this basic equipment kit if funds don't allow you to get everything in one go. The most obvious saving would be to buy fewer brushes. You could use only Gel medium and turpentine; find your own receptacles to hold them in and use a piece of old Formica or varnished plywood for a palette.

When working outdoors the only additions you will need are a stool, a portable easel and a carrying box. Incidentally, the one illustrated in fig. 7 can be bought empty and the paints and brushes etc. can be of your choice.

Fig. 8

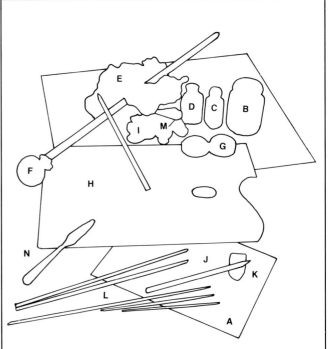

KEY   A — Painting Board   B — Jar for washing brushes
C — Low Odour Oil Painting Thinners   D — Alkyd Medium
E — Rag   F — Mahlstick   G — Double dipper   H — Palette
I — Paints   J — Pencil   K — Plastic eraser   L — Brushes
M — Gel Medium   N — Palette knife

GETTING TO KNOW OIL PAINT

At last you can start to paint. But don't get too excited and rush ahead without first going through these early exercises, even though they may look simple. Although these exercises may appear easy, for most beginners this is the hardest part of learning to paint – just the simple act of putting paint onto canvas. It doesn't matter what shapes they paint, or the size or colour, they are afraid of making a fool of themselves in front of their family or friends.

This of course is very natural. They are trying to do something that is new and alien to them. I find that a beginner is most vulnerable at this stage. Because we all want to show off what we can do, we tend to take on too much, too early. Beginners will want to have a go at painting a picture, anything from mountains to large snowscapes, forests – in fact the type of picture that inspires them. A man who is inspired to drive in a Grand Prix motor race knows that he can't do it until he has learnt to drive a car first. In the same way, no one can paint a full-blooded landscape until he or she has learnt the basics of handling paint.

I think that for a real beginner – this is the most important point I can make – your first real painting must be of a subject that is very, very simple. Then the chances of success are very great and we all know that success breeds success, and therefore you will approach your next painting with confidence. The more confident you become the better your paintings will be, and the more enjoyment you will get from painting. So we will take things from the very beginning, in a steady progressive order.

FIRST DOODLES

The first thing I want you to do is to play with your paint and mediums. We couldn't start more simply than that! I suggest you use a cheap form of support to work on; try oil painting paper. Put some paint on your palette and off you go.

Try painting over a large area with only paint, then try it with Alkyd medium added. See what happens when you add only oil painting medium or turpentine to the paint. Smudge one colour into another with your finger – a very useful painting tool! Add white to your colours to make them lighter. Try your small sable and nylon brushes and feel the difference between those and the hoghair brushes. Paint thinly, and also try your paint thick. Look at what I have done in fig. 9. It makes a strange picture, but it is good practice.

It doesn't matter how long you doodle in this way; in fact, the more you do, the more familiar you will become with oil colours, brushes and mediums. Because you are not worried about shapes (drawing), colours and creating an atmosphere in your work while you are playing with paint, all your learning power is concentrated on the application of paint to canvas.

Fig. 9

Paint with Low Odour Oil Painting
Thinners added
Thursday 3.45 pm DRY 4.30 pm

Paint only (thin)
Thursday 3.50 pm DRY Friday 2 pm

Paint with Alkyd White added
Thursday 3.50 pm DRY Sat 11 am

Paint with 50% Gel medium added
Thursday 3.56 pm DRY 9 pm (thin areas)
(thick areas dry Sat 9 am)

Paint with 25% Alkyd medium added
Thursday 4 pm DRY 11.30 pm

Paint only (thick) Thursday 4.10 pm
DRY thin Sunday 3 pm
DRY thick approx. 2 weeks

Fig. 10 Approximate drying timetable

WORKING WITH OIL

As you have been playing with paint, one thing you must have noticed is that the paint has not dried while you have been working. You have been painting 'wet on wet'. This is something you are going to have to come to terms with and learn how to work your paint while it's wet. You will find that you can get some lovely soft edges and merging of colours and tones, but you will have more difficulty in getting hard edges. This will come with experience.

'Alla prima' is the name given to a method of painting in which paint is worked directly onto the canvas, usually on a white ground, without underpainting first or using glazes later during the painting. It is a direct way of painting, relatively unsophisticated and simplified, made popular over the last century by the many amateurs who took up oil painting. Basically, you are painting wet on wet throughout the picture.

There are variations; for instance, you could underpaint with a thin turpentine and colour wash first and then work over the top in a direct way. You could start a picture in this way, and leave it to dry, then work on it again, adding paint over dry paint to finish the picture. I have talked about alla prima because to me it is the basic way of oil painting, with variations, for beginners to start.

Questions I am often asked by students are: 'Do I have to wait for the paint to dry?' 'Do I use thick paint or thin paint?' 'Can I do a painting in one sitting?' 'Do I have to underpaint first?' These are very important questions and painting in a direct way (alla prima) in fact answers them all. If you were to go out into the countryside to paint a scene and you were there for the day but knew you would not be going back, you would have to paint your picture in one sitting. In the process of painting you would use thin and thick paint to get variation of texture and depth of tone, and you would have to work wet on wet to finish the painting in one sitting. If you were using mediums with drying agents added you might find that some parts of the picture would be dry enough (as the day progressed) to overpaint without pulling up the paint underneath. You could then take it a stage further by adding some dark or light accents or even, after the painting was dry, change some small passages at home to finish it off. But beware, too much work at home, away from the real life scene, can ruin a painting done on the spot. Experience is the only answer here.

MAKING TIME FOR DRYING

You might find you paint as far as you can working wet on wet and then have to let certain parts dry to be able to paint over them to continue the picture. Don't worry about this; it is a natural way of painting in oil. I could write about all the variations on what parts of a picture could be left to dry or painted wet on wet for the rest of this book, but the best way is to work at it and find out what happens in practice.

As the drying time of the paint is so crucial to our way of painting, I suggest you make yourself a drying timetable. This will give you first-hand experience of paint drying time and a reference for the future, until it becomes second nature. Prepare this drying timetable on a durable surface (painting board or hardboard) and copy what I have done in fig. 10. Naturally, add some more combinations to your chart if you want; remember, your chart is a working tool for your painting. After playing with the paint earlier you will know just how liquid or stiff you want your colours to be. Therefore the amounts of medium that you put in will be very personal to you.

PAINTING DEFINITE SHAPES

The most important skill to learn is to be able to paint up to a particular area of your painting and have control of the brush, so that it will keep within the boundaries you want. If you were painting the hull of a boat, you would want it to stay that shape and not become one dictated to you by an uncontrollable brush! So it is very important to practise with your brushwork until it becomes second nature to you; in fact, your brush will become an extension of your eye. What shapes you can see, your brush will be able to create on your canvas.

In fig. 11 you will see the two types of arrow I have used in various places in the book to help you to understand the movement of the brush strokes. The solid black arrow shows the direction of the brush stroke, and the outline arrow indicates the movement of the brush in relation to the canvas, i.e. working from top to bottom, or side to side.

We will start by painting up to a straight line, as shown in fig. 11. Practise on all these exercises, using different-sized brushes, because during a painting you have to paint shapes of different sizes, and it may not be practical to change to your brush size at that time. When you are painting up to a definite line, after loading your brush let your first brush stroke start to the right of the line. This ensures your paint is 'running' well out of the brush in the right consistency, and it also gives you a 'practice run'. Then repeat this stroke, getting closer to the line, and finally let your brush stroke hit the line you are painting up to.

Naturally, there are times when you can't start working your brush on the canvas before you paint up to a line but, by practising in this way, when the occasion does arise you will be pretty confident to go straight in and hit the line the first time. Also practise painting up to a line on its left. You will find this more difficult as it is an awkward movement (unless, of course, you are left-handed), but with a little patience you will be able to do it.

Now we will work to a curved line and paint a solid circle (fig. 12). With an HB pencil, draw round something to create a circle on your canvas. Then start at the top and work down the left side to the bottom, letting the bristles follow the brush movement, i.e. pulling the brush down. Remember, as with the straight line, work a couple of practice runs before you hit the line.

Now start at the top again and paint the right-hand side of the circle. As with the straight line, when you paint up to the left side of the line you will find it more difficult, but it will come with practice. When you have done this, simply fill in the centre with the same brush.

The next exercise, a kitchen spatula (fig. 13, see page 178) is a little more difficult. The shape is more complicated and you have to fill it in first and then paint in the background, working up to the edges of the spatula with the background colour. It is a silhouette, and we are using it only to illustrate shapes, not trying to paint it as a three-dimensional object.

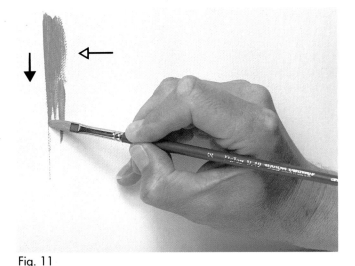

Fig. 11

Fig. 12

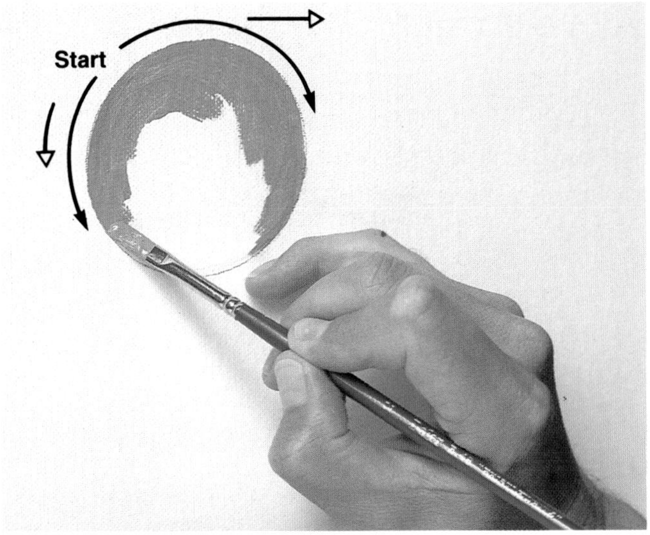

HOLDING THE BRUSH

There are two basic ways of holding the brush. As you have been working on the previous exercises, I would imagine that 99 per cent of you have been holding your brush as you would hold a pencil. Well, for the exercises you have been doing, this is correct. However, where you have to work over wet areas of paint and you want to steady your hand for careful brush control, then you use a mahlstick.

This is a long stick – mine is 455mm (18in) long – and the end has a lump of rag fastened onto it. Hold it in your left hand and rest the padded end on the edge of the canvas, or on any part of the easel that will support it. Then you can rest your hand on the stick to give it support (fig. 14). The position shown in fig. 15 is for painting more freely and over larger areas. The brush is placed across the palm of the hand and held firmly by the thumb and first finger.

Fig. 13

Naturally there is a variety of ways to hold a brush. You might be perfectly happy holding it one way, while for someone else it could be uncomfortable. If you start by practising these two important basic positions, through experience you will find your 'natural' way of working your brush.

Fig. 16 shows how to paint a horizontal line. Hold the brush in the 'detail' position, turn the hand half round to the right and drag the brush across the canvas from left to right. Remember, when you are drawing a line like this, to make sure your paint is 'runny' enough. If not, add Alkyd medium or turpentine to thin it. The curved lines above the horizontal were drawn in exactly the same way, except the hand moved up and down to create the curves. Practise painting both the horizontal and curved lines.

DRY BRUSH TECHNIQUE

This is a very traditional brush stroke and is used with all types of paint. It gives a lot of movement and life to an area. It can create the illusion of dappled sunlight on water, a rough earth field, texture on a plaster wall, etc.

Don't fill your brush to capacity, fill it about one quarter full and then drag it across from left to right, lifting (less pressure) the brush as it travels along (fig. 17). You will find that the paint will hit and miss the canvas, leaving areas unpainted. Then have a go at the harder way – right to left! As you practise the dry brush stroke you will find your own ways of creating this very useful and versatile technique.

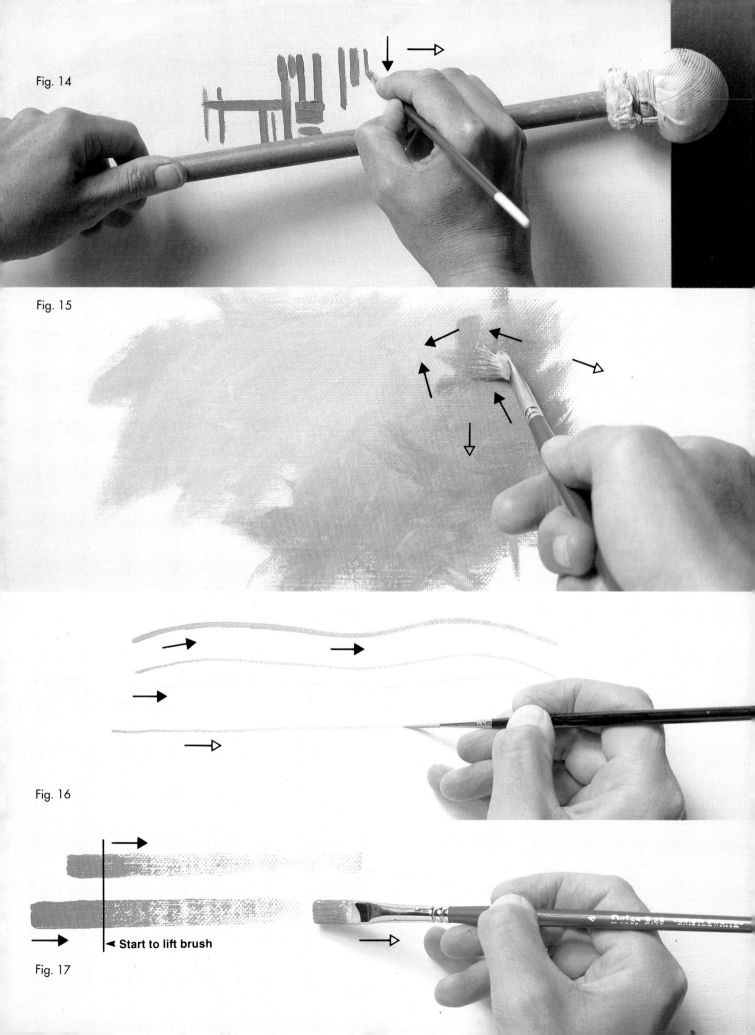

Fig. 14

Fig. 15

Fig. 16

◄ Start to lift brush

Fig. 17

DRAWING YOUR PICTURE

I am constantly asked by students how important drawing is when you are painting. The answer is that it is very important, yet you can paint without being a draughtsman.

Let me first make it absolutely clear that to have the skill of drawing is a bonus for any aspiring student, and using it to plan and draw your picture before painting will give the picture a foundation upon which you can work with confidence right from the beginning. But painting is not just drawing shapes to make a picture. It is a combination of colours, tones and shapes that eventually all build together to produce the picture. It is more important to get the colour and tonal values correct than to produce a perfect drawing. A picture that is weak on drawing but strong on colour and tone will look good, but the end result of one where the colour and tonal values are weak, no matter how good the drawing, will be a poor painting.

Taking good drawing at one end of a scale and good colour and tonal values at the other end, naturally there are many places in between that will produce good paintings. After all, how good is 'good drawing' and how good is 'good colour and tonal work'? If you want to be a very realistic and detailed painter, then you must be able to draw well, as the results you are looking for with your finished paintings are largely dictated by careful observation and drawing.

You will find, when you are oil painting, that you will cover up some of your drawing with paint. This is inevitable and you will therefore have to re-draw with paint; so it is important that, until you gain experience, you always have a reference to work from, e.g. a still-life object, a real life scene, a sketch, and so on. You can then refer back to this during the painting of your picture. If you are without a constant reference, your picture could quite easily wander away from its original concept. Some experienced artists work this way, and let the creation of the picture unfold as they work. It's a bit too early at this stage for you to try working like that.

Finally, whatever your skill or lack of it at drawing, don't let it put you off painting. It is a natural course of things that the more you paint, the better your drawing will become. If you feel you need more experience, then draw objects in your home as extra exercises. Spend just half-an-hour a day practising and you will notice the difference.

DRAWING ON CANVAS
To apply the drawing to the canvas you can use charcoal, pencil or paint. I have never used charcoal, because it is messy, and the 'dust' it leaves on the canvas surface can mix with your paint and discolour it. I find pencil all right, except that you can easily lose the image when you are painting.

Fig. 18

Finally, you can use a small sable brush – I use a Rigger – with a mixture of turpentine and colour.

I work two ways. If there is a lot of careful drawing to be done in a picture, I draw it first with an HB pencil, then paint over the lines with Cobalt Blue diluted with plenty of turpentine. I feel more relaxed doing the drawing carefully with pencil. The reason why I then paint over the pencil is that the paint line will not disappear when you paint the picture as the pencil line could. When I work over with the paint drawing I do not try to copy my pencil lines exactly, or the freedom would go out of the drawing; in fact I very consciously loosen up the drawing.

When you are drawing on the canvas, don't draw carefully laboured lines. You must put character into them: be bold and free (fig.18). Feel and experience the picture as you draw it. If a picture needs only a little drawing, then I will use just a pencil or a brush, or even start painting without drawing at all, especially if it is a small picture.

CREATING FORM – 3-D EFFECT

Painting is really creating an illusion of 3-D objects on a flat two-dimensional surface, and one of the ways of doing this is by adding light and shade (dark against light, light against dark) to our painted objects. For instance, if you look at fig. 19 you can only see a flat yellow panel. If you now look at fig. 20 you can see a yellow box. This all seems very obvious, but it holds one of the vital keys to painting.

Fig. 19 is a yellow background, that has a yellow box painted on it, but without any light. Therefore there are no shadows, no light against dark, and consequently we can't see the box. In fig. 20 a light is positioned top left, and you can see the box because of the shadows and tones cast by the light. Through light and shade we can see forms and shapes of objects.

A most essential part of painting from nature, whether it is from a still life indoors or a landscape outdoors, is to screw up your eyes as you look at the subject you are painting. You will find that the middle tones disappear and you see the darks and lights of the scene quite clearly. This helps you to see shapes and forms, but also to know where your real darkest darks and lightest lights are situated. Get into this habit quickly; it is very important.

When you start any painting, always make a positive effort to remember from what direction the source of light is coming – obviously where the light hits an object directly will be the 'light side', and the opposite side will be the dark or shadow side.

Fig. 19

Fig. 20

Fig. 21

UNDERPAINTING

The next stage for a painting, after drawing, is to underpaint it. The object of underpainting (also called blocking in) is to get light and shade (three dimensions) into your picture, so before you start worrying about colour you create your picture in monochrome (just one colour) (fig. 21). You have worked out where your light and dark areas are to be placed, the drawing has been done and then you have a firm foundation on which to work.

Underpainting is done with one colour mixed with plenty of turpentine (don't add white to it), almost like applying watercolour to paper. This can be applied with a brush, or a rag on your finger, or just your finger. The light areas are shown by leaving white canvas, the dark areas shown by adding more pigment (paint) to the turpentine. As this mixture is applied thinly, it does not take long to dry (if you tried it on your drying chart you will know roughly how long) and you can then paint the picture. You can also start working your paint when the underpainting is not quite dry, but only experience will tell you when and how to work over it.

Some artists take the underpainting a stage further and add additional colour to it. I can't see anything wrong with this at all; in fact, you are another stage closer to the finished painting. You can use any colour you like for your underpainting except, of course, a light colour that will be difficult to see on the canvas. Raw Umber dries quickly and is therefore a good colour to use for underpainting and for

drawing the picture with a brush, but I mostly use only the Cobalt Blue.

There is one other way of underpainting that the old masters could not do, and that is to use acrylic paints (only introduced as a painting medium in the early 1960s). The advantage is that acrylics dry very quickly and do not have any effect on the oil paint when it is worked over the top. Note: the acrylic must be dry before you start in oils, and you must not put acrylic paint over oil paint.

Naturally if you try this way of underpainting, use sensible precautions, e.g. use a brush for acrylics only, and keep it washed out or it will harden very quickly. Keep your acrylic paints totally separate from your oil paints. You can't afford to get the two mediums mixed up by accident as water (acrylic paints are water-based) does not mix with oil! I find it a good way to work. Fig. 22 is a drawing and underpainting worked in acrylics.

USING A COLOURED GROUND

After a support has been primed (white), a common way of working is to then put a wash (turpentine plus colour) all over the support to cover the white primer. Sometimes it's a cool blue, or a warm brown, orange or yellow ochre. This helps to give an all-over hue to the painting, because small areas of the background will be left unpainted when they are missed by the brush as you paint the picture. Also, where you work the paint thinly, the coloured ground will shine through.

Fig. 22

COMPOSITION

Composition or design in painting is a very complex subject. One person could think a painting was a good composition; another would think it weak. I will go through some basic 'rules' which will be sufficient for you to apply to your paintings, but as you work you will learn more about design through your own experience of painting.

Some people have a natural talent for design and composition, while others find it difficult, just as some students find drawing or colour mixing easy, and so on. I believe that everyone has a natural strong point and once you find yours you can then concentrate on some of your weaker areas.

Composition or design in painting means the same to me, namely, the positioning of objects on paper in a happy way that enables you to tell a story visually to the onlooker. Since any painting will finish up on a piece of paper or canvas with an edge around it, it obviously has to be designed within those boundaries. Let us then look at some basic, but important rules.

Look at fig. 23, I have divided the paper (canvas) vertically and horizontally into thirds. Where the lines cross at a, b, c and d are the focal points. If your centre of interest is positioned on or around a focal point, then you should have a good design. Don't have your centre of interest in the middle of the picture, as it will look too symmetrical (fig. 24, left). Placed at the focal point b, however, it becomes a good design (fig. 24 right). Look at fig. 25 and you can see how the church positioned at b gives the picture a happy look (by which I mean that it works well on paper).

To give the centre of interest more importance to the picture, you can add colour either brighter, stronger, darker or lighter than its surroundings, or add an odd or unexpected colour.

The space between objects is also important to good design. An ugly space between objects can spoil a picture, but a pleasing shape can enhance it. Try to avoid two objects just touching; it can be difficult for the eye to separate them in a picture. The golden rule is to let important objects either 'hit' or 'miss' each other (fig. 26).

After going through these basic rules, don't feel you have to stick to them rigidly; they are a general guide from which you can work. A deviation from the expected to a more personal approach can create an original and sometimes unusual painting. When you wander around an exhibition, look at paintings and the way they have been designed. You will learn a lot from them, whether you are looking at old masters or modern artists' work.

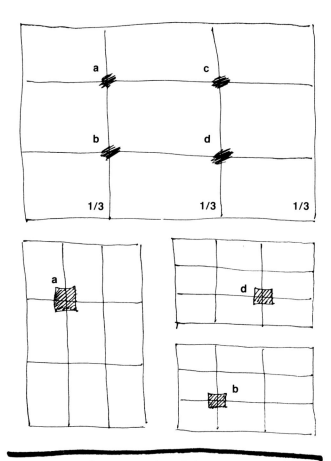

Figs. 23 and 24 (above), 25 and 26 (below)

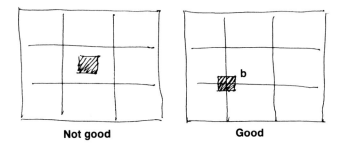

Not good   Good

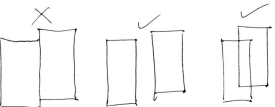

MIXING COLOURS

Now we come to what must be one of the most important aspects of painting: mixing colours. Wherever you are, everything you see is made up of colour. To a beginner, the thought of mixing all those thousands of colours and shades must be very daunting, especially when you can only buy between fifty and sixty ready-made colours. And even if you had them all on your palette, you would find that you never had the perfect colour you wanted.

As with watercolour and acrylic painting, you can mix all the colours you need from a basic three – the primary colours red, yellow and blue. In fig. 27 (top) I have shown you Crimson Alizarin, Cadmium Yellow and Cobalt Blue. Of course, there are other reds, yellows and blues, and they can vary greatly in tone. For instance, Cadmium Yellow, Cadmium Yellow Pale, Lemon Yellow and Yellow Ochre are all yellows, but look different when compared to each other. This means that although you are restricted to the primaries you still have a choice of colours.

You will no doubt have found out by now, that if you want a bright red, and the primary red you are using is Crimson Alizarin, then this won't give you a bright red colour and you will have to use Cadmium Red, for instance, instead. The point I am making here is that although you mix your colours using just the three primaries, you will find that to get some colours you need a different red, yellow and blue on your palette to help achieve the shade you want.

My most important rule for mixing colours is always to put the main colour of the mix onto your palette first. For instance, if you want to mix a yellowy orange, then you would put yellow first and add red to the yellow, gradually mixing in the amount of red you need to make your yellowy orange. If you put the red on the palette first then the emphasis would be on red, and you would have to add a lot of yellow to make a yellowy orange. This is very vital to mixing the colours you want. First, learn to mix with just the primaries (red, yellow and blue), then you will be able to cope with almost any colour you see.

There are other colours that we use besides the three primary colours, and these help with our mixing. Gradually, as you progress, introduce some of these to your palette and you will find them very useful. Until you gain experience, use the colours I have used for the exercises in the book.

VARYING YOUR COLOUR MIXES

With oil paint, to make colours lighter we add white. When you are mixing a pale colour it is essential that you put white onto your palette first and then mix in the other colours. You can choose between Flake White and Titanium White. Flake White has more body (is thicker) and dries a little more quickly, but I prefer to use Titanium White. Don't forget Alkyd White, which dries twice as fast as the previous two: it may suit you, and it is another aid to quicker drying.

Look at the colour chart on the opposite page (fig. 27). In the first three columns I have painted different colours, using the three primary colours. First I have made each primary colour paler by adding white; then I have added one other primary colour; finally, to the resulting colour I have added more white to make the progression paler. In the fourth column I have mixed the three primary colours together to obtain the 'black' and then added variations of the primary colours plus white to obtain the other colours. Copy this chart and try to match my colours, and then try mixing your own colours and make your own chart.

Some colours jump out from the canvas, while others seem to stay in the background. It is the warm colours – reds – that 'jump', and the cool colours – blues – that recede. Not only does this happen on the canvas, it does this in nature. That is why, looking at a landscape, the distance colour is overall blue, and the foreground colours are stronger and warmer. Next time you are out, look at the distance while you cover up the middle distance and foreground with your hand (look over the top of your hand) for about one minute. Then quickly take your hand away and look at both the distance and the foreground together. You will be surprised just how 'blue' the distance is, how colourful the foreground is, and how much warmer are the foreground colours.

Notice that the warm and cool variations can be applied to neutral colours as well as the more colourful hues. In fig. 27 (top right) I have mixed a warm (reddish) grey and a cool (bluish) grey. This helps you to enliven your more subtle colour mixes.

You can't paint a picture, no matter how small, without mixing colours, so you will get better with every painting you do. Nevertheless do practise your mixing; you will get a tremendous thrill when you achieve the colours you were trying for. Make everything a personal challenge and you will enjoy even the most mundane of tasks.

Fig. 27

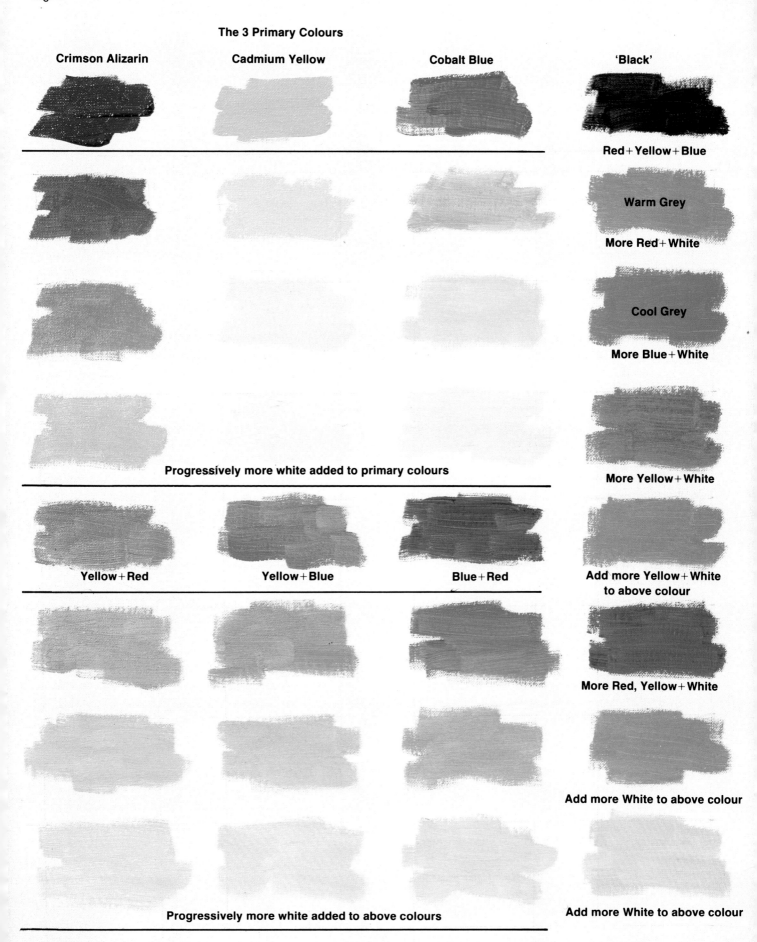

The 3 Primary Colours

Crimson Alizarin	Cadmium Yellow	Cobalt Blue	'Black'

Red+Yellow+Blue

Warm Grey

More Red+White

Cool Grey

More Blue+White

More Yellow+White

Progressively more white added to primary colours

Yellow+Red	Yellow+Blue	Blue+Red

Add more Yellow+White
to above colour

More Red, Yellow+White

Add more White to above colour

Progressively more white added to above colours

Add more White to above colour

PAINTING WITH THREE COLOURS

Well, at last we are here! If you have been working page by page and not jumping forward, this will be your first real attempt at a painting. I have chosen a banana for the first exercise (fig. 28) because it can be long, short, fat or thin; greeny yellow, bright yellow or orangy yellow; in fact, from a painting point of view, one banana can look quite different to another. This is important. Your drawing might not be quite accurate or your colours not exactly like mine but, because of the way bananas vary, your painting will still look like a banana.

If your first painting had been, say, a scene of boats moored in a harbour (not a simple subject), then your drawing, your colours and inexperience could have combined to make it a disaster. It is far better to paint something simple first and be seen as someone who paints simple things well, than someone who paints complicated scenes badly, and is humoured by their friends. Time and practice will get you to the harbour.

Copying these exercises will give you confidence for when you begin to paint from life. However, don't try to copy my pictures exactly, as you will be too concerned over the drawing and find yourself getting inhibited. Before you start, look at the stages and see how I did the painting, so that you are familiar with the subject. Don't forget to keep each exercise simple, but if you find you go wrong or you can't get the effect you are after, leave it alone, go onto another exercise and come back with a fresh eye. The chances are you will be able to cope with it. When you have followed these exercises, try painting the real-life objects.

I have used only three colours for these exercises, a red, a yellow and a blue (plus Titanium White). They are not always the same red, yellow and blue, but the colour names are shown at the bottom of each exercise. Throughout all the exercises it is most important to mix your colours in the order that I specify in the text or as they are indicated in the illustration captions. Generally speaking, each colour you add will be less in quantity than its predecessor. If it is a very pale colour then it will have a large proportion of white as its first colour.

For all the exercises I have used low odour oil painting thinners instead of genuine turpentine, although naturally you can use either. I will refer to these thinners as turps. I have also mixed Alkyd medium with my paint, to help it spread and to speed up the drying time. All the exercises in this section were painted one quarter larger than they are

reproduced, except fig. 29 (see page 188), that finished painting being 145 x 125 mm (5$\frac{3}{4}$ x 5in).

PAINTING A BANANA

First draw the banana (fig. 28) with an HB pencil; this will make you feel more confident when you paint over the pencil with Cobalt Blue mixed with turps (first stage). Use your Series B48 No. 1 hoghair brush. Next, paint in the banana with your hoghair No. 2 brush. You may find you want the drawing to dry; I let mine dry and it took 20 minutes. For the third stage, mix a brown and paint in the dark marks and the stalk. This is painting wet on wet, as naturally the yellow is still very wet. Now, with the same brush, paint in the shadow using the colours indicated. Finally, mix up a light colour of a thick juicy consistency and in one stroke, working away from the banana, paint in the broken end of the stalk, still using your No. 2 brush.

Until you have gained experience do not apply your paint thickly, unless to show definite brush strokes to help illustrate form, as you did for the broken end of the stalk. If your paint is thick you will have great difficulty in painting over it with more colour, and your picture could easily turn into a muddy, shapeless mess. You will find that the art of applying thick paint will happen in a natural way as you get used to the medium. As a guide, use thin paint for dark and shadow colours and thick paint for bright and highlight colours. The banana was painted on a canvas panel.

A PAIR OF EGGS

For this exercise (fig. 29) I used the smooth side of hardboard and painted on two coats of primer. Using your Series B48 No. 1 brush, draw in the eggs with a mix of Cobalt Blue and turps. If you feel happier, draw with your HB pencil first. Now, with your No. 2 hoghair brush, using Cobalt Blue, paint in the background and shadows, and with your finger smudge in the soft shadows on the eggs.

Mix the colours for the eggs and paint them in. Remember as they are very light-coloured, put white on the palette first and mix your colour into it. Then paint in the background, using your Series B48 No. 4 brush. Finally, still using your No. 4 brush, paint in the shadows on the table with a mix of Cobalt Blue, Titanium White, Crimson Alizarin and a little Cadmium Yellow, and then paint the table. 'Clean up' the edges of the eggs with your Rigger No. 1 brush.

Fig. 28

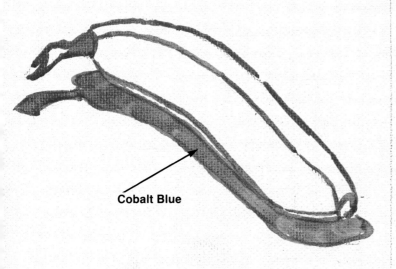

Cobalt Blue

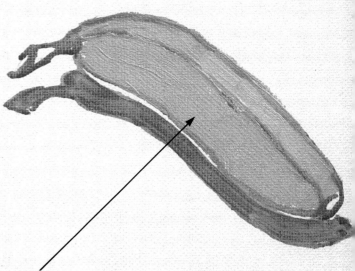

Cadmium Yellow, Crimson Alizarin and Titanium White

Crimson Alizarin, Cadmium Yellow, plus a little Cobalt Blue and Titanium White

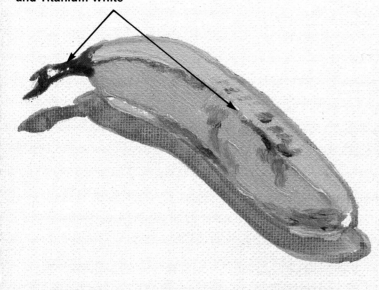

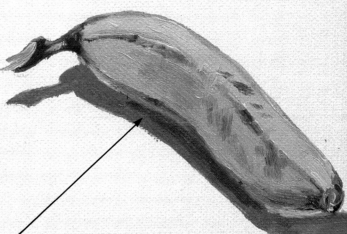

Cobalt Blue, Crimson Alizarin, Cadmium Yellow plus a little Titanium White

Crimson Alizarin

Cadmium Yellow

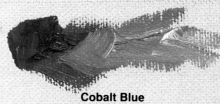

Cobalt Blue

Plus Titanium White

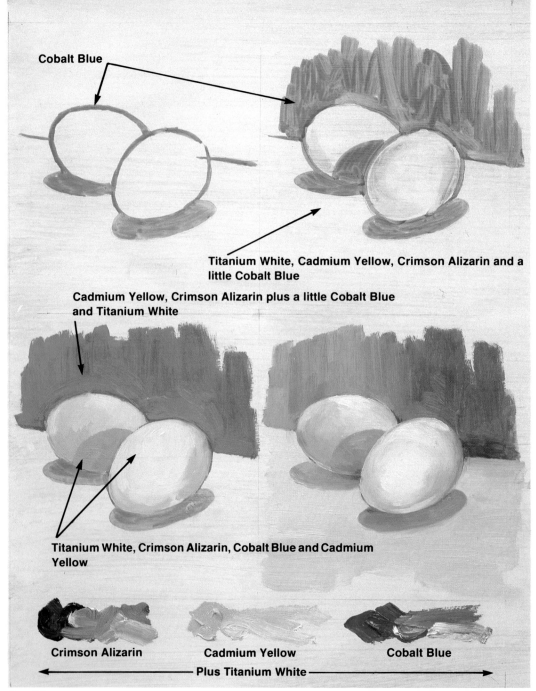

Cobalt Blue

Titanium White, Cadmium Yellow, Crimson Alizarin and a little Cobalt Blue

Cadmium Yellow, Crimson Alizarin plus a little Cobalt Blue and Titanium White

Titanium White, Crimson Alizarin, Cobalt Blue and Cadmium Yellow

Crimson Alizarin   **Cadmium Yellow**   **Cobalt Blue**

◀─────────── **Plus Titanium White** ───────────▶

Fig. 29

JAM JAR

Beginners are always afraid of painting glass because they think it is too advanced and too difficult to paint. The secret is to observe. Observation means looking very carefully, but understanding what you are seeing. Put a drinking glass in front of you and you see glass! Now look at it again and ask yourself, what is behind the glass? What makes those shapes? By looking carefully you will see that, for instance, a table-edge or an apple from the fruit bowl can be seen through the glass. Look at each shape against the next and, if you do this for a few minutes, you will find that you are not looking at a glass, but at shapes that are through the glass.

At this point you are capable of painting your glass. The way to do it is to paint the shapes you see, then half-close your eyes and look for the shadows and highlights on the glass, and put them in. There is one very important rule to remember: the colours of the shapes seen through the glass are usually darker than the ones seen outside the glass. Notice the 'black' background on the top left in fig. 30. I have painted it lighter inside the jar – it appeared that way. I drew it in with my Rigger No. 1 brush and used my Series B48 No. 4 for the rest of the picture, except for detail work in the last stage, where I used my Series B48 No. 1 and Rigger No. 1. I painted this exercise on a canvas.

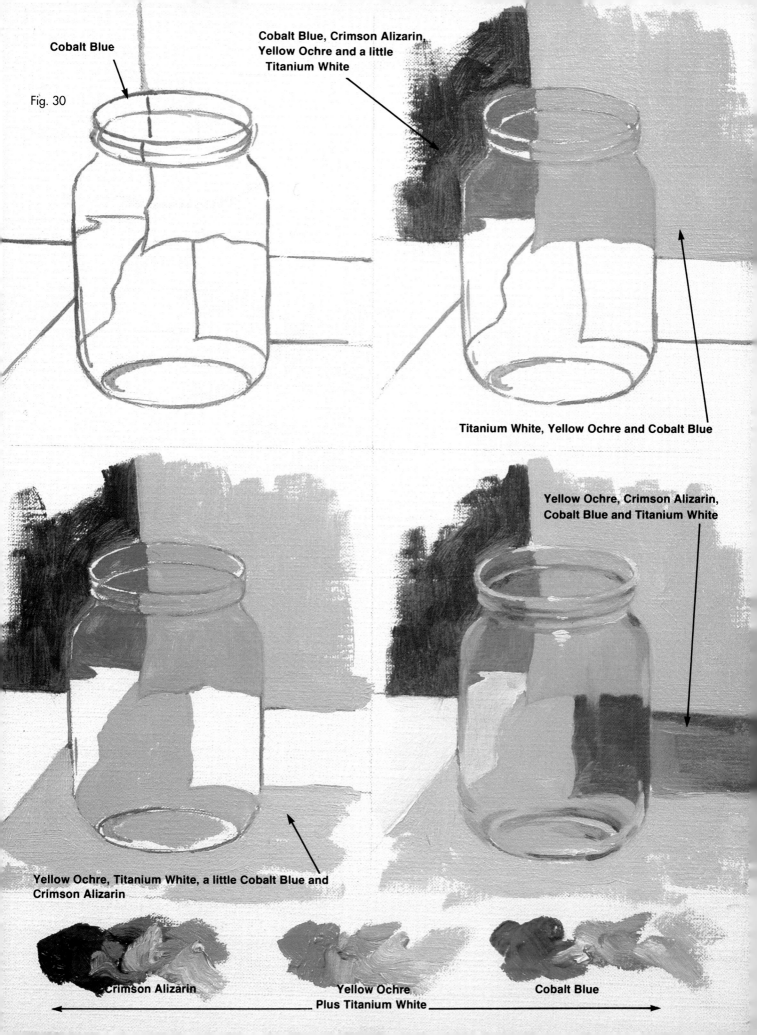

Cobalt Blue

Cobalt Blue, Crimson Alizarin, Yellow Ochre and a little Titanium White

Fig. 30

Titanium White, Yellow Ochre and Cobalt Blue

Yellow Ochre, Crimson Alizarin, Cobalt Blue and Titanium White

Yellow Ochre, Titanium White, a little Cobalt Blue and Crimson Alizarin

Crimson Alizarin

Yellow Ochre
Plus Titanium White

Cobalt Blue

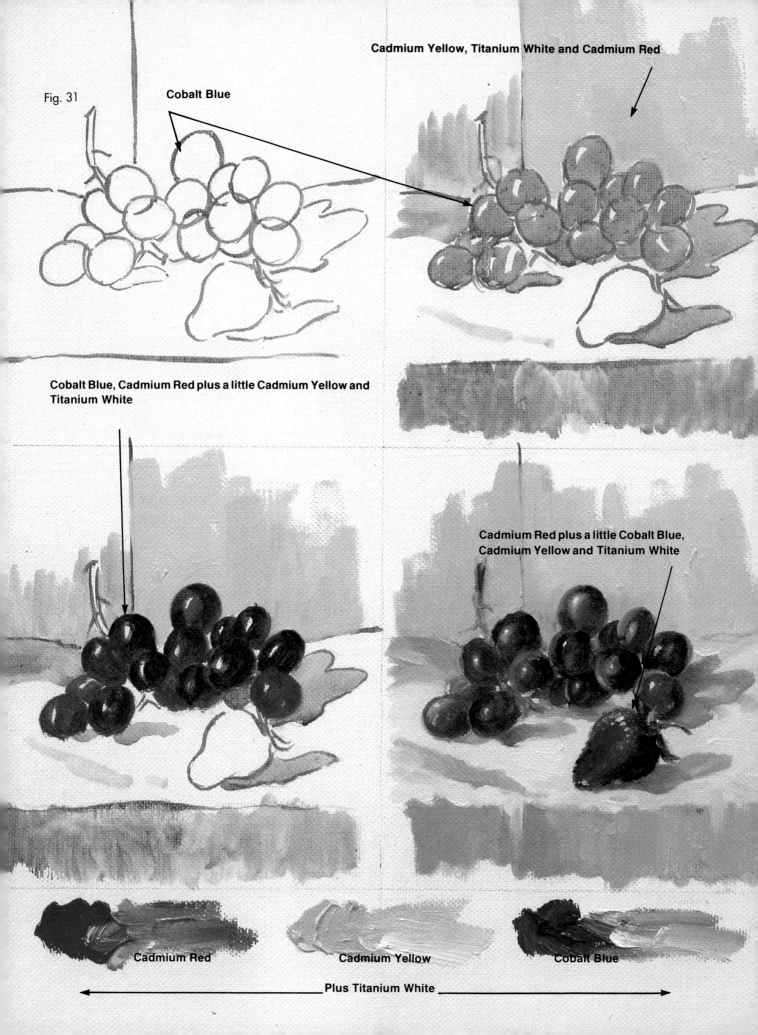

Fig. 31

Cobalt Blue

Cadmium Yellow, Titanium White and Cadmium Red

Cobalt Blue, Cadmium Red plus a little Cadmium Yellow and Titanium White

Cadmium Red plus a little Cobalt Blue, Cadmium Yellow and Titanium White

Cadmium Red

Cadmium Yellow

Cobalt Blue

Plus Titanium White

Fig. 32

STRAWBERRY WITH GRAPES

I have changed one of the primary colours for this exercise (fig. 31), which I painted on a canvas panel. I have used Cadmium Red, Cadmium Yellow and Cobalt Blue. The reason for the new red is because Crimson Alizarin would not be the colour for a strawberry.

Start by drawing in the picture with your Rigger No. 1 using Cobalt Blue mixed with turps. (Draw it in pencil first if you prefer.) Then, with the same colour, paint in the shadows and grapes, using your Series B48 No. 2 brush. Next, with your Series B48 No. 4 brush, paint in the background with a mixture of Cadmium Yellow and a touch of Titanium White and Cadmium Red. Note how I left highlights on the grapes when I painted them in blue, and how they follow the curve of the grape.

With your No. 2 hoghair brush, paint in the grapes, leaving the existing highlights unpainted. Paint in the strawberry, using pure Cadmium Red then, with a very little touch of Cadmium Yellow and Titanium White added, paint over the light tones; add a little Cobalt Blue to Cadmium Red for the dark areas.

Now put a light blue-grey over the highlights on the grapes, and then in the middle of the highlight put a bright spot of Titanium White with a touch of Cadmium Yellow mixed in. Next, paint in the grey background and yellow/white tablecloth with shadows. Paint the stalks of the grapes and strawberry. Finally, clean up and add accents of dark and light where you feel necessary.

PRAWNS ON A PLATE

I did this exercise (fig. 32) on canvas using the same three primary colours as for the last exercise. Start as you did there, by drawing in with a mix of Cobalt Blue and turps, using your Rigger No. 1.

Now paint in the top prawn with your Series B48 No. 1 brush. Let the brush strokes follow the shapes of the scales on the back of the prawn. Here is a very important rule to remember. Always paint your brush stroke in the direction that the object is growing or going. For instance, if clouds are moving from left to right, then paint them with brush strokes working from left to right. Naturally there are times when this can't be done, but get into the habit whenever possible; it will give your pictures tremendous life and movement.

Next, paint in the plate and carry on painting the other two prawns. Leave their feelers, or areas where the feelers will cross, until the background is finished; e.g. the feelers of the bottom left-hand prawn overlay the bottom right-hand prawn and therefore can't be painted in until that one is finished. Now paint in the shadows and finally paint in the feelers, using your Rigger No. 1.

Cobalt Blue

Cadmium Yellow, Cadmium Red, Titanium White and a little Cobalt Blue

Titanium White, Cadmium Yellow and Cadmium Red

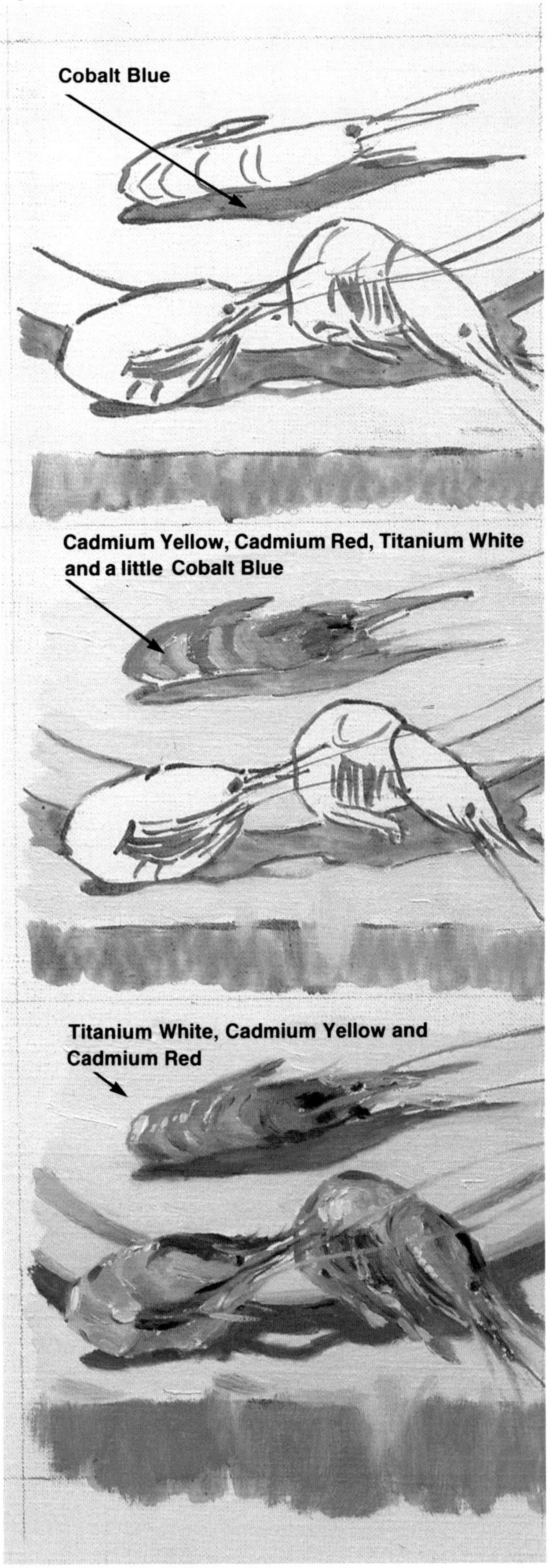

Using A Palette Knife

For most of us, when we think of palette knife painting we visualize thick juicy paint being mixed and spread over a canvas or painting board. We expect the finished painting to be very colourful and impressionistic, with lots of thick paint standing out in relief off the canvas. Well, that is one way of working with a painting knife and, as you can imagine, a very exhilarating and exciting way. You can really let loose your passion for a subject as you move the thick paint around the canvas, feeling your way, making shapes and mixing colours. One word of warning: make sure you have enough paint before you start, as it goes very quickly working this way!

Working the paint thickly is one way of using the painting knife, and another is to work the paint with the knife as you would with a brush, and gradually use thicker paint for important areas, or where thick paint will help to tell the story in the painting. In fig. 35 the sea is very thin – in fact,

Fig. 33

Fig. 34 Pencil sketch of fig. 35

Fig. 35 *From the Cliffs*

you can see the grain of the oil sketching paper through the paint in most areas, but I have used thicker paint for the cliffs and rocks.

Once you have mastered using palette knives you will be surprised at the amount of detail that you can get into your painting. Naturally, the mixing of colours, the design, choice of subject and the general 'rules' of painting apply to palette knife painting in the same way as painting with a brush: the difference is the instrument with which you apply the paint, and the marks it makes.

WORKING METHODS

There are different palette knives as there are different brushes, and the choice is personal. But to start you off I suggest you use the three knives with which I worked on fig. 35. This is a painting I did from a pencil sketch worked on the spot (fig. 34). Use these knives until you gain experience

and then, if you want, add to them from your own choice. The three are: No. 521 short trowel shape, No. 524 small pear shape, and No. 554 cranked blade 75mm (3in).

Start by experimenting (doodle) on a piece of canvas paper like you did with your brushes (see fig. 33, top left). Try using paint very thick, getting different marks from the blades. Scrape the paint off to allow the grain of the paper to show through. Make marks with the edge of the blade, or simply try anything you can think of.

Now begin the exercise (fig. 33). This was worked on oil sketching paper and the size that I painted the picture was 280mm (11in) wide. Draw it in first with your Series B48 No. 1 brush with a mix of turps and Cobalt Blue, then work through the stages. On the last stage I used plenty of paint and, in the foreground, did a lot of mixing on the paper. Add Gel medium to the paint, it helps it dry more quickly and can help you to spread the paint. Good luck!

WORKING FROM PENCIL SKETCHES

There are many times when it is impractical to take your oil painting equipment with you to paint outdoors. The only way around this is to make some pencil sketches and copy from these at home. Make colour notes on your sketch, or on the back of it. You will find that you can very easily devise your own code system to save time and space. For instance, S = sun, GR = green, P = pale, etc.

There is still another aid to help your pencil sketch: the camera. But please take note: photographs can never take the place of working directly from nature, or be a short cut to your own personal observation and experience of landscape. Having said that, how can the camera help? If you were to sketch a scene in pencil and then photograph the same scene, you would have an indication of colours to help with your memory and notes. The photograph would also show details of subjects, where the sketch was inadequate. A photograph is also a perfect trigger to remind you of parts of the scene, the type of day, and many other incidents, that help to add more information to your sketch, which in turn will enable you to use the sketch to produce an oil painting.

Start by sketching simple subjects to work from. Remember, don't run before you can walk, and use the camera sparingly and wisely.

STRAW BALES

This first exercise (fig. 36) was sketched very simply, using a 2B pencil on cartridge paper. There are no details drawn in, apart from the suggestion of the birds; it is all broad tone work. I painted the picture 280mm (11in) deep x 200mm (8in) wide. Before I started, I painted a watery wash of acrylic Cadmium Yellow and Crimson Alizarin over the canvas to give me a warm base on which to work. It was the type of warm summer day when storm clouds keep threatening rain but it never comes.

Make sure the acrylic paint is absolutely dry and then, using your Series B48 No. 1 brush, with a mix of turps and Cobalt Blue, draw in and fill in the first stage using your sketch as a reference. Now paint in the blue sky, using your No. 4 brush and a mix of Titanium White, Cobalt Blue and Crimson Alizarin. Then paint in the dark clouds, using Cobalt Blue, Crimson Alizarin, a little Yellow Ochre and a little Titanium White.

Paint the trees with your Series B48 No. 2 brush, using a mix of Cadmium Yellow, Cobalt Blue and Crimson Alizarin; then add a little Titanium White to the trees on the left of the dark one. For the corn stubble and straw bales use Yellow Ochre, a touch of Crimson Alizarin, Titanium White and a little touch of Cobalt Blue. For the highlights on the bales and the field use Titanium White and Cadmium Yellow.

Notice in the field how some of the underpainting shows through. Paint the straw bales with your No. 2 brush, and use your No. 4 brush for the field. The shadow in the foreground is mixed with Cobalt Blue, Crimson Alizarin, Yellow Ochre and a little Titanium White.

HARTFORD WOODS

This next exercise (fig. 37) is a little more complicated than the last one, but I have tried to simplify it by keeping my pencil sketch unfussy. It was done on cartridge paper with a 2B pencil and is nearly all tonal shading, like the straw bales exercise.

First, draw the painting in with your Series B48 No. 1 brush, and then, using your No. 4 brush, fill in the solid area. As usual, use a mix of Cobalt Blue and turps. Paint the sky in next with Cobalt Blue, Titanium White and Crimson Alizarin using your Series B48 No. 2 brush.

With the same brush and a mix of Cobalt Blue, Viridian, a little Crimson Alizarin and Cadmium Yellow, paint in the 'dark blue' background trees and the foreground trees. Still using your No. 2 brush, now paint in the tree trunks with a mix of Titanium White, Cadmium Yellow, Cobalt Blue and a little Crimson Alizarin. Use less Titanium White with this mix for the shadows on the trunks. With the same colour, using your Rigger No. 1, paint in the thin branches.

Finally, work the ground, using Titanium White, Viridian, Cadmium Yellow and Crimson Alizarin. Paint up to the existing shadows (underpainting) with your colours and then, adding more Cobalt Blue to the ground colours, paint over the existing shadow areas, and add a few more shadows in the distance. Using your Series B48 No. 2 brush, without paint, rest the bristles on the grass below the long shadow and 'flick' the brush upwards and off the canvas almost at the same time. This gives the illusion that the shadows and the grass in front of them are interspersed. It is a good idea to practise on a piece of paper painting ground and grass effects. It's an important part of landscape painting.

Titanium White, Cobalt Blue and Crimson Alizarin

Cobalt Blue, Crimson Alizarin, Yellow Ochre and a little Titanium White

Yellow Ochre, Crimson Alizarin, Titanium White and Cobalt Blue

Fig. 36

COCKEREL

I did pencil sketches of the chickens and cockerel (fig. 38) with a 2B pencil on cartridge paper and also took photographs of them to help me with the colours.

In the first stage, after drawing in with my Rigger No. 1, I painted the foreground using my Series B48 No. 4 brush and also my finger. I used my Series B48 No. 2 brush for the cockerel, and Rigger No. 1 for the eye. Start by putting a very turpsy wash of Cadmium Yellow and Cadmium Red

over the cockerel except the tail. Then work from the head to the tail, making sure your brush strokes follow the shape and direction of the feathers: be bold. I painted the background in last, but I also reshaped some feathers over the background. Use various mixes of Cobalt Blue, Viridian and Cadmium Red for the black feathers, and various mixes of Cadmium Red, Crimson Alizarin, Cadmium Yellow and Cobalt Blue for the brown feathers. Add Titanium White to both where necessary.

Fig. 37

Cobalt Blue, Titanium White and Crimson Alizarin

Cobalt Blue

Cobalt Blue, Viridian, Crimson Alizarin and Cadmium Yellow

Titanium White, Viridian, Cadmium Yellow and Crimson Alizarin

Fig. 38

Cobalt Blue

Cadmium Yellow and Cadmium Red

Cobalt Blue, Viridian, a little Cadmium Red and Titanium White

Cadmium Red, Crimson Alizarin, Cadmium Yellow, Cobalt Blue and Titanium White

OIL SKETCHING OUTDOORS

When you feel confident painting indoors, then it's time that you took your paints outside and worked at nature first hand. Every painting you do from nature adds more information into the 'store cupboard' of your brain, which will make your next painting easier. More important, you will find it easier the next time you work indoors from a pencil sketch.

Let me make it clear that an oil sketch can be accepted as a finished painting and hung in any gallery, just as a large detailed painting can. A painting is a statement that you have made in paint on canvas and the size or the amount of time or work you have put into it doesn't matter. However, when an artist sets out to do a sketch outdoors, usually the prime objective is to get information to use at a later date in the studio for painting a larger or more finished picture; whereas a painting done outdoors is simply a picture that you start and know you will finish as a painting in its own right.

There is no size barrier for a sketch; it can be as small or as large as you want. However, an oil sketch (used for information) has one major drawback, and that is the amount of detail that cannot be painted in. This, of course, is because of the very nature of the paint. For instance, it is very difficult to paint thin lines over wet paint. The answer is to go for the atmosphere of the scene, 'the feel of it'. Make sure you get the tones of objects correct in relation to other objects. Remember that it helps if you half-close your eyes to do this. Look for shapes rather than detail. If you feel you will not be able to carry the detail in your head, then make pencil notes in your sketchbook, either written or drawn ones.

WORKING OUTDOORS

Here are some very important ground rules. Make sure you take enough clothing to keep warm – you can always take some off, but you can't put any extra on if you don't have it with you. Take a comfortable fold-up seat on which to work. You must try to be as comfortable working outside as when you are inside. Don't have too much equipment to carry or, when you find your spot, all you'll be fit for is a long rest, not painting! If you are going by car you can carry more equipment than you need, and it gives you a base to draw from if you forget or run out of any, or spill your bottle of turps!

Don't spend all morning looking for a 'better' place to paint (we all do, including me), or your painting time will disappear. The answer to this age-old problem is to paint the first scene that inspires you and not to think that there must be a better one round the corner, and then, when you have walked round the corner, to think there may be a better one

still round the next corner, and on and on it can go. As soon as you are inspired – paint!

If possible, check that the subject you are going to paint will stay there. If you are painting a tractor, a boat or any working object, workmen can move it. Also make sure you are not obstructing any normal workday duties – or you will be moved on. If you are not sure, then ask someone. Remember the country code: close all gates after you; if a gate is open, leave it open.

SKETCHING EXERCISES

I drew figs. 39-42 and 45-48 the same size as they are reproduced here. This gives you an indication of the formation of the brush strokes. I drew figs. 43 and 44 at 125 x 180mm (5 x 7in). I have done them all in two stages to show how I started them, and they are small to show how a small oil painting can be as exciting to do as a large one.

ST MICHAEL'S MOUNT

This exercise (figs 39 and 40) was worked on oil sketching paper (smooth). Colours: Cobalt Blue, Crimson Alizarin and Yellow Ochre.

Paint over the paper first with a turps and Cobalt Blue wash. When it is dry, draw in the main areas with an HB pencil. Use your Series B48 No. 4 brush for the whole of the picture, except the boat and men; for these use your Rigger No. 1. The bright sunlight in the clouds over the sea was added with thick paint when everything else was finished. Notice how I left some of the Cobalt Blue underpainting showing through.

THE WHITE FARM

This picture (figs. 41 and 42) was worked on an oil painting board and first painted over with a turps and Raw Umber wash. Colours: Cobalt Blue, Yellow Ochre, Cadmium Yellow, Crimson Alizarin and Titanium White.

Draw in the picture with an HB pencil and then, with your Series B48 No. 1 brush, use a turps and Cobalt Blue mix to draw over the pencil and fill in the dark tonal areas. Then paint the sky with your Series B48 No. 4 brush. Next, with your No. 2 brush, paint over the dark trees in the middle distance and then, with your No. 4 brush very dry, paint the feathery branches of the large tree. Now, with your No. 2 brush again, paint in the house and fields. Use thick paint for the 'white' clouds and sunlit side of the farmhouse.

Fig. 39 (above) *St Michael's Mount,* first stage   Fig. 40 (below) Finished stage

Fig. 41 (above) *The White Farm,* first stage　　Fig. 42 (below)　Finished stage

Fig. 43 (above) *Beach,* first stage   Fig. 44 (below) Finished stage

BEACH

For this exercise (figs. 43 and 44) I painted one coat of white emulsion paint over a sheet of cartridge drawing paper. When this was dry, I painted a wash of acrylic colour, Raw Umber and Crimson Alizarin, over the emulsion paint. Remember, you can paint oil over acrylic paint – when it is dry – but never acrylic over oil paint. Colours: Cobalt Blue, Yellow Ochre, Cadmium Yellow, Crimson Alizarin and Titanium White.

Draw in the scene with your HB pencil, then paint in the sky with your Series B48 No. 4 brush and use this brush for all the sketch except for the seagulls and figures. For these use your Rigger No. 1. Don't get fussy with the rocks, keep them simple. Thick Titanium White and a little

Cadmium Yellow were used to get the breaking waves and surf under the rocks. What is very important with this sketch is that if it were not for the three people on the rocks, there would be no reference to scale in the picture. The cliffs could be 4.5 metres (15 feet) or 152 metres (500 feet) high. Scale is very important in any painting, so that we can relate to the scene.

TWO BOATS

I used oil-primed canvas for this sketch (figs. 45 and 46). Colours: Cobalt Blue, Viridian, Crimson Alizarin, Yellow Ochre, Cadmium Yellow, and Titanium White.

Draw in with pencil first and then using your Rigger No. 1 brush, paint in the boats with turps and Cobalt Blue.

Fig. 45 (above) *Two Boats,* first stage   Fig. 46 (below) Finished stage

Fig. 47 (above) *Sky,* first stage   Fig. 48 (below) Finished stage

Fig. 49 Sky studies

Next, using your Series B48 No. 2 brush and the same colours, paint in the dark areas. With your No. 4 brush, work on the harbour wall, then paint in the reflections. Now, using your No. 2 brush again, work on the boats but don't get over-fussy with them. Next, paint the harbour quayside and finally, using thicker paint, work in the sunlit water.

SKY

The sky is the most important part of a landscape painting. It sets the mood of the scene, therefore it is important to practise and to learn to paint it well. Do try to copy from life as much as possible. Clouds move, and as you start to paint your subject will change shape or even disappear. The secret is to sit and watch the sky and the clouds for a while, until you have observed the movement and pattern they make. Then, as you see a section you like, start to sketch it quickly. Some sky formations can last long enough to paint them before they change, but don't just practise on these – try the difficult ones as well! Always put some form of land object – distant hills, tops of trees, or, as in fig. 48, rooftops – to give the scale and the angle of direction from which you are seeing the sky.

When you are working outside, mix your main colours first before you start to paint, or your clouds will have moved on before you are ready! The sky in figs. 47 and 48 was painted on emulsion-primed (one coat) cartridge paper, and the colours used were Cobalt Blue, Yellow Ochre, Crimson Alizarin and Titanium White.

Before you start working from life, copy the six sky sketches I have done (fig. 49). I did each painting at the same size, 180 x 148mm (7 x 5⅝in), on canvas. By copying these first it will give you more confidence to work at a moving sky from life. These are the colours that I used, but not necessarily all on one painting: Cobalt Blue, Cadmium Red, Crimson Alizarin, Yellow Ochre, Cadmium Yellow and Titanium White.

SNOW LANDSCAPE

Fig. 50 was painted on canvas with a turps, Cadmium Yellow and Crimson Alizarin wash, and the picture size was 180 x 205mm (7 x 8in).

When the background wash is dry, paint in the trees and foreground shadows with your Series B48 No. 1 brush. Now paint in the sky around the two main trees, and then the background trees and field. When you paint the sky, don't go over the underpainting of the middle distance trees or you will have difficulty in painting your dark trees on top. You can always add sky colour into your trees later to help make the shapes. Next, paint in the two main trees with Cobalt Blue, Crimson Alizarin, Cadmium Yellow and a

Fig. 50 Snow landscape

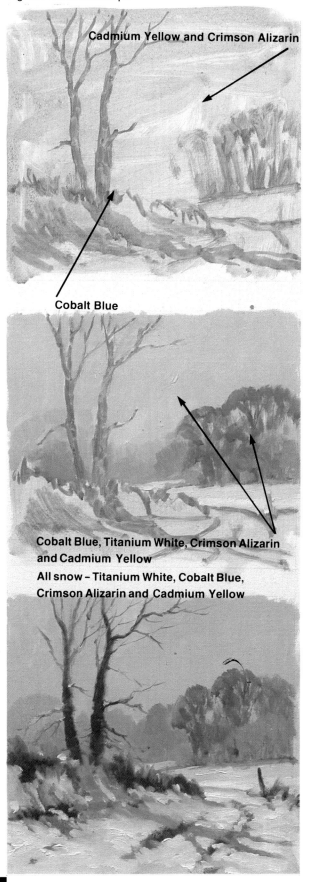

Cadmium Yellow and Crimson Alizarin

Cobalt Blue

Cobalt Blue, Titanium White, Crimson Alizarin and Cadmium Yellow

All snow – Titanium White, Cobalt Blue, Crimson Alizarin and Cadmium Yellow

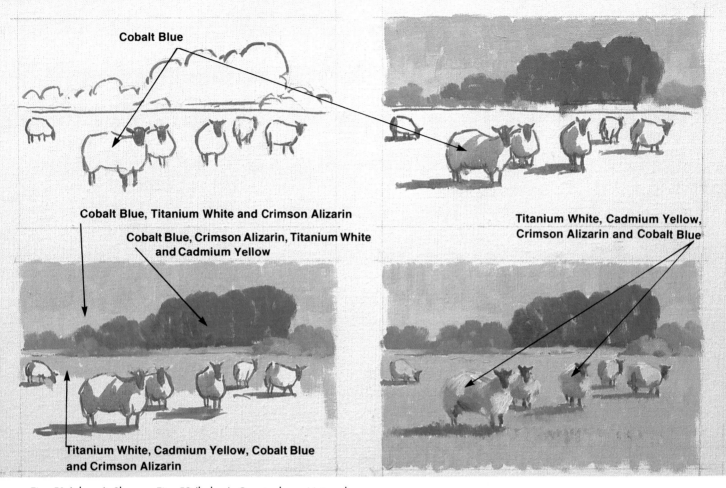

Cobalt Blue

Cobalt Blue, Titanium White and Crimson Alizarin

Cobalt Blue, Crimson Alizarin, Titanium White and Cadmium Yellow

Titanium White, Cadmium Yellow, Crimson Alizarin and Cobalt Blue

Titanium White, Cadmium Yellow, Cobalt Blue and Crimson Alizarin

Fig. 51 (above) Sheep   Fig. 52 (below) Country lane, Metcombe

Add to Titanium White: Cobalt Blue, Crimson Alizarin and Cadmium Yellow

Cobalt Blue, Crimson Alizarin, Cadmium Yellow and Titanium White

little Titanium White, and use your Dalon Series D99 No. 2 brush for the small branches. Put in the hedge, shadows and cart tracks using the same colours, in different mixes, as for the two trees and, finally, paint in the foreground snow, using thick paint.

SHEEP

You have the same problem with animals as you do with the sky – they will not keep still! When I paint animals, I usually start with one, get halfway through and it moves on. I then look for another in roughly the same position and carry on, or even improvise the finish. You can only become proficient at animal subjects by sketching and getting to know them, through constant work and observation. A camera can help, because you can study your photographs and see how the animals are formed. Until you are confident, keep them at a distance in your painting, where you will not have to suggest too much detail.

In fig. 51 the sheep are not detailed; I have only painted their overall shape and character, and in fact their heads are just dark shapes. They were painted on oil-primed canvas 115 x 180mm (4 x 7in). Colours: Cobalt Blue, Crimson Alizarin, Cadmium Yellow and Titanium White.

COUNTRY LANE, METCOMBE

This view (fig. 52) has always excited me. I walk past it many times and its fascination is in the very dark shadows forming an archway with the trees and a strong sunlit landscape beyond. I painted this on an oil-primed canvas panel, picture size 230 x 185mm (9¼ x 7¼in).

After drawing, paint in the sky and distant landscape. The brightness of the landscape will not become apparent until you have painted in the dark trees (light against dark). At first I painted all the trees dark, but found it overpowering, so I suggested sunlight on the two trees on the left. This made a tremendous difference: it seemed to give life and atmosphere to the picture. I used my Series B48 Nos. 2 and 4 brushes and my Dalon Series D99 No. 2 brush for the small branches.

RYE, SUSSEX

I painted this exercise (fig. 53) on oil-primed canvas, picture size 180 x 205mm (7 x 8in). Colours: Cobalt Blue, Crimson Alizarin, Cadmium Yellow and Titanium White.

Use your Rigger No. 1 to draw in with and then paint in the sky; using your Series B48 No. 4 brush, work thick paint for the clouds. Now paint in the main shadow areas of the town. Apart from the sky, use your Series B48 No. 2 brush for all the picture, except the chimneypots and suggestion of tree trunks, for which use your Rigger No. 1. Paint the foreground thinly, as this is not so important as the skyline which is the inspiration and composition for this picture.

Fig. 53 Rye, Sussex

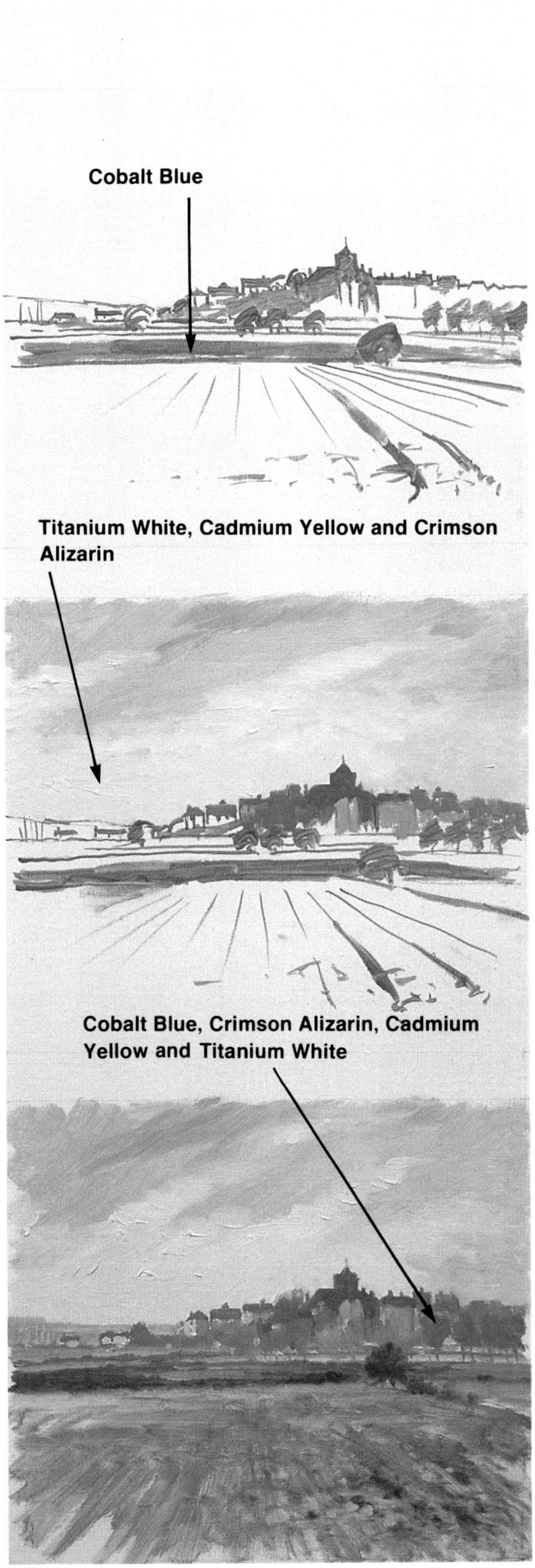

Cobalt Blue

Titanium White, Cadmium Yellow and Crimson Alizarin

Cobalt Blue, Crimson Alizarin, Cadmium Yellow and Titanium White

WORKING FROM AN OIL SKETCH

It is interesting to see a pencil sketch, an oil sketch and the finished painting reproduced together, all approximately the same size. Normally you only see them in their true life sizes. In this case the pencil sketch (fig. 54) was done on an A4 sketch pad, the oil sketch (fig. 55), worked on oil sketching paper, was painted 125 x 180mm (5 x 7in), and the finished painting (fig. 56) was done on oil-primed canvas, 410 x 610mm (16 x 24in).

When you go outside to make a sketch from which to work a larger painting at home, what you put into the sketch is really up to you. It is you who will have to copy from it and therefore you will know what information you require. But, as I said earlier, a sketch painted in oil has its limitations for showing detail (small brush work) information. There is a limit to how much detail can be worked (a) over wet paint and (b) working on a small scale.

However, the one great advantage that oil paint has on a small scale is to enable you to capture the atmosphere of the scene and this is what you must aim for. Any detail work can be recorded either by making notes, or by doing a pencil sketch and putting in the detail that you require. In a complicated scene this could be two pages of careful drawings of the various objects which you will want to paint in detail in the finished picture. You can also take photographs of the whole scene and its details.

When you start work on the painting at home, use the mood you created in the sketch as your main inspiration. If your painting changes from your sketch while you are working, to whatever degree, don't worry. Remember that you are only using the sketch as your source of inspiration; let your creative instincts have full rein when you paint the final work.

Fig. 54 Pencil sketch

Fig. 55 (above) Oil sketch   Fig. 56 (below) Finished painting

EXERCISE ONE
SUMMER LANDSCAPE

Summer is a wonderful season for painting landscapes. Because the trees are covered with leaves and the flowers are in bloom, everywhere seems cosy and happy. The colours are soft and warm, and most of the hard shapes of winter have melted away. The picture in this exercise was sketched on a warm summer's day a few miles from where I live, and I used the sketch to work from in my studio.

In this exercise and the ones to follow, it is important to remember when mixing your colours to start with the one I have listed first, then add to it the other colours, usually in smaller amounts. The first colour of your mix should be the main one. For instance, if you wanted to mix a pale blue, you would start with white and mix small amounts of blue into it until the required 'pale blue' is reached.

In these exercises I have tried to give you a detailed account of the way I have worked. Naturally I can't give you a brush stroke by brush stroke account as there is insufficient space in the book, but I have explained the important features. The photographs taken at various stages of the work enable you to see how the painting develops until it is finished. Incidentally, the paintings in the exercises were done in one sitting. I didn't wait for areas to dry.

The actual size of each painting is indicated next to the finished stage, as it is important for you to know the scale to

which to work. The close-up illustrations are reproduced the same size as I painted them, so you can see some of the brush strokes. I have also illustrated the method I used for certain parts of the paintings, with the arrows indicating the direction of the brush strokes and the movement of the brush.

I have painted these subjects in my own style which has evolved over the years. The way I paint in this book is the way I work; I haven't made the paintings work differently for the book. This is very important. We all have a creative style of our own and this will emerge naturally. Whatever you do, let your own style come to the fore.

FIRST STAGE

I used oil-primed canvas and painted it over with a turpsy wash of Cadmium Yellow mixed with Crimson Alizarin. When your turpsy wash is dry, start by drawing in the main features of the picture with an HB pencil and then, using your Rigger No. 1 with a mix of Cobalt Blue and Crimson Alizarin thinned with turps, draw over the pencil.

SECOND STAGE

For the whole of this stage use your Series B48 No. 2 brush. Incidentally, if the 'drawing in' paint is still wet, don't worry. It can mix with the underpainting colour. Starting from the top, using the same colours as for the drawing in the first stage, paint in the picture to arrive at its overall tonal values. This means that you will need dark and light tones of your colour. Do not use white to lighten the colour, use turps. For those of you who use watercolour, it is just the same as painting in watercolour.

Notice how the brush strokes help to form the shape of objects. Remember that your brush strokes should always follow the direction that objects grow or go. For instance, trees grow upwards and therefore brush strokes should work up trees. Look at the large dark trees, even in this stage they look like growing trees in full leaf. Can you imagine what they would look like if they had been painted in horizontal brush strokes?

Movement is also depicted by your brush stroke. For instance, if you are painting clouds and they are travelling from left to right, then let your brush strokes work from left to right. Use this method as much as possible on your paintings, from the largest mountain to the smallest blade of grass – it will help to make your paintings come 'alive'.

MID/DISTANT TREES
Titanium White
Cobalt Blue
Crimson Alizarin
Cadmium Yellow

FIELDS
Titanium White
Cadmium Yellow
Cobalt Blue
Crimson Alizarin
Viridian
Yellow Ochre

TREES
Cobalt Blue
Cadmium Yellow
Crimson Alizarin
Viridian
Titanium White

First stage

Second stage

Third stage

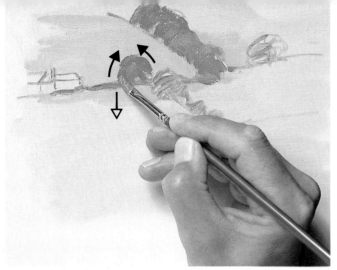

Brushwork detail

Fourth stage

Up to now I have always suggested you draw with pencil, then with paint, and then add your underpainting. It is at this point that you are ready to paint. One reason I have told you to draw your picture twice, i.e. pencil and paint, has been to give you confidence. But once you are confident, you can work directly with your colours onto a surface without underpainting or drawing. Or, of course, you can use only paint to draw in with, or work straight in with your underpainting with no drawing. The choice is yours.

THIRD STAGE
Throughout this stage use your Series B48 No. 4 brush. First, paint in the sky, using a mix of Titanium White, Cobalt Blue and Crimson Alizarin. Next, paint in the long line of trees in the distance, using a mix of Titanium White, Cobalt Blue, Crimson Alizarin and a little Cadmium Yellow.

Now paint in the two top fields, using Titanium White, Cadmium Yellow, a little Cobalt Blue and Crimson Alizarin. Paint in the trees behind the church, and the ones that separate the top fields next, using the same colour as the fields, but adding a little Viridian. Work the fields to the left and right of the church. Add Yellow Ochre to your field colour for the field on the extreme right. For the field behind the main dark trees, add Viridian and more Titanium White.

FOURTH STAGE
With your Series B48 No. 2 brush, start by painting in the shadows and roofs of the church and house to the right. Use Titanium White, Cobalt Blue, Crimson Alizarin and a touch of Yellow Ochre. Using the same colour, but a little warmer (more red), paint in the dark roofs behind the dark trees. Using the same brush and a mix of Titanium White, Cobalt Blue, Crimson Alizarin and a touch of Yellow Ochre, paint the roofs of the large white house. With the same colour but a little cooler (add blue), paint the light colour of the roofs behind the trees. Now paint the sunlit side of the church with a mix of Titanium White, Yellow Ochre and a touch of Crimson Alizarin.

Add a little more Titanium White and paint in the sunny side of the house next to the church. With the same colour, paint in the walls of the large white house. The main body of trees comes next. Mix various colours and tones of green, using Cobalt Blue, Cadmium Yellow, Crimson Alizarin and Viridian, adding Titanium White where you want the green to be lighter, then, using your No. 4 brush, follow my painting and paint in the trees.

Now paint the roofs and chimney of the foreground buildings using Cobalt Blue, Crimson Alizarin, Yellow Ochre and a touch of Titanium White. Use the same colours for the walls in shadow. For the wall leading to the large white house and the white wall of the left-hand building, use Titanium White mixed with Cobalt Blue, Crimson Alizarin and a touch of Yellow Ochre. Now, with your No. 2 brush, paint in the small tree in the foreground with your tree colours.

FINISHED STAGE
Start by painting the foreground field, using your No. 4 brush with a mix of Titanium White, Viridian, Cadmium Yellow and Crimson Alizarin. When you paint the field, don't paint over the shadows. Notice how the brush strokes on the right of the path go in perspective towards the bottom of the field. This helps to give direction and make the field look flat. Next work the path, using Titanium White, Yellow Ochre, Crimson Alizarin, and some of your field colour.

Now you can paint in the shadows on the field with a mix of Titanium White, Cobalt Blue, Crimson Alizarin and a touch of Yellow Ochre.

At this stage leave your painting for a break and come back with a fresh eye to see what detail it needs to complete it. I put in the church clock, a shadow on the house wall next to the church, a cool grey on the distant farm houses, and a small tree in front of the large white house with its shadow cast onto the wall of the house. Then I added chimney pots and accents where necessary, and finally painted in some birds over the trees.

Finished stage 305 x 410mm (12 x 16in)

Detail from finished stage

EXERCISE TWO
FLOWERS

Flower painting is very much like still life painting. If you are not capable of working outside, then these can always be painted indoors. The subject can be selected to suit your ability, or creative mood. For instance, if you are a beginner, you can put one simple bloom on a table and paint it, or if you are brimming over with confidence you can fill a large vase with all the flowers you can find in the garden, creating a subject full of delicate life and colour.

One word of advice: throughout the book I have suggested using few colours, and for this exercise I have chosen Dog Daisies, as these can be painted with the colours that we are using (see below). When painting flowers, however, you will usually find it easier and get better results if you add more colours to your palette. These will be decided by the flowers you are painting. If you are painting a flower predominantly lemon yellow, then use a Lemon Yellow paint as your main colour; or if a flower were purple, then buy a purple paint and use it as the main colour.

FIRST STAGE

I painted these flowers on an oil-primed canvas over which I put a turpsy wash of Yellow Ochre before I started the drawing. I did this with a rag over my finger.

FLOWERS
Titanium White
Cobalt Blue
Crimson Alizarin
Yellow Ochre
Cadmium Yellow

BACKGROUND
Titanium White
Yellow Ochre
Cobalt Blue
Crimson Alizarin

VASE
Titanium White
Yellow Ochre
Cadmium Yellow
Crimson Alizarin
Cobalt Blue

When this is dry, draw first with an HB pencil, then use your Series 43 No. 4 sable and draw over the pencil, using a mix of Cobalt Blue and a little Crimson Alizarin. If you look closely at the first stage picture you will see on the right-hand side that I changed the flower positions from the pencil drawing when I painted them in with the sable brush. I have pointed this out because even at the very beginning – the drawing stage – a picture develops and is changing, sometimes very subtly, at other times radically. So never be afraid if your picture is changing direction as it progresses at any stage, but make sure any change is for the better!

SECOND STAGE

Use your Series B48 No. 4 brush for the underpainting of the background and vase (I used my fingers in places). Use a turpsy mix of Yellow Ochre, Crimson Alizarin and Cobalt Blue. When you are painting the background don't paint over the flowers. Then, with your No. 1 hoghair brush, using a mix of Cobalt Blue and Crimson Alizarin, paint in the shadows on the flowers.

THIRD STAGE

Now paint in the background with your Series B48 No. 4 brush, using a mix of Titanium White, Yellow Ochre, Crimson Alizarin and a little Cobalt Blue. Don't worry if some of the underpainting is still wet; let it mix with your paint as you work. Work up to the flower petals. If your background colour goes over onto the petals, it doesn't matter, because you will be painting over the petals to give them their colour and final shape later.

Next, paint in the shadows on the flowers; use your Series B48 No. 1 brush and work each brush stroke to represent a petal. Use a mixture of Titanium White, Cobalt Blue, Crimson Alizarin and a touch of Yellow Ochre. With the same brush, using Titanium White, a little touch of Crimson Alizarin and Cadmium Yellow, paint in the middle tones of the petals. While you are doing this, with the same brush pick up some of the background colour that is on your palette and work it into the petals. This reflects the background colour into the white of the flowers and helps to give a uniformity of colour to the picture.

Now put in the flower centres, using Titanium White, Cadmium Yellow and Crimson Alizarin. For the shadow side

Second stage (above)   Third stage (below)

First stage

add a little Cobalt Blue. Finally, on the flowers, paint in the lightest petals using Titanium White and a touch of Cadmium Yellow. Notice how the bottom right-hand flower has a very 'white' petal that has caught the light. This works well because the light petal is against dark background and dark petals. Remember light against dark shows form and it can also create the illusion of an area being lighter, or darker, in a picture.

Finally, with your Series 43 No. 4 sable, paint in the stems, using Cobalt Blue, Crimson Alizarin, Cadmium Yellow and a little Titanium White.

During this stage the flowers were changing position in the vase quite alarmingly. Some had drooped well over the vase, some had opened more and others had moved over and covered other blooms. When you are working from nature it is always on the move, and you have to learn to cope with it.

FINISHED STAGE

Use your Series B48 No. 4 brush to work on the light-coloured area of the vase. Mix Titanium White, Yellow Ochre, Cadmium Yellow, Crimson Alizarin, and Cobalt Blue. For the dark colour on the vase, mix Cobalt Blue, Crimson Alizarin, Yellow Ochre and a little Titanium

215

Details from the finished stage (above and below)

Brush work detail

White. Let your brush strokes follow the shape of the vase; this will help to make it look more three-dimensional. Then, using the same colours, work on the table, with your brush strokes painted horizontally.

Work some cool highlights on the vase, using Titanium White, Cobalt Blue and a little Crimson Alizarin. Notice the highlight on the bottom right-hand side of the base. This is a reflected light and it helps to make the vase appear round. On the light brown side of the vase also paint some warm highlights by adding Cadmium Yellow to Titanium White. With your Series 43 No. 4 sable, add some highlights to the stems of the flowers and the small dried leaves on the stems.

Finally, look at your picture and decide where you may need some dark or light accents to help the painting. Although you have copied my painting, your picture will have its own little areas of beauty, and by now I hope your own style will be showing itself.

216

Finished stage 410 x 305mm (16 x 12in)

EXERCISE THREE
BOATS

Last summer I did some painting in Scotland, the first time I had ever been there. It's an exciting place for the painter with its beautiful mountains and lochs. One thing I did notice was how cool the light was compared to where I live in Devon. Compare the finished picture on page 223 with Summer Landscape on page 213, which is warm and mellow where this one is cool, crisp and clear. I painted a watercolour 355 x 455mm (14 x 18in) (page 222) of this scene sitting on the quay and I have used that painting in the studio to help me work the oil painting for this exercise.

I have made this the final exercise, because I feel it is the most ambitious painting in the book. There is a lot of 'drawing', and that crisp, clear atmosphere to capture. But by now, if you have worked hard you should be capable of doing this painting. Good luck!

FIRST STAGE

I painted this on oil-primed canvas. Draw in first with an HB pencil. Then, using your Rigger No. 1 brush with a mixture of Cobalt Blue and Crimson Alizarin, work over the pencil.

SKY/WATER
Titanium White
Cobalt Blue
Crimson Alizarin
Yellow Ochre
Cadmium Yellow

MOUNTAINS
Titanium White
Cobalt Blue
Crimson Alizarin
Yellow Ochre
Viridian
Cadmium Yellow

TREES
Cobalt Blue
Crimson Alizarin
Cadmium Yellow
Viridian
Titanium White

SECOND STAGE

Now the underpainting. Use Cobalt Blue and Crimson Alizarin, as usual, mixed with plenty of turps. Start at the top of the canvas and, with a rag over your finger, paint in the sky, mountains and trees. Then use your Series B48 No. 2 brush and work the tonal values of the buildings and boats. Use the rag to paint in the foreground quay.

THIRD STAGE

Using your Series B48 No. 4 brush, start working on the sky. Paint in the blue areas first, starting at the top and working down, using Titanium White, Cobalt Blue and Crimson Alizarin. Then work the light-coloured clouds, using Titanium White, Yellow Ochre and a touch of Crimson Alizarin, and paint over the mountain tops on the right. Add some Cobalt Blue to your mix and paint in the dark cloud hanging over the mountain. Now paint the mountains, using Titanium White, Cobalt Blue, Crimson Alizarin and Yellow Ochre. Start at the left and work to the right. Paint into the clouds that are now over the mountains; don't paint over the two green 'fields' on the mountain or behind the large trees.

Then, with a mixture of Titanium White, Viridian and Cadmium Yellow, paint in the two green 'fields' on the mountain. Now merge the cloud back over the mountain into the wet 'mountain paint'. This will help to soften the edges of the clouds and also give them the appearance of being over the mountain. Now, with your Series B48 No. 1 brush, using Cobalt Blue, Crimson Alizarin, a little Cadmium Yellow, a little Viridian and a little Titanium White, paint in the distant trees and the large group behind the single white house.

FOURTH STAGE

Start by painting the sunlit field in the distance. Use your Series B48 No. 1 brush with a mix of Titanium White and a little Viridian and Cadmium Yellow. Darken the field to the left and in front (behind the boats) by adding a little Cobalt Blue. Now paint in the shadow side of the white house with a little touch of 'mountain colour' (which should still be on your palette) and Titanium White, then paint the sunlit side with Titanium White with a dash of Crimson Alizarin.

First stage (above)   Second stage (below)

Detail from finished stage

Next paint in the dark lock gates with Cobalt Blue, Crimson Alizarin and Yellow Ochre. With your field colour, adding a little Crimson Alizarin, paint in the bank to the right of the lock gates and then, using your lock-gates colour, the dark edge to the bank. Now paint in the houses on the left: for the sunlit roofs use Titanium White, Cobalt Blue and a touch of Crimson Alizarin and Yellow Ochre, and for the ones in shadow use the same colours but less Titanium White.

Use Titanium White and Yellow Ochre for the sunlit walls and add a little Cobalt Blue and Crimson Alizarin for the walls in shadow. With this colour still on the brush, drag it across the buildings underneath the gutters to show a shadow. Now with a dark colour, using downward brush strokes, paint in the solid fence in front of the furthest house. Next, paint in the two small trees in front of the first house, using your tree colour.

Next work the boats. Use Cobalt Blue, Crimson Alizarin, Yellow Ochre and just a touch of Titanium White for the dark boats; use Cadmium Red and Crimson Alizarin for the red line on the nearest boat and the sail on the white boat. For the white super-structure and white boat use Titanium White, Cobalt Blue, Crimson Alizarin and a touch of Yellow Ochre. Paint these boats with your Series B48 No. 1 brush, but don't go for detail. All you want at this stage is the form of the boats.

Now paint in the quay in front of the houses, using Titanium White, Yellow Ochre and Crimson Alizarin for the top half and adding Cobalt Blue and less Titanium White for the bottom half. Finally, paint in the masts, using your Rigger No. 1.

FINISHED STAGE

Now the water. Use your Series B48 No. 2 brush and paint in the dark reflection, using Cobalt Blue, Crimson Alizarin, and Yellow Ochre, adding a little 'tree colour' where the reflection is under the large trees. Then, with plenty of Titanium White mixed with Cobalt Blue and Crimson Alizarin, paint the 'blue' water and work it back into the dark reflection to show water movement.

With a mix of Titanium White, Cadmium Yellow and Crimson Alizarin, work from the light blue to the harbour wall, getting lighter as you get to the edge of the wall. Then work some of this colour back into the blue with horizontal, broken brush strokes to represent water movement. Now, using your Series B48 No. 4 brush, paint in the foreground, using Yellow Ochre, Crimson Alizarin, Cobalt Blue and a little Titanium White. Then paint the black and white post.

To finish the picture you have to put in the detail, or the illusion of detail. Suggest the figures on the quayside using your Series 43 No. 4 sable; paint in the 'white' of the white yacht using Titanium White and Cadmium Yellow. With your Rigger No. 1, paint in the railings over the lock gates;

Third stage (above)   Fourth stage (below)

with the same brush, paint in the rigging lines on the boats and then the lines on the quayside to represent the stone edges. With your No. 4 sable, paint in the shadow of the post and, finally, using your Rigger No. 1 with Titanium White and Cadmium Yellow mixed, paint in the seagulls over the fishing boat.

Now have a break and come back to your painting with a fresh eye and add or subtract anything that you feel will help it. I am sure that now you have completed all three exercises you will be feeling very pleased with yourself – brimming over with confidence and waiting to show your pictures to the next person who comes to your home. Well, this is the way it should be. It is far better to create a picture for other people to enjoy than just for yourself. You are sharing your pleasure with others. However, while it is easy to accept admiration, do be prepared to respect criticism. Do not let it deflate you or your hard-earned confidence, but accept it in the spirit it is given and you will probably learn something to help you in your next picture. The all-important factor is that, from a white, blank canvas, you have created a picture – be proud of it, continue to paint and, above all, enjoy your painting.

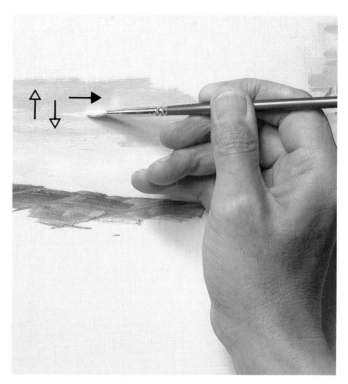

Brush work detail

Watercolour painted on location used for reference (below)

Finished stage, 300 x 410mm (12 x 16in)   Detail from finished stage (below)

VARNISHING

Now that you have progressed through the book, you should have quite a few exercises and paintings all finished and taking pride of place on various walls throughout your home. And we haven't yet talked about varnishing the paintings. The reasons for varnishing are (a) it protects the pigment from atmospheric impurities that could discolour your painting, and (b) varnish will restore colours to their original brilliance. You will have noticed by now that on some parts of the paintings the colours have gone greyer or dull, and other parts are shiny. This is the way paintings dry but varnish will bring them back to their original colours.

However, a painting should not be varnished for at least six to nine months after it has been painted as, during this time, considerable changes are occurring within the paint film structure and the application of varnish would inhibit some of these changes. This, in turn, could have an adverse effect on the oil painting in the long term.

If you want to exhibit a painting, or you want it to look its best before it is time to varnish, you can use a Retouching Varnish as a temporary measure, varnishing straight on top of your paint. This can be bought from your local art supplier, as can the normal varnish. With the normal varnish, however, you need to 'wash' your picture in the following way before varnishing. Clean the surface of the picture with a piece of cotton wool dipped into soapy water and squeezed out (you do not want to 'soak' your painting). This is to take off any grease and dirt that has accumulated over the past months. Then, with clean water, wipe over again to get rid of any traces of soap. Finally, dry the painting with cotton wool and make sure you don't leave any cotton wool fibres on the surface. When it is absolutely dry, you can varnish it.

I use Artists' Clear Picture Varnish. Use the varnish brush illustrated on page 171. Start at the top of the painting and work down and across, brushing the varnish in well. You must do the whole painting in one operation. If you only varnished part of the painting and the varnish started to dry, when you came back to finish it you would get a thick edge where the two varnishes joined up. You must also do your varnishing in a room where there is as little dust as possible.